François Hédélin

The whole art of the stage

François Hédélin

The whole art of the stage

ISBN/EAN: 9783742893888

Manufactured in Europe, USA, Canada, Australia, Japa

Cover: Foto ©Thomas Meinert / pixelio.de

Manufactured and distributed by brebook publishing software
(www.brebook.com)

François Hédélin

The whole art of the stage

THE
Whole ART
OF THE
STAGE.

CONTAINING

Not only the Rules of the *Drammatick Art*, but many curious Observations about it.

Which may be of great use to the Authors, Actors, and Spectators of Plays.

Together with much Critical Learning about the Stage and Plays of the Antients.

Written in French by the command of Cardinal *Richelieu*.

By Monsieur *Hedelin*, Abbot of *Aubignac*, and now made English.

LONDON,

Printed for the Author, and sold by *William Cadman* at the *Pope's-Head* in the *New Exchange* ; *Rich. Bentley*, in *Ruffel-ftreet*, *Covent-Garden*; *Sam. Smith* at the *Prince's Arms* in St.*Paul*'s Church-Yard; & *T.Fox* in *Weftminfter-Hall.* 1684.

The Translator's

PREFACE.

Some may wonder that this being a work of such use, and replenished with such judicious Remarks, as well as deep learning, in the whole course of it, has hitherto scaped the pen of our Translators out of a Language that has almost tyr'd our Presses with continual productions. But the reason of that may be that it was published in a time when we were Embroiled in civil Wars here in England, and that having laid aside all those Inno-

A 2

cent

The Translator's Preface.

cent _Theatral Reprefentations_ the whole _Kingdom_ was become the _Stage_ of real _Tragedies_ ; So that till his _Majefties_ happy _Reftauration_, with whom the _Mufes feemed_ to have been banifhed this _Ifland_, it could not be expected that a book of this nature could meet with any kind reception in the world ; but by that time I fuppofe the _Impreffions_ were all fold off, and it was to be met with no where but in the _Libraries_ of the curious. It was by _Communication_ from a _Perfon_ of that fort that the _Tranflator_ firft had the thoughts of making it _Englifh_, which he obtained leifure to do, by an unhappy confinement to a retir'd life for his health fake from more folid ftudies and bufinefs which his profeffion elfe involves him in. So _Reader_ thou haft here the whole _Art_ of the _Stage_,

of

The Tranſlator's Preface.

of which there needs little to be ſaid, the Book being its own Commendation ; As for the Author he was a perſon of a good Family in **Paris**, and of Exquiſite Learning in Antiquity; much cheriſhed by Cardinal **Richelieu** that great **Mæcenas** of Ingenious men, and by him for his deſerts made Abbot of **Aubignac** & deſign'd Overſeer or Super-Intendant General of the Theatres in **France**, if the project of reſtoring them to their Ancient glory (of which you will ſee an abſtract at the end of the book) had gone on, and not been Interrupted by the Cardinals Death.

The Tranſlator has made ſome Alterations in the Authors method & order of his Chapters, for the Author having promiſcuouſly placed much of the crabbed Antiquity Learning among the other Obſervations upon the Drammatick

The Tranſlator's Preface.

tick Art; and that being likely to diſguſt ſome Readers The Tranſlator has
put it all in one Book at the latter
end, where thoſe who love that critical
Learning may have it altogether, and
the others who delight in a ſmoother
career of Reaſons and Obſervations
may go on in the firſt three Parts without too ſtrong an Application in matters of ſome Intricacy.

There is nothing more, but that thou
excuſe the Errata, which by the negligence of the Printer are but too many.

THE

THE
CONTENTS.

Book I.

Book III.

The Contents.

Book III.

THE

THE

Whole Art

OF THE

STAGE.

The First BOOK.

CHAP. I.

Being instead of a Preface to the whole Work , wherein is treated of the necessity of Publick Spectacles, of the Esteem the Ancients had them in , and in what state they are now amongst us.

ALL those Incomparable and Famous Genius's which, from time to time, Heaven Designs for the Government of Mankind , do not only indeavour to make the Nations subject to their Conduct, Triumph with victorious Arms over their Enemies, and thereby become Formidable

B ·   to

to the World ; but also having enriched them with all
the wonders of Nature and Art, by the means of Commerce with Foreign Nations, they do strive to soften
and sweeten their Dispositions, by all the Noble Sciences that Mankind is capable of; and considering that
Nature its self in its Noblest Productions, after having
adorned them with all Qualities necessary to their Perfection, gives them a certain Contentment and Rejoycing in them, which is the greatest of its Favours ;
these great Politicians, in imitation of her, do use to
Crown all their Endeavours for the publick safety, with
publick Pleasures and Entertainments, making their
own glorious Labours either the means or the pretexts
of all general Diversions.   Their Victories are noted
by days of Rejoycing and publick Games ; and all the
Spoils and Riches of Foreign Nations, are brought from
the extremity of the Earth, only to compose the Pomp
and Decoration of their Spectacles, as well as the most
curious Sciences are Cultivated to produce men capable
of inventing new Entertainments.

And to say Truth, what greater marks can there be
of a flourishing Greatness in any State, than to see many of these Diversions ? Thereby in Peace appears the
Superfluity of its Riches, the Abundance of its People, who without being a Charge to the Publick, can
spare many days to their Pleasure, from those Employments which are necessary to the subsistance of the
great Body of the People ; and besides, the Number of
rare Wits busied in the publick Diversion, with all sorts
of Inventions, and the greater number of excellent Artificers, employed to execute the ingenious thoughts of
the first, cannot but be a great Ornament to a Nation.

All the Common-wealths of *Greece*, had each their
publick Games, where their Neighbours were as it
were

were obliged to affift, that they might all appear equal in Magnificency, as well as in Power and Authority : And if the Common-wealths of *Italy* were forced to come fhort of the Grandeur of *Rome* in that point, yet by their particular Cirk's and Theatres they have fhew- ed the World that they yielded only to the Miftr... of it, and not to one another.

But whenever in the midft of War all thefe D. verfi- ons are continued in a ftate , 'tis giving an evident de- monftration, that the Riches of it are without meafure, and the People inexhauftible, when the dangers and la- bours of a Campaigne paffed in the toyls of War, and the profpect of one to come, does neither change the Hu- mour nor the Courage of thofe that compofe the Ar- mies, nor of thofe that ftay at home ; that they un- dertake with Joy in Summer thofe glorious actions, of which they fee an Image upon the Stage in Winter with fo much Pleafure ; and that the Advantages their Enemies reap from the War, are fo inconfiderable as not to difquiet, or interrupt the publick Joy.

Thus the *Athenians,* having received in the very Theatre the news of an entire defeat of their Army be- fore *Syracufa,* would not fo much as interrupt the pub- *lick* Games, but went on with thofe Spectacles as they had begun ; and Foreign Embaffadours, who themfelves were by, and Spectators of this undaunted Generofity, admired it more than their real Power, as thinking it harder to fubdue. And to come nearer our times, if we confider what has paffed at *Vienna* and *Paris* , the Heads of two Rival Empires, under the Miniftry of the great Cardinal *Richelieu ;* we muft confefs that thefe two Capitols feem'd by the Magnificencies of their Plays, Bal- lets, and other publick Entertainments, to try to perfwade the World, that the Event of the War, which fo warm-

ly

ly they carried on againſt each other, was indifferent to them, both as to their good or evil Fortune.

We are not nevertheleſs to imagine that theſe pub-lick Spectacles afford nothing but a vain Splendour, without any real Utility ; for they are a ſecret Inſtru-ſtruction to the People of many things, which it would be very hard to inſinuate into them any other way. As for Example, Thoſe publick Diverſions where there is any image of War, do inſenſibly make them acquaint-ed with Arms, and make thoſe Inſtruments of Death familiar to them, inſpiring them at the ſame time with Courage and Intrepedity againſt all dangers ; beſides, Vanity often prevails more with us than Reaſon ; and that Jealous humour, of which our Nature can hardly ever well diveſt it ſelf, does continually foment within us a certain deſire of Conpuering, which often carries us to overcome all our natural Weakneſſes, and go be-yond our ſelves in great Attempts. Thus the Glory which one receives in publick for ſome handſom action ; and the recital or repreſentation of the Heroick Virtues of thoſe who are not even in being, at the time we hear them, does nevertheleſs raiſe in us a preſumptuous be-lief that we are able to perform the like ; and this pre-ſumption becoming a nobler ſort of Envy, called Emula-tion, produces in us an inſatiable deſire of Honour, and elevates our Courage to undertake any thing that may effect that Glorious Deſign.

As for thoſe Spectacles which conſiſt as much in Diſ-courſe as Action, ſuch as formerly were the Diſputes upon the Stage between the *Epick* and *Drammatick* Po-ets : They are not only uſeful but abſolutely neceſſary to inſtruct the People, and give them ſome tincture of Moral Virtues.

The minds of thoſe who are of the meaneſt Rank

and

and Condition in a State, are generally so little acquainted with any notions of Morality, that the most general Maximes of it are hardly known to them ; 'tis in vain therefore to make fine Discourses, full of convincing Reasons, and strengthened with Examples to them, they can neither understand the first, nor have any deference for the latter. All the elevated Truths of Philosophy are lights too strong for their weak Eyes: Tell them of these Maximes, that Happiness consists less in the possession of worldly things, than in the despising of them ; that Virtue ought to seek its recompence in its self; that there is no Interest in the World considerable enough to oblige a man of Honour to do a base thing ; all these, I say, are Paradoxes to them, which makes them suspect Philosophy it self, and turn it into Ridicule ; they must therefore be instructed by a more sensible way, which may fall more under their senses ; and such are the Representations of the Stage, which may therefore properly be called the Peoples School.

One of the chiefest, and indeed the most indispensible Rule of Drammatick Poems, is, that in them Virtues always ought to be rewarded, or at least commended, in spight of all the Injuries of Fortune ; and that likewise Vices be always punished, or at least detested with Horrour, though they triumph upon the Stage for that time. The Stage being thus regulated, what can Philosophy teach that won't become much more sensibly touching by Representation ; 'tis there that the meanest Capacities may visibly see, that favours of Fortune are not real Enjoyments, when they see the ruin of the Royal Family of *Priamus*; all that they hear from the Mouth of *Hecuba* seems very probable, having before their Eyes the sad Example of her Calamities ; 'tis there that they are convinced that Heaven punishes the horrid Crimes of
the

the Guilty with the remorse of them; when they see
Orestes tormented by his own Conscience, and driven
about by Furies within his own Breast; 'tis there that
Ambition seems to them a very dangerous Passion,
when they see a man engaged in Crimes, to attain his
Ends, and after having violated the Laws of Heaven
and Earth, fall into Misfortunes as great as those he had
overwhelmed others in, and more tormented by himself than by his Enemies: 'Tis there again that Cove-
tousness appears a Disease of the Soul, when they see a
Covetous man persecuted with continual Restlesness, and
fears of want in the midst of all his Riches. And
lastly, 'tis there that a Man, by Representation, makes
them penetrate into the most hidden secrets of Humane
Nature, while they seem to touch and feel in this living Picture, those Truths which else they would scarce
be capable of: But that which is most remarkable, is,
That they never go from the Theatre without carrying
along with them the idea of the Persons represented;
the knowledge of those Virtues and Vices, of which
they have seen the Examples; their memory repeating
continually to them those Lessons which have been de-
rived to them, from sensible and present Objects.

Besides, in all Governments there is a number of idle
People, either because they hate taking pains, or because they need not do it to live; this idleness carries them generally to many Debaucheries, where they
consume in a very little time, what might suffice for
the keeping of their Families many Months,
and are then forced upon ill actions for a supply to their
present wants. Now, I think nothing worthier the
care of a Great Prince, than to prevent, if possible, his
Subjects from taking these extravagant Courses; and as
it would be too severe to enjoyn them perpetual labour,
so

*Comœdiæ &
Tragœdiæ o-
tiosis d mus:
nemo enim in
Theatrum venit
qui non libens
velit id tempo-
ris amittere.
Scalig. l. 3 c.
2 l. 190.*

fo I think that publick Spectacles and Entertainments would moft innocently amufe thofe who have no other employment; their own pleafure would carry them thither without conftraint, their hours would flide away without regret, and their very idlenefs being bufie, they would there lofe all the thoughts of doing ill.

Thus whether out of the confideration of procuring that Joy and Content to Mankind, which makes their greateft Felicity, and without which they can relifh no other Happinefs; or whether to fhew the greatnefs of a State, either in Peace or War; to infpire the People with Courage, or to inftruct them in the knowledge and practice of Virtue; or laftly, to prevent Idlenefs, (one of the greateft mifchiefs of a State) Princes can never do any thing more advantageous for their own Glory, nor for their Peoples Happinefs, than to found, fettle, and maintain at their own Charges, publick Spectacles, Games, and other Diverfions, in the greateft Order, and the nobleft Magnificence that their Crown will afford.

And without doubt they have always been thought very important to the very Political part of the Government, fince the Philofophy of the *Greeks*, and the Majefty and Wifdom of the *Romans*, did equally concern their Magiftrates, in making them Venerable, Noble, and Magnificent. They made them Venerable, by Confecrating them always to fome of their Gods, and by putting them under the direction of their Chief Magiftrates; and they were beyond meafure Magnificent, becaufe the Expence was allowed out of the publick Treafure; and the liberal Contributions of their greateft Men in employment, who endeavoured to furpafs each other in Magnificence, that they might make the time of their Adminiftration more memorable. Very often

often the Chief of the Nobility were at the whole Expence, only to gain the Peoples Favour; and they obliged all the Eminent Artificers in all kinds, to shew their Excellency in them: they did use to send to the remoteft Nations for Men, Beasts, or any Rarity that could increase the Pleasure of their Spectacles; and laft of all, they had Crowns for the Conquerors in all Exercises, and Statues for thofe, who with any extraordinary Magnificence had been at the charge of them.

It had been neverthelefs little for thefe two Noble Nations to enjoy thefe Pleafures alone, if they had not propagated them to all the others of their Knowledge. The *Greeks* filled *Afia* with them, and the *Romans* carried them all over *Africa* and *Europe*, and after they had Conquered the beft part of the known World, to shew that their Domination was Gentle, and not Tyrannical; they received the Gods, and the Religions of all Nations into *Rome*, and fent them the Games, Spectacles, and Diverfions of that famous Capitol, to let them fee that they had not made War upon them to opprefs them, but to increafe their Happinefs, by fharing their Felicity with them. The Theatre of *Sardis* in *Afia*, that of *Carthage* in *Africa*, and thofe of *Douay*, *Nifmes*, and *Autun* in *France*, are convincing Teftimonies of this, though ruinous ones; and when *Conftantine* carried the Siege of the Empire to the City of his Name, he made there fuch publick Buildings for Spectacles, as shewed he would make it the Seat of his Pleafures, as well as of his Power.

But the Ancients did not only aim at obliging the prefent Age with their Noble Structures, but endeavoured to endear Pofterity to them, by making of them, as much as in them lay, immortal: Thus their Cirques, their
Theatres,

Theatres, and Amphitheatres, were built with the most polish'd and lasting Marble, and with so much Art, that if any thing they might resist the suppression of Time; but alas! as if man imprinted the Character of his own Mortality upon all his Works, these Glorious Monuments of their greatness have yielded to the same destiny; the Torrent of Time which overwhelms and destroys all things, has scarce left us the Image of them in some old ruines, half demolish'd. And Reason and Custom seem to have join'd with Time in abolishing many of the Ancient Spectacles. Those Bloody Combats of Gladiators against each other, and of Men against Beasts, till certain Death followed, have not been deriv'd to us, because they are contrary to that Humanity which the Law of the Gospel recommends, as the Foundation of Christian Charity. Something of that consideration made their Naumachia's or Naval Battels, in which sometimes there were fifteen or sixteen thousand men engag'd, be left of; but indeed the Expence of that was such, as nothing but the *Roman* Empire could ever furnish. The Courses of their Chariots, and the Races of their Horses, with the other Games of the Cirque, have been neglected as useless. And the running at the Ring in Turnaments, and fighting on Foot at the Barriere, which succeeded them in our Ancestors Days, have been likewise laid aside; Lances being as little in use with us in War, as Chariots: For as to the Courses of Bulls and Horses, which yet remain in *Italy*, they are rather to be numbred among the ridiculous Sights of our Age, than compared to the Spectacles of the Ancients.

The Javelin is of little use neither; and therefore.

C   we

we have neglected the Art of throwing it with flight in War.

Agonot. Fabr.
.. c. 6.

The Difcus or Coite is onely a diverfion of the meaner fort of People. Boxing or fighting with Cudgels or Clubs, becomes the roughnefs of none but Savages, and it would in my Opinion be a very fcurvy Diverfion in the Gallantry of the *French* Court.

Tennis, or Playing at Balls, which the Ancients called *Sphæromachia*, has nothing of its firft manner and glory, but is fo chang'd as hardly to be known, and there being no Crowns nor Rewards for the Actors, it is only become a voluntary Diverfion.

Petr. Fabr. in
Agon. paffim.
Suetom. in De-
mit. c. 4. &
pugnas femina-
rum dedit, &c.
Mart. l. 1.
Stat. Sylv. &
Juvenal. Sa-
tyr.

As for Wraftlers, they are in fome of our Provinces, but very few : Firft, becaufe it is againft the Rules of Modefty to fee not only Men, but Women naked, try their Strength and Skill againft one another, (for fo both Sexes did formerly) but now the Women are banifh'd from that Immodeft Exercife: And befides there was a necefity of being Dieted,and living up to the ftrictnefs of certain Rules of Health, which has made it be forfaken ; and having nothing Noble left in it, is onely become the Diverfion of the meaner fort.

Noftri feculi
Ludicra nihil
cum antiquis
fimile, quum
incondite, ine-
pte nulla in
conficiendis
arte, fed tu-
multuariè, &
fine ullo figu-
re artificio
fiant &c. Onu.
in Lud. Cirs.
l. 2. c. 18.

The fame thing has befallen the Amphitheatres, where from all Parts of the Earth were brought wild Beafts to fight againft one another: For to fee, as we do fometimes, a Fellow lead a Lyon about to be Worried by a Dog of his Acquaintance, is a ridiculous fight; and fo are thofe other Combats of Beafts, which are yet in *Italy,* unworthy the greatnefs or care of a State.

Bonfires and Fireworks have had a better deftiny;

ny ; for if ours do not obſerve that Order and Art
which the Ancients did in theirs, they are not at all In-
feriour to them in Magnificence. I may ſay the ſame
of our Balls and Balets, of which we have happily
maintained the Splendour, though our way of Dancing has nothing in it like that of the *Greeks* and
Romans : But ſtill thoſe which we have ſeen at *Paris,* and which have deſerved the Admiration and
Applauſe of the two greateſt Kings in *Europe,* and of
their Courts ; theſe Balets, I ſay, in which twice the
whole Machine of this World, the Heavens, the Sea,
the Earth, and Hell the bottom of it, were repreſented, ſurpaſs in my Opinion any thing that we
can by reading obſerve of that kind among the Ancients.

As for the Theatre, or Stage, it has not been much
happier than the Cirque. For not to ſpeak of thoſe
other Diverſions which were given the People in it,
the Art of compoſing Drammatick Poems, and re-
preſenting of them, ſeems to have had the ſame De-
ſtiny with thoſe Famous Structures where they
were Acted. It has lain long buried with the Ruines of *Athens* and *Rome* : And when at laſt it was
reſtor'd in ſome ſmall meaſure amongſt us, it ſtill appear'd like a Carcaſs taken out of the Grave, without any Shape or Vigour. All the firſt Pieces of the
Stage were without either Art or Learning, or any
other Ornament than that of Novelty ; the Compoſition was without Skill, and the Verſes without any
Politeneſs ; the Actours no waies underſtood their buſineſs, and the whole Repreſentation was defective all
over ; inſomuch that they had not a painted Cloth to
hide thoſe who were to go off the Stage ; but they
were reputed abſent who did not preſent themſelves
to ſpeak.   C 2   'Tis

'Tis true, that in our Age our Poets having recovered the Way to *Parnaſſus,* upon the Footſteps of *Euripides* and *Terence,* and there happening to be Actours amongſt us, who might in *Rome* it ſelf have match'd with *Æſopus* the famous Tragedian, and *Roſcius* the no leſs Renown'd Comedian, the Stage has got a new Face, and the Wrinckles that were upon that Old one have begun to grow ſmooth, and altogether to look with leſs deformity. Happy in this, that the greateſt Genius of our Time, the great Cardinal *Richelieu,* ſmil'd upon her. It was by his Liberality that ſhe firſt receiv'd new Strength, and began to challenge her Old Rights, her Beauty, Nobility and Splendour; and it was by his care that moſt of what was either Ingenious, Learned, or Magnificent among the Ancients, was ſeen by degrees upon our Theatre: And yet after all, we muſt own that the Stage was fallen from ſo high a degree of Glory, into ſo much contempt and abjectneſs, that it was impoſſible to heal entirely thoſe Wounds which it had received in its fall, nor to reſtore it, but after much Labour and Time. But ſince the ſame hand, which begun the Cure, has not been able to finiſh it, 'tis to be feared that the Drammatick Art will never arrive to its perfection, and I doubt will hardly maintain it ſelf in the ſtate it is, any long time. And if ſo, its relapſe will be ſo much the more dangerous, becauſe it is not every Age that produces Genius's both underſtanding and Liberal, and accompliſh'd with all the Qualities neceſſary to ſo great a Deſign. The Life of this great man has form'd an Age of great and new things: but all thoſe which did not arrive to perfection, according to their Nature, in his time, will hardly meet with an Opportunity to do it after his Death. And indeed it belong'd to no body more to adorn the Kingdom with all delightful Spectacles, than to him; who every day encreas'd our Victories, and Crown'd us with new Lawrels. 'Twas but reasonable that he, who was in War so like *Cæsar* and *Pompey*, should imitate them likewise in the restoring of Theatres, and other Princely Diversions; and in a Word, the magnificence of Publick Spectacles could not be better deriv'd than from him, who was himself the most glorious and noble Spectacle in the World.

It was to please him that I Compil'd this Practice of the Stage, which he most passionately had wish'd for; in hopes it would ease our Poets of the great labour, they must else have undergone, if with great Expence of Time they would have collected these Observations, which I have made ready for them, out of the different Authors, and from nice and accurate Remarks on the Stage it self. It was likewise by his Order, that I made a Project of restoring the *French* Theatre to the Splendour of that of the Ancients, and what Remedies were to be used against all our Impediments. He had conceiv'd such hopes of succeeding in this design, that he made me treat to the whole extent of the matter, upon that which I had first but summarily touch'd, and was resolv'd to employ all his Power and Liberality in compassing this Noble Enterprise. The Death of that great man made those two Works miscarry, but here is the first, which as it is I give to the publick, upon the sollicitation of my Friends. As for the second, I shall only Communicate to the World the Project of it, it not being proper to Expose any more of it,

since

fince there were not above five or feven Chapters of
it Writ, which are imperfect too, and out of Order.

C H A P. II.

The Defign of the whole Work.

THE Glory to which the *French* Theatre is
arriv'd, may perhaps make fome think that
this Difcourfe is ufelefs, fince our Poets, having given
to the World fo many compleat Poems, with a general Approbation, may be thought to be above thofe
Inftructions, which feem to be the Remedy for
Faults to which they are no longer fubject ; I will
not therefore be guilty of fo great a Vanity, as to
fay that the Scope of this Work is to inform them
of things which we fee they Practice every day with
fuccefs, but it is to let the World know the Excellency of their Art, and to give People fubject to admire them fo much the more, in fhewing what Learning, Invention, Abilities, and Care there are requir'd to finifh thofe Poems which make one of the
greateft of our Pleafures, while they only give the
Players the Trouble of reciting them. And in this
I fhall not onely raife the Fame of our Poets, but
contribute confiderably to encreafe the Pleafure we
take in feeing and reading their Works: For it is natural to every body to relifh any agreeable object fo
much

Much the more, by how much they are capable of difcovering the Reafons that render it agreeable ; and as we have more Value for Precious Stones, when befides their noble natural Qualities, we confider to what dangers they expofe themfelves, who bring them from the remoteft Parts of the Earth ; fo I think we fhall feel fo much the more admiration and joy in the Reprefentation of Theatral Diverfions, if by the knowledge of the Rules of the Art we are able to penetrate all the Beauties of them, and to confider what Meditations, Pains, and Study they have coft to be brought to that Perfection. So noble and fo vaft a defign requir'd, I confefs, a Genius much fuperior to mine, and a Body more capable of fupporting the Fatigue of ftudy and application. But I think that this being rather a Summary, than a compleat Treatife, and as it were rather a Collection of my own Obfervations, than a profound Differtation, full of knotty Difputes and Contestations with our modern Authors, whofe Opinions are it may be more reafonable than mine, I may be the eafilier Excufed.   All that will be feen here is but the Compendium of thofe Matters which I had once refolv'd to treat at large, if many Confiderations had not taken from me both the defire and power of performing it : If by chance it be obferv'd, that fome Places are touch'd with more Strength, and better Finifh'd than others, it is becaufe I deliver'd thefe Memoires to my Friends as they were, unequal and unpolifh'd, according to thofe Heats and Colds which accompany all Writers, who following the firft ardour of their Projects, do not review with Care the whole Product of their Endeavours.

If

If any thing appear reafonable and pleafing, that will be enough to hinder me from repenting the reprieve I have given my Book from thofe Flames to which I had once refolutely Condemn'd it; and at leaft, though my matter and Order be not approv'd, yet fome one more laborious, finding the way open, and having the Affiftance of fome Illuftrious Protectour, will purfue to the utmoft Perfection that which I have but hinted, and as it were flightly imagin'd.

CHAP.

C H A P. III.

What is to be understood by the Art *of the Stage.*

IT may seem very rash, or at least superfluous, to treat of Poetry, after that so many Authors both Ancient and modern have given us Books upon that Subject, full of Learning ; and more particularly have taken Pains to make Observations upon Drammatick Poetry, as being the most agreeable, and yet the hardest to succeed in.   But if we may believe, with *Seneca*, that all Truths have not been yet spoken, we may assure it in the Subject which I undertake ; for all I have seen yet that concerns the Stage, contains only the general Maximes of Drammatick Poetry, which is properly the Theory of the Art ; but as for the Practice and Application of those Instructions, I never met with any thing of that kind hitherto ; all the Discourses that are upon that Subject, being only Paraphrases and Commentaries upon *Aristotle*, with great obscurity and little Novelty.

I do not pretend here to trouble my self about satisfying the Criticisms of Grammarians, or the Scruples of Logicians, who it may be will nor freely admit of this distinction in an Art, whose Rules seem all to tend to practice : I am sure all the rational and

polite

polite Learning will not oppofe me in it, fince 'tis
natural in all Arts to diftinguifh the knowledge of
the Maxims, and the Ufe of them; befides that in the
Execution of all general Rules, there are obfervations
to be made, of which there is no mention, when
one teaches only the Theory, and which neverthelefs are of great importance. Thus Architecture teach-
eth the beauty and fymmetry of Buildings, their noble
Proportions, and all the reft of their magnificent Appearance, but does not defcend to exprefs a thoufand neceffary Contrivances, of which the Mafter
of the Houfe is to take care, when he puts his hand
to the Work.   If the Art of playing upon the Lute
were reduc'd into Rules, it could teach onely gene-
al things, as the number of the ftrings and touches,
the manner of making the Accords, the meafures,
paffages, quavers, &c. but ftill one would be forc'd
to have recourfe to the Mafter himfelf, to learn, in the
Execution of all this, the niceft way of touching the
ftrings, the changing of the meafures, the moft
graceful way how to give a good motion to ones
playing, and many more particulars, which could
not well be committed to writing, and fo muft either
be neglected or learned of the Mafters themfelves.

The fame thing has happened to the Stage. There
has been ample Treatifes of Drammatick Poems,
the original of them, their progrefs, definition, fpe-
cies, the unity of action, meafure of time, the beauty
of their contrivance, the thoughts, manners, language,
which is fitteft for them, and many other fuch matters, but only in general ; and that I call the Theory
of the Stage ; but for the Obfervations to be made
upon thofe general Rules, as how to prepare the Incidents, to unite times and places ; the continuity of
the

the Theatral Action, the Connexion of the Scenes, the intervals of the Acts, and a thousand other particulars, of which there is nothing left in Antiquity, of which all the Moderns have said so little, that it is next to nothing ; all this, I say, is that which I call the Art or Practice of the Stage.   As for the Ancients, if they have writ nothing about it, as to the practical part, it is because that perhaps in their time it was so common, that they could not believe any body capable of not knowing it ; and indeed if one look into their works, and make but the least reflection upon the Art they use, one may perceive it almost every where.

But for the Moderns; they for the most part have been entirely ignorant of it, because they have neglected the reading the Poems of those great Masters; or if they have read them, it was without taking notice of the nicest beauties with which they are adorn'd ; therefore it must be set down for a Maxime out of conteft, that 'tis impossible to understand Drammatick Poetry without the help of the Ancients, and a thorough meditation upon their Works.

D 2   CHAP.

C H A P. IV.

Of the Rules of the Ancients.

I was, I muſt confeſs, extremely ſurpriz'd ſome years ago, to ſee ſome Plays in great eſteem both in *Paris*, and at Court, in which there was ſcarce a Scene, that did not in ſome meaſure offend the Rules of Decency and Probability ; but I was much more aſtoniſh'd, when going about to ſay ſomething of thoſe Rules, and to Explain the ways how to obſerve them, I was taken for an Hypochondriack, who had ſtrange ſingular fancies of his own, of things that never were, nor could be. All the Rules of the Ancients, by which I pretended Poets were to be guided in the conduct of their Plays, were look'd upon as dangerous innovations, like thoſe in Government, or in Religion. There was no asking, what time the action repreſented took up, and in what place the things expos'd to our view were ſuppos'd to be perform'd, nor how many Acts a Play had ? I was anſwer'd preſently, that the Play had laſted three hours, that the Action had been all upon the Stage, and that the Fiddles had mark'd the Intervals of the Acts ; in a word, 'twas enough to pleaſe, to have the name of Commedy given to a

great

great many Verſes put together, and recited upon the Stage. But at laſt having grown acquainted with ſome of the learned men of our Age, I found amongſt them many very well acquainted with the Art of the Stage, particularly in the Theory and the Maxims of *Ariſtotle*, and ſome too, who did apply themſelves to the conſideration of the Practical part. All theſe were of my opinion, and condemning the voluntary blindneſs of our times, did extremly help me to confound the ſtubbornneſs of thoſe, who refus'd to yield to Reaſon.

Thus by little and little the face of the Theatre has been entirely changed, and is at laſt come to that perfection, that one of our moſt celebrated Authors has publickly confeſs'd, and that often, that in looking over ſome of his own Plays, which had been acted with great approbation of the Town, about ten or twelve years ago, that he was much aſham'd of himſelf, and did extremly, pity thoſe who had applauded him. I have neverthelefs had the misfortune to incur the diſgrace of ſome little Authors, who having neither Genius, nor Learning enough, to come up to theſe Rules in the excellency which they propounded, ſided with part of the Players, to run me down. As for theſe latter, their deſign being only to gain by their Profeſſion, and not to excel in it, they thought that the ſtrictneſs and ſeverity of theſe Rules would frighten all the young Authors, and deter them from writing; by which means they thought themſelves in danger of being forc'd to leave the Stage, to ſeek for ſome other Employment, for want of new Plays: but the Event has confounded this piece of Ignorance, for there were never ſeen more Drammatick Poems, nor more agreeable ones, than

than fince ; although we have not for Actours fuch as *Valeran*, *Veautray*, and *Mondory* were.

But yet fince fome perfons of Judgment, for want of being well vers'd in Antiquity, have endeavour'd with fome appearance of Reafon to maintain the errours of our Age, I think my felf oblig'd to anfwer their fcruples, and to fatisfie a great number, who yet feem unwilling to be undeceiv'd. Therefore here are five Objections which have been ordinarily made to me, againft the Rules of the Ancients.

Firft, That we are not to make Laws to our felves from Cuftom and Example, but from Reafon ; which ought to prevail over any Authority.

Secondly, That the Ancients themfelves have often violated their own Rules.

Thirdly, That divers Poems of the Ancients had been tranflated, and acted upon our Stage with very ill fuccefs.

Fourthly, That divers of our modern Plays, though quite contrary to thefe Rules, had been acted with great applaufe.

And laft of all, That if thefe rigorous Maxims fhould be followed, we fhould very often lofe the greateft beauty of all true Stories. Their Incidents having moft commonly happened at different times, and in different places

As to the firft Objection, I anfwer, That the Rules of the Stage are not founded upon Authority, but upon Reafon ; they are not fo much fettled by Example, as by the natural judgment of Mankind ; and if we call them the Rules and the Art of the Ancients, 'tis only becaufe They have practis'd them with great regularity, and much to their Glory ; having

¶

firft

firſt made many Obſervations upon the Nature of Moral Actions, and upon the probability of Humane Accidents in this life, and thereby drawing the Pictures after the truth of the Original, and obſerving all due circumſtances, they reduc'd to an Art this kind of Poem, whoſe Progreſs was very ſlow, though it were much in uſe among them, and much admir'd all the world over. But however I am very ſparing of citing their Poems, and when I do it, it is only to ſhew with what agreeable Artifice they kept to theſe Rules, and not to buoy up my opinion by their Authority.

As for the ſecond Objection, it ſeems not conſiderable; for Reaſon, being alike all the world over, does equally require every bodies ſubmiſſion to it; and if our modern Authors, cannot without offence be diſpens'd from the Rules of the Stage, no more could the Ancients; and where they have fail'd, I do not pretend to excuſe them. My Obſervations upon *Plautus*, ſhew very well that I do propoſe the Ancients for Models, only in ſuch things as they ſhall appear to have followed Reaſon in; and their Example will alwaies be an ill pretext for faults, for there is no excuſe againſt Reaſon. In things which are founded only in Cuſtom, as in Grammar, or in the Art of making a Verſe with long or ſhort ſyllables, the Learned may often uſe a licenſe againſt the receiv'd practice, and be imitated in it by others, becauſe Cuſtom may often have countenanc'd a thing not well of it ſelf. But in all that depends upon common ſence and reaſon, ſuch as are the Rules of the Stage, there to take a licenſe, is a crime; becauſe it offends not Cuſtom, but Natural light, which ought never to ſuffer an Eclipſe.

Non omnia ad Hem rum referenda tanquam ad normam cenſeo, ſed & ipſum ad normam. Scalig. l. 1. c. 5.

I

I muſt not omit, for the Glory of the Ancients, that if they have ſometimes violated the Art of Drammatick Poems, they have done it for ſome more powerful and inducing Reaſon, than all the Intereſt of the Play could amount to. As for Example, *Euripides*, in the *Suppliants*, has preferr'd the glory of his Country to that of his Art, of which I have ſpoken elſewhere.

The third Objection has no force, but in the Ignorance of thoſe that alledge it. For if ſome Poems of the Ancients, and even thoſe which were moſt in Eſteem with them, have not ſucceeded upon our Stage, the Subject, and not the want of Art, has been the cauſe of it; And ſometimes likewiſe the Changes made by the Tranſlators, which deſtroyed all the Graces of the Original: They have added improbable Scenes between Princes, and have ſhew'd out of time that which the Ancients had carefully conceal'd with Art ; and very often changed a fine Relation, into an impertinent ridiculous Spectacle. But That which is more worthy our conſideration, is, that there were certain Stories, fitted for the Stage of *Athens* with great Ornaments, which would be in abomination upon Ours: For Example, the Story of *Thyeſtes*; ſo that we may ſay, that either the Moderns have corrupted the Ancients, by changing their whole Oeconomy, or the Imperfection of the Matter ſtifled the excellency of the Art.

To deſtroy the 4th Objection, we need only to remember, that thoſe Plays of ours, which took with the people, and with the Court, were not lik'd in all their parts; but only in thoſe things which were reaſonable, and in which they were

con-

conformable to the Rules: When there were any
paſſionate Scenes, they were prais'd; and when
there was any great Appearance or noble Spectacle, it was eſteem'd; and if ſome notable
Event was well manag'd, there was great ſatisfaction ſhewn; but if in the reſt of the Play, or even
in theſe beauties of it, any irregularities were diſcover'd, or any fault againſt Probability and Decency,
either in the perſons, time, or place, or as to the
ſtate of the things repreſented, they were condemned as Faults.   And all the favour that was ſhewed
the Poet, was, that out of the deſire of preſerving
what was fine, the Spectatours were ſomewhat more
indulgent to what was amiſs.

Therefore that ſucceſs ſo much bragg'd on, is ſo
far from contradicting the Rules of the Stage, that
quite contrary it eſtabliſhes their Authority.   For
theſe Rules being nothing but an Art to cauſe the
fineſt Incidents to pleaſe with decency and probability, it ſufficiently appears how neceſſary they
are, ſince by common conſent, all that comes up to
them is approved of, and all that varies from them is in
ſome meaſure condemn'd.   Examples would extremely illuſtrate this truth, if I were not afraid to
anger ſome of our Poets, by inſtructing the others
at their coſt.

The 5th Objection is abſolutely ridiculous.   For
the Rules of the Stage do not at all reject the moſt
notable Incidents of any Story, but they furniſh us
with Inventions, how ſo to adjuſt the Circumſtances
of the Action, Time, and Place, as not to go againſt

all probable appearance, and yet not to reprefent them always as they are in Story, but fuch as they ought to be, to have nothing but what's agreeable in them. 'Tis That then that we are to feek, and of which in the following Difcourfe I fhall communicate my Thoughts.

CHAP.

CHAP. V.

How they ought to Inſtruct themſelves, who intend to write a Drammatick Poem.

IN the Univerſities, the Drammatick Poets, as well as others, are given to young Scholars to read and ſtudy, and they affording great variety by moral Sentences, of which they are full, and by the Dialogues of different perſons conteſting with paſſion, as alſo by the imagination of thoſe Machines, which one muſt neceſſarily ſuppoſe to have been employed in the repreſentation of them; to which may be added the ſudden Turns and Events of the Stage, they cannot but procure an Extrem delight to theſe young Students, and make a ſtrong impreſſion in their minds; and though the whole, it may be, is both ill explain'd by thoſe that Inſtruct them, and as ill underſtood by Them; yet they have infinite ſatisfaction in the thing.

It may be after this, they ſee ſome Play compos'd by their Maſter, and acted in the ſame Schools; and though that be done by very ill Actors, and carry with it in all its circumſtances the true Character of

pedantry,

pedantry, neverthelefs this is perform'd with fo much noife, buftle, and preparation, that they conceive a mighty Idea of it, having feen nothing better, and being incapable of finding out the faults of the piece.

If then there happens to be amongft thefe Youths a fiery Lad with Fancy, and fome Inclination to Poetry, finding himfelf at leifure to employ his parts his own way, he fixes upon Drammatick Poetry; and out comes a piece of his. To make which he generally follows this method; he pitches upon fome ftory that pleafes him, without confidering, whether it be fit for the Scene or no, or ever reflecting what is to be avoided in it, or what Ornaments may be added; he is refolv'd to hide under the Curtain any thing that fhall incommode him, to put *France* at one corner of the Stage, *Turkey* at the other, and *Spain* in the middle, his Actours fhall be fometimes in the *Louvre*, then in a Wood, or High-way, and then in a Garden full of Flowers, and no body knows how they came there; and if any body is to pafs by Sea from *Denmark* to *France*, 'tis done with the drawing of a Scene. Having thus fill'd every thing with ridiculous Imaginations, and things oppofite to all probability, he makes his firft Scene; which he has no fooner done, but finding himfelf at a ftand, he repairs to fome of the Theatres, to fee if he can fteal any Invention from them, that fhall pleafe him. Then he gets into the company of fome celebrated Poet or Critick, and from them he is fupplyed with fome new thought, or paffionate incident, or fome flight of the Art, which he immediatly employes quite contrary,

and

and out of all time; and having thus with the help of some *Songs* and *Elegies,* made formerly for *Cloris,* muster'd up three or four hundred Verses, he resolves to call it an Act. Thus going on in the same method, he gets to the death or marriage of some Prince, and then 'tis privately whisper'd among his Friends, that he has made a very pretty Play: The Ladies desire to see it, and 'tis by the Author red to them in secret, they are charmed with some Florid Expressions, or smart Repartees, and call in the Gentlemen of their acquaintance to hear it. Every body applauds and flatters the Author, reserving to themselves the privilege of laughing at him, as soon as his back's turn'd; and in short, he acquires thus the honourable title of a Poet.

Without doubt, not only one must have prodigious good fortune, but more than that, an infus'd science, like *Adam's,* to make at first and by such methods a piece (not comparable, I say, to those whom twenty Ages have reverenced) but to make a thing like that of the Poet *Rhodophilus,* of whom *Scaliger* says, that his *Comedie* rather excited pity than mirth. To say truth, the Complaisance or Ignorance of the Spectatours is extreme, when they condemn others, as too severe, who cannot applaud such stuff, as this is. There is no Mechanick trade in the World that does not oblige to a long Apprentiship under a Master, and when the Artists set up for themselves, they are examin'd by the Company, to whom they must produce some Master-piece of their own making. And shall we then think, that to succeed in the greatest Art that is, in which the mind has all the share,

Extat illius Comædia, q a nihil aversum magis a comitate; adeo enim insulsa est, ut misericordiam potius quàm risum excitet. Scal. l. 6. c. 3.

Diu non nisi optimus quisque, & qui creden-

and

tem sibi minime fallit, legendus est; sed diligenter aut pene ad scribendi solicitudinem, nec per partes modo scrutanda omnia; sed perlectus liber utique ex integro resumendus. Quintil. l. 10. cap. 1.

and which is not only the hardest, but the least understood Art that we have, there needs nothing, but to have the Impudence to undertake it; no certainly, there goes a great deal more to it, and therefore I will now counsel, as well as I can, any body that undertakes to be a Poet, and tell him, what he is to do.

In the first place, let our Poet suppress all those impetuous desires of glory and applause, and leave thinking, that to make a good Play, 'tis enough to have a vein for Poetry. He must begin with applying himself to the reading of *Aristotle's* Poeticks, and those of *Horace*, and he must read them attentively, and meditate upon them; then he must turn over those that have made Commentaries upon them, as *Castelvetro* in *Italian*, who in his Jargon says very fine things, *Hieronymus Vida*, *Heinsius*, *Vossius*, *la Menardiere*, and a great many more; and let him remember, that *Scaliger* alone says more than all the rest; but he must not lose a word in him, for all his words are of weight and importance. As for the book of *Boulenger*, he must value him only for his Collection of Passages out of other Authors, and not mind the Consequences he draws from them; for I believe for my part that the things he has writ, came into his head just as he was writing them, and without any precedent Meditation.

Horat. de art. poet. verf. 268. Vos exemplaria Græca Nocturnâ versate manu, versate diurnâ.

I add to these Authors *Plutarch*, *Athenæus*, and *Lilius Giraldus*, who all in many places have touch'd the chief Maxims of the Stage; in a word, he must not let slip any thing of the Ancients, without examining every period of them; for very often

a

a word thrown out by the by, and out of the fubject of the Stage, contains in their books fome
important fecret, and the refolution of fome great
difficulty.

Having thus ftudied the Theory, he muft read all
the Greek and Latin Drammatick Poems, which by
good fortune have been preferv'd to our times, as
likewife their old Scholiafts or Commentators, but
ftill take the liberty to examin them impartially,
for they are fubject to a great many Errours, and
delight in falfe and vain fubtleties of no ufe at all;
and all along one muft be fure to make conftant reflexions, and examine why a Poet has rather done
one thing than another, and he may obferve that
often a word ingenioufly caft out by an Actour, to
prepare fome Incident, or to explain the Circumftances of place or time, is not a thing flightly to be pafs'd
over ; and if after all, I durft be fo vain, as to make one
amongft his Mafters, I could wifh he would join
the Precepts of this practical part of the Art, to
what he may difcover in the Ancient or Modern
Poets; for though I cannot brag of giving him confiderable and important fuccours in his Defign, yet I
am fure I fhall not be ufelefs or incommodious to
him, and though it fhould appear that I am miftaken,
yet I am fure he will thank me for the very means I
afford him of inftructing himfelf better.

Our Poet having thus acquir'd a perfect Notion of
the Art of the Stage, may much more certainly,
and with greater fuccefs undertake fome noble
defign.

As

As for me, without repeating here what may be learnt in *Ariftotle*, and his Interpreters, both Ancient and Modern, I will only endeavour to treat of new matters, or at leaft to give new Inftructions upon thofe things, which have been treated of by others.

CHAP.

C H A P. VI.

*Of the Spectators, and how they are
to be confidered by the Poet.*

MY Intention is not here to teach the Spectators
of a Play, the attention that they ought to
have, nor the filence that they ought to keep, no
more than the caution they ought to obferve in judging of the Play ; nor what they fhould do to avoid
thofe Errours which Complaifance, or a Prejudice
againft the Author, often runs them into ; though
all this might be ufefully enough, and to good purpofe, treated of here.

But I onely mention the Spectators in reference
to the Poet, that is, how he ought to confider them
when he is making a Play.

I borrow here the Comparifon of a Picture, of
which I fhall often make ufe in this Treatife ; and I
fay that my Picture may be confidered two
ways.

Firft, as a Picture ; that is, as the work of the Ar-
tift ; where there are Colours, and not real things ;
fhadows, and not fubftances ; artificial lights, falfe
elevations, profpective diftances, or lontananzas, de-
ceiving fhortnings, and in a word, appearances of
things that really are not in the Picture.

F

Secondly,

Secondly, It may be confider'd as containing a Story painted, whether a true one, or fuppos'd to be fo; whereof the Place is certain, the Qualities natural, the Actions undoubtedly true, and all the Circumftances of them obferv'd accordingto order and reafon.

This may be all applyed to Drammatick Poems: One may at firft confider the Shew and Reprefentation of things, where Art gives you Images of them which really are not. There are Princes in appearance; Palaces upon painted cloth, dead men in fhew; and 'tis for this that the Actors carry all the Marks of thofe whom they reprefent. The Decoration of the Stage, is the Image of thofe places where the thing is fuppos'd to be tranfacted. There are Spectators, and the perfons that appear upon the Stage talk in the Mother Tongue of the Audience, all things being to be made fenfible and plain to them. 'Tis to arrive to this Reprefentation of the thing, that the Poet caufes fometimes one, fometimes another Actor to appear, and difcourfe upon the Stage: making recitals of things that ought to be known, and yet ought not to appear; and Employing Machines, and other Contrivances, for the appearance of thofe things which are to be fhew'd to the Audience.

Thus *Efchylus* makes the Palace of *Clytemneftra* open, that the body of *Agamemnon* may be feen upon the Step of the inward door, where a dead man lies along upon the Threfhold. In *Ajax*, *Tecmeffa* opens his Tent to fhew his madnefs, by the number of the dead fheep which lye round about him. In *Euripides*, *Hecuba* fwouns away upon the Stage, to exprefs the greatnefs of her Mifery: And in *Plautus*, the

the Captives exprefs their condition of flavery, by
being bound, and having an appearance of Guards
about them; and after this the difcourfes made
by the Actors, upon thefe different Appearances,
perfect the Reprefentation.

Or elfe we may confider in thefe Dramatick
Poems, the true Hiftory, or that which is fuppo-
fed true, and of which all the Adventures have really come to pafs, in that order, time, and place,
and according to thofe Intrigues which appear to
us. The perfons are there confider'd according to
their different Characters, of their Condition, Age
and Sex; and the things they fay, as having been
really pronounced by them, as well as perform'd
in their actions; and in a word, all things as we
fee them upon the Stage.

I know very well that the Poet is the Mafter,
and that he difpofes the order of his Poem as he
thinks fit; taking the time, which he lengthens or
fhortens as he pleafes; chufing likewife what place
he will in the whole world; and for the Plot he
Invents it according to the ftrength and finenefs
of his own fancy; and in a word, he gives what
form he pleafes to the matter he has in hand; but ftill
'tis certain, that all thefe things muft be fo adjufted,
as to feem to have naturally both the rife, progrefs,
and end which he gives them; fo that though he
be the Author, yet he muft write the whole with
fuch Art, that it may not fo much as appear that
it was by him Invented. So in *Efchylus*'s Trage-
die of *Agamemnon*, all things appear as if really
Agamemnon had been murder'd; and in *Sophocles*,
as if *Ajax* were really furious; and fo of all the
other Pieces of the Ancients. And likewife when

we

we judge of any Play on our Stage, we suppose the thing either true, or that ought to be so, and might be so; and upon that supposition we ap- prove of all the Words or Actions that are done or said by those who speak or act; and of all those E- vents which might probably follow the first Ap- pearances; because that in this case we believe that things might really happen as they seem, nay that they have happened, and ought to happen so. And on the contrary, we condemn all that ought not to be done, or said, according to the qualities of the persons, the place, the time, and the first appearances of the Play.

Now to understand how the Poet is to govern himself, with regard to the Spectators, and when they are to be considerable to him, or not so, we need but reflect upon what we have said of a Pi- cture; for looking upon it only as the Work of the Artist, the Painter does what he can to make it Excellent, because it will be seen, and that he ex- pects to be known and admir'd by it; but if he consider it as a Story painted, he keeps us close as he can to the Nature of the thing he represents, and does nothing but what will seem probable in all its Circumstances, because it is all to be consi- der'd as true, and suppos'd so. For example, if he will draw *Mary Magdelen* in her penitent retire- ment, he will not omit any of the most important parts of her Story, because if he shou'd do other- wise, they that should see it would hardly know it. He must place her in a decent posture, else she will be a disagreeable Object. He will not draw her prostrate and groveling with her face upon the ground, because that would hide the finest part of

her,

her, but rather he muſt ſet her upon her knees.
He ought not to cover her all over with a Cilice, or
haircloth, but leave her half naked, that the Charm
of her beauty may appear the more. He muſt not
place her in the bottom of a deep Cavern, for then
ſhe cannot be ſuppos'd to be ſeen, but at the entrance of it, with ſo much light as is juſt neceſſary;
and this he muſt do, becauſe he conſiders his work
as a Picture which ought to fall under the Senſes,
and pleaſe at the ſame time.

But when he conſiders this Picture the other way,
that is, keeping to the truth of the Story, he muſt
give her a Complexion pale and wan, becauſe it is
not credible it could be otherwiſe in the midſt of
ſo much auſterity; ſhe ſhall not have a Crown before her, but a Croſs; ſhe muſt not be plac'd upon
a rich embroider'd Bed, but upon the ground;
there ſhall not be a Palace near her, but a horrid
Wilderneſs; he muſt not environ her with Pages,
and Women Attendants, but rather with wild Beaſts,
but they muſt be in a quiet poſture, that ſhe may
be ſuppos'd to live among them; the Cave ſhall be
cover'd with Moſs, not gilded and finely ſet out.
The very trees are not to be made full of Flowers and Fruits, but rather half-dryed, and wither'd;
and all the Country about them barren and wild.
And in a word, he ſhall adorn his work with all
thoſe things which probably might become the
ſtate of penitence, according to the perſon, place,
and other dependencies of the Story, becauſe here
he conſiders the truth of what he is to repreſent.

In the ſame manner, the Poet conſidering in
his Play the Repreſentation or Spectacle of it, does
all that he can to make it agreeable to the Spectators;

tors; for his bufinefs is to pleafe them. And therefore he fhall preferve all the nobleft Incidents of his Story, he fhall make all his Actors appear with the beft Characters he can, he fhall employ the fineft Figures of Rhetorick, and the Moving'ft Paffions, obferving to hide nothing that ought to be known and pleafe, and to fhew nothing that ought to be hid, and may offend.; and in fine, he fhall try all means to gain the efteem and admiration of the Audience.

But when he confiders in his Play the true Story of it, or that which is fuppos'd to be fo, he muft particularly have a care to obferve the Rules of probability in every thing, and to make all the Intrigues, Actions, Words, as if they had in reality come to pafs; he muft give fit thoughts and defigns, according to the perfons that are employed, he muft unite the Times with Places, and the Beginning with the Confequences; and in a word, he follows the Nature of things fo, as not to contradict neither the State, nor the Order, nor the Effects, nor the Property of them; and indeed has no other Guide but Probability and Decency, and rejects all that has not that Character upon it. He muft contrive every thing as if there were no Spectators; that is, all the Perfons in the Play are to act and fpeak as if they were truly (for example) a King, and not *Mondoroy* or *Bellerofe*; as if they

Two famous Players.

really were in the Palace of *Horatius* in *Rome*, and not at *Paris* in the *Hoftel de Bourgogne*; and as if no body faw them, or heard them, but thofe who are acting with them upon the Stage. And by this Rule it is that they often fay that they are alone, that no body fees them, nor hears them,
that

that they need not fear being interrupted, or di-
fturb'd in their Solitude, no more than hindred in
their defigns ; though all this is fpoken in the prefence of it may be two thoufand perfons; becaufe in
this the Nature of the Action is followed according
to truth, for then the Spectators were not by ;
and this onght to be ftrictly obferv'd, for all that is
affected in favour of the Spectators is falfe and
faulty.

I know very well that the Poet does not work upon the Action as true, but only fo far as it is fit
for Reprefentation, and therefore it may feem that
there may be fome mixture of thefe two Confiderations, therefore I fhall propound the way how he
fhall diftinguifh them.   He examines firft all that he
defigns to make known to the Audience, either by
their Eyes or their Ears, and accordingly refolves
either to let them fee it, or to inftruct them by fome
recital of the thing which they ought to know.
But he does not make thefe Recitals or Spectacles
onely becaufe the Spectators ought to know or fee.
How then ? Why he muft find in the Action,
which is confider'd as true, fome motive, colour, or
apparent Reafon, for which it may appear that thefe
Shews or Recitals did probably happen, and ought
to come to pafs ; and I may fay that the greateft Art
of the Stage confifts in finding out thefe Motives
or Colours.   An Actor muft come upon the Stage,
becaufe the Spectator muft know his Defigns and
Paffions. There muft be a Narration made of things
paft, becaufe elfe the Spectator being ignorant of
them, would not underftand what's prefent, and under reprefentation.   There muft be a Shew or Spectacle, to move the Audience with pity or admi-
rations ;

ration; and that is working upon the action as reprefented; and it is his duty as well as his chief defign ;
but he muft hide this under fome colour drawn from
the truth of the Action it felf; infomuch, that the
perfon who is to inftruct the Audience, muft come
upon the Stage upon the pretext of looking for
fome body there; or to meet one who had given him an Affignation. So the perfon who is to
make a Narration of things paft, muft do it fo as it
may feem neceffary, and done to advife about fomething in agitation at prefent, for which there is fome
help wanting. If there be a Spectacle, it muft be
to fome end, as to excite fome body to be reveng'd,
or fo; and this is call'd working upon the truth of
the Action, without minding the Spectators ; becaufe 'tis probable, that, taking things only in themfelves. all this might fall out fo.

Let us come to the Examples alledg'd before. *Æfchylus* caufes *Agamemnon* to be murder'd in his Palace; but the Audience muft know this, and how
does he inform them of it? He makes that Unfortunate Prince cry out like a man that expires under
the violence of thofe who murder him. *Sophocles*
obferves the fame thing in the murder of *Clitem-
neftra* by the hand of *Oreftes*. And I cannot but admire at fome who tax both thofe Poets of having
defil'd the Stage with blood, when 'tis apparent
that they are kill'd in the Houfes reprefented upon
the Stage, and out of the fight of the Spectators,
who only hear their cries and lamentations, and fee
the body afterwards when 'tis dead.

In the fame *Sophocles*, *Ajax* is outragioufly furious,
and yet there is a neceffity of his appearing upon
the Stage with *Ulyffes*, without hurting him, and

¶   to

to that end *Minerva* brings him out of his Tent, and suspends for a while his fit of madness.

In *Euripides* the Spectators must know that *Polydorus* is dead, that *Hecuba* may receive a new heightning to her afflictions ; and to do it with appearance of reason, one of her Women goes to fetch water at the Sea side, to wash and purifie the dead body of her Daughter *Polyxena*, whose Funeral she was to perform, where she finds, as it were by chance, the body of the unhappy young Prince, which she brings to his more unhappy Mother, and so discovers very handsomely the series of all that sad Adventure. (And by the by it appears, how much they are mistaken, who think that the Poet sends *Hecuba* her self to the Sea side, and that there she had found the Body of her Son). But we should be bound to too tedious an enumeration, if we would by Examples shew the conduct of the Ancients in this point.

For upon their Stage there is not a Recital, a Passion, nor an Intrigue, that has not its colour ; if you take the Story as true, though it be a Fable invented by the Poet only for Representation. In a word, the Spectators are not considerable to the Poet, in the Truth of the Action, but only in the Representation ; and upon this Maxim, if we examine the best part of our Modern Poets, we may easily perceive, that they go against all probability, even in those things which have been esteem'd the most; Because the Authors, when they expos'd them to the people, did it without any colour that might make us suppose them reasonable. Thus in the truth of the Action it happens that a man makes a necessary Narration, that's well, for the Spectators ought not

G   to

to be ignorant of it ; but this man could not know the very thing he tells, then 'tis against probability for him to make this recital. A Lover appears upon the Stage in a violent passion to please the Spectatours ; but he could not naturally make these complaints in the place represented by the Stage ; there must then some colour be found out for his being there extraordinarily, or else you go against probability : As much may be said of a thousand other Adventures which appear upon our Stages, where every day we have Images of thing s that never were, never can be, and by consequent ought not to be.

CHAP.

CHAP. VII.

Of the Mixture of Representation with the Truth of the Theatral Action.

I Believe the Title of this Chapter will be at firſt ſight ſeverely cenſur'd, becauſe it may be it will not be underſtood; but when I ſhall have explain'd my meaning, I hope all the judicious will be reconcil'd to the Terms, as well as to my Sentiments about the thing.

I call Truth of the Theatral Action, the whole Story of the Play, ſo far as it is conſider'd as a true one, and that all the Adventures in it are look'd upon as being come to paſs. But I call Repreſentation, the Collection of all thoſe things which may ſerve to repreſent a Drammatick Poem, conſider'd in themſelves and in their own Nature, as the Players, the Scenes, the Muſick, the Spectators, and a great many other things. As for Example, in the Play of *Cinna*, made by Monſieur *Corneille*; that that *Cinna*, who appears upon the Stage, ſpeaks like a *Roman*, that he loves *Æmilia*, counſels *Auguſtus Cæſar* to keep the Empire, conſpires againſt him, and is pardon'd by him; all this I ſay, is the truth of the Theatral Action. That the ſame *Æmilia* hates

Auguſtus,

Auguftns, and loves *Cinna*, that fhe defires to be reveng'd, and yet apprehends the Event of fo great an Undertaking; all this too is of the truth of the Action. That *Auguftus* propofes his thoughts of leaving the Empire to two perfidious Friends, and that one advifes him to keep it, and the other to leave it, is likewife of the truth of the Action. In a word, all that in the Play either is confider'd as a part, or has a neceffary dependence upon the Story, ought to be of the truth of the Action; and 'tis by this Rule that one ought to Examine the probability of all that's done in the Play; as the fitnefs and decency of the Expreffions, the connexion of the Intrigue, the patnefs of the Events, &c. And one naturally approves of all that ought to have been don according to the truth, though it be a fuppos'd Story, and one condemns all that one thinks contrary to truth, or not becoming the actions of life.

But that *Floridor* or *Beauchafteau* act the part of *Cinna*, that they are good or ill Actors, well or ill drefs'd, that they are feparated from the people by a Stage, which is adorn'd with painted cloth, reprefenting Palaces and Gardens, that the Intervals of the Acts are mark'd by ill Fidlers, or excellent Mufick; that an Actor goes behind the Stage, when he fays he goes into the Kings Clofet, and fpeaks to his Wife, inftead of fpeaking to a Queen, that there are Spectatours, and thofe either from the Court, or the City; that they are filent or make a noife, that there are quarrels in the Pit, or none, all thefe things are, and do depend on the Reprefentation.

Therefore *Floridor* and *Beauchafteau* are to be look'd

look'd upon as reprefenting, and that *Cinna* or *Horatius*, whom they reprefent, are to be confider'd as real aud true perfons, acting and fpeaking as *Cinna*, and *Horatius*, and not as thofe who reprefent them, and *Floridor* and *Beauchafteau* muft be look'd upon as transform'd into thofe men, whofe names and concerns they take upon them, fo that part of the *Hoftel de Bourgogne* which is rais'd and adorn'd for a Stage, is the place reprefenting, and the Image of another place which is reprefented at that time, whether the Palace of *Auguftus* or *Horatius*; and it muft in the Play be look'd upon as the true place where all things pafs, fo the time which is employed in the Reprefentation, being a part of our natural currant year, is but a reprefenting time, but the day reprefented, and in which one fuppofes the action of the Stage to come to pafs, ought to be taken for a real true time in regard to the Action.

I fay then that one ought never to mingle together what concerns the Reprefentation of a Play, with the true Action of the Story reprefented.

It would not be well lik'd off, that *Floridor*, while he is reprefenting *Cinna*, fhould talk of his own domeftick affairs, or of the lofs and gains of the Playhoufe; or that while he is repeating the Speech made by *Cinna* to the Confpirators at *Rome*, he fhould addrefs himfelf to the People of *Paris*, and make fome Reflections upon them; or that while he is examining the hatred and haughtinefs of *Æmilia*, he fhould go about to talk of the fweetnefs and good breeding of our Ladies; In a word, he would not be endur'd to confound *Rome* and *Paris*, nor actions pafs'd fo many years ago, with prefent Adventures,

ventures ; becaufe that is not only offending againft all the Rules of decency, but thofe of common fenfe.

I know very well that our Modern Poets have not hitherto been very guilty of this fault, but becaufe the Ancients, whom I generally propofe for Examples, have been fo indulgent to the Peoples pleafure, as not to take care to avoid this Errour, I thought it would not be amifs to fay fomething of it, left our Poets fhould follow their Example, after the rate of that fcurvy Orator, whom *Cicero* fpeaks of in *Brutus*, for never imitating the great men in any thing, but fuch things where they were faulty. * *Ariftotle* fays that ill Poets fall into Errors, becaufe they are ignorant of the means of doing better, and that good ones do the fame thing out of Complaifance to the Players, and for the Diverfion of the Audience ; but I think that a true Poet ought not to feek any other way of being profitable to the firft, nor of pleafing the laft, but by the excellence of his Play.

Comedy in its rife, and when it firft begun to be acted, as Tragedy was, by fet Actors, was nothing but a Satyrical Poem, which by little and litle, under pretext of inftructing the People, by inveighing at their Vices, came at laft to be fo bitter and fcandalous, as not onely to expofe the moft Eminent Citizens, but not to fpare the Magiftrates themfelves, nor the moft Illuftrious Perfons of the State, whofe Names, Faces, and actions were brought upon the Stage ; and this was that the Authors call Old Comedy.

Not but that at firft even this was much more innocent than afterwards ; for under *Epicharmus*, and the firſt Comicks who ſucceeded him, Comedy was merry and laughing, but not injurious and affronting; it had Salt and Railleries, but not Gall and Vinegar; but at laſt that liberty degenerated into ſo much libertiniſme, that *Ariſtophanes*'s Plays did not a little contribute to the death of the famous *Socrates* by exciting the People againſt him. The Repreſentation in thoſe days was ſo confounded with the Truth of Action, that they were almoſt the ſame thing; and that which was ſaid againſt the *Socrates* upon the Stage, was often applicable to the *Socrates* who was in the Pit. 'Tis but reading *Ariſtophanes*'s firſt Plays, and you ſhall ſee that all along he confounds the intereſt of the Actors with thoſe of the Spectators, and even the Hiſtory repreſented with the Publick Affairs of the State, upon which he founds his Jeſts and Railleries; In a word, his Plays are down-right Libels, containing the Names, Qualities, Actions, and viſible Portraicts of thoſe whom the Poet undertook to expoſe; and that without any other conduct or rule, but that of his Satyrical wit and paſſion; ſo far were they from being ingenious rational Poems, regulated by Art; and the Magiſtrates foreſeeing the dangerous Effects of ſuch licenſe, forbid them any more naming particular perſons in their Plays.

But as one is always Ingenious in miſchief, the Poets found means, though they left out the Name, to repreſent the Perſon ſo livelily, that every body knew preſently, who they meant; and this was ſince call'd Middle Comedy; and ſuch were the laſt Plays of *Ariſtophanes*.

But this way of Satyr, though ſomewhat milder than the other, was ſtill thought to be of as

ill

ill Confequence, and by the Magiftrates accordingly prohibited. This put the Poets to fome ſtand, and forc'd them at laſt to invent not only the Names, but likewife the Adventures of their Stage, and then Comedy, being an ingenious Product of wit and Art, was regulated upon the model of Tragedy, and became (to define it rightly) the true Picture and Imitation of the Common Actions of life. Then the Reprefentation was no longer confounded with the Truth of the Action, and all that was done upon the Stage was confider'd as a true Story, in which neither the State, nor the Spectators, were ſuppos'd to have any part. The Adventures were generally taken from fome remote Country, with which the place where they were reprefented had little communication, and the Actors feem'd to act only by the confideration of thofe things, which were reprefented. Thus that which came to be call'd New Comedy was made, of which *Terence* was one of the firſt that gave us a Model, and that fo good a one, that it is ne-

Parùm ſeriò res agi videtur, ſi Actores ipſi populum com-pellent. Voſſ. lib. 2. c. 26. ſect. 15. Poet.

ver feen that he ever confounds the Reprefentation with the Truth of the Theatral Action. *Plautus* who went before him, and was nearer the time of Middle Comedy, is not fo regular, but does fo often fall into that inconvenience, that the reading him becomes tedious, and not feldom his Plays are confus'd and obfcure by it.

Act. 3. Sc. 1. Nunc huc hono-ris veſtri ve-nio gratiâ, ne hanc inchoa-tam tranſigam Comædiam, ſi-mul Alcumenæ quam vir &c.

In his *Amphytrion*, *Jupiter* is ſuppos'd to be at *Thebes* in the time that *Hercules* is born, and when he appears under the form of *Amphytrion*, he tells the Spectators, *I am Jupiter, and I am chang'd to* Amphytrion *when I pleafe, which I do,* (fays he to the Spectators) *to oblige you by Continuing this Play,*

and

and for the love of Alcmena that she may appear Inno-
cent. Where we fee he mingles the concerns of the
Actors with the Intereſt of the Spectators, and makes
an Interfering of *Romans* who were preſent, with
thoſe who were ſuppos'd to act in *Greece*, which certainly cannot be but very ridiculous, and muſt confound the underſtanding of the Spectators, by for-
cing them to imagine a man double, and to diſtinguiſh in him both words and ſentiments very different, without any neceſſity or reaſon for it. Certainly when a man appears before us with the
Clothes, Countenance, Words, and Geiture of a
perſon, whom he repreſents, he is not to be conſider'd otherwiſe than according to that Image, which
from our Eyes we imprint in our mind ; and therefore all that unmasks him, to ſhew him, as he really
is, ſuch a Player, whoſe Name is ſo or ſo, confounds
the Attention of the Audience, who expect nothing
from that Actor, but things proper to the perſon
whoſe Appearance he takes.

In his *Aulularia, Euclio* is at *Athens*, where he has
been rob'd, and while he is ſeeking the man that ran
away with his Treaſure, he ſays ſuch things to expreſs his deſpair, that the Audience falls a laughing ;
upon which *Euclio* turning to them, ſays, *why do*
you laugh, I know you all well enough, and know that
amongſt you there are Thieves enough. Now *Euclio*
is ſuppos'd to be at *Athens*, where no *Romans* could
be for Spectators, much leſs could they be ſuſpected
to conceal among them the man that had ſtoln
his Money. He is ſo full of theſe faults, that
there is ſcarce a Play of his without them ; but in
two places the raillery is ſo ingenious, and ſo plac'd

at the end of the Play, without being interwoven in the Story, that it may very well be excused.

Bal. Te sequor, quin vocas Spectatores simul? Pf. Hercle me isti haud solent vccare, neque :rgo ego istos; verùm si voltis applaudere atque approbare hunc gregem & fabulam, in crastinum vos vocabo. Pseudol. Act.5.Sc. 2.

The first is at the end of *Pseudolus,* where his witty Slave having invited *Ballio* to drink with him, he answers, *Why don't you likewise invite these Gentlemen?* pointing to the Spectators ; to which *Pseudolus* replies, *I don't use to invite them, nor they me; but Gentlemen, if you will say that our House and Play pleases you, I invite you again to morrow.*

Spectatores vos quoque ad scenam vocem, ni daturus nihil simyneque sit quicquam polluctizi domi, néue adeò vocatos credam vos esse ad cænam foras. Verùm si Voletis plausum fabulæ huic clarum dare, Comissatum omnes venitote ad me ad annos sexdecim.

The other is at the end of his *Rudens,* where *Dæmones* having invited *Labrax* to Supper, tells the Spectators. *I would invite you too, Gentlemen, but I have little to give him ; and besides I hope you are all engaged; but if you please to give your approbation to this Play, I will Invite you all to sup with me this day sixteen year.*

In these cases, the Action of the Stage being over, the Railleries that are made can no longer confound the *Ideas* of the Spectators.

As for Tragedies, as their subject is more noble and serious, they are seldom infected with this corrupt way; except in *Euripides*'s Prologues, where often the chief Actor, or a God in some Machine, makes a Narration of things happened before the the opening of the Stage. Which I must confess I cannot approve of, because often these things are clear enough in the thread of the Story ; and when Poets do not explain their Subject, by the

Mouth

Mouth and Actions of their Actors, 'tis a fault without excuse, and Prologues are but ill shifts to repair such a neglect. *Sophocles* never does it, and I cannot but advise all Poets to follow him in this.

H 2   CHAP,

C H A P. VIII.

How the Poet muſt make his Decorations, and other Neceſſary Actions in the Play, known to the Audience.

THE moſt remarkable and indeed an eſſential difference between Epick and Dramatick Poems, is, that in the firſt, the Poet ſpeaks alone, the perſons that he produces all uttering themſelves by his mouth ; 'tis he that ſays, that ſuch and ſuch people made ſuch and ſuch diſcourſes, and not they that come and make them themſelves. But in the Dramatick Poem, the Poet is ſilent, and none but the perſons introduc'd by him, do ſpeak ; and during all the Theatral Action, he appears no more than if the perſons were really thoſe whom they repreſent.

Therefore in the Epick Poem, the Poet makes all the deſcriptions that may grace his work, when and where he pleaſes. If he has a mind to ſhew a Temple or a Palace, he frames the Architecture of it according to his own fancy. If there be a ſhipwrack, he expreſſes as he pleaſes the horror of the

Tempeſt

Tempeſt, the fear of the Seamen, the cryes of thoſe who are caſt away, and the conſtancy of his Hero, and for all this he chuſes that place in his Poem, which he thinks fitteſt for theſe or other Deſcriptions.   But in a Dramatick Poem, the Poet muſt ſpeak by the mouth of his Actors, he cannot employ any other means, and what they omit, can no ways be ſupplyed by any induſtry of his ; if there be a Shipwrack, the Actors muſt explain it, and ſpeak of the misfortune of thoſe who have been caſt away; and ſo for any Ornament or Action extraordinary :   They muſt all be explain'd by thoſe whom he brings upon his Stage.   The Ancient Poets have been very exact and judicious in this pàrticular, but our Modern Authors have committed ſuch faults in it, as have much disfigur'd their Plays.

A Play may be regarded two ways; it is made to be acted by perſons, who are to do every thing, as if they were the true perſons repreſented; and likewiſe Plays are made to be read by people, who without ſeeing them acted, can by their imagination, and the ſtrength of the impreſſions the Poet gives, make thoſe perſons as it were preſent to their Idea.   Now whether a Play be acted or read, it muſt be underſtood by the Spectators, and by the Reader ; it cannot be known to the Spectators, but juſt as the Actors ſhall make it ſo ; and the Reader can underſtand no more of it, than the Verſes or Expreſſions do inform him, ſo that either way all the Decorations, Clothes, or neceſſary Motions, for the underſtanding the Play, muſt be had in the Verſes, or other expreſſions in Proſe, which are by the Actors recited.

                                                        To

To this may be said, that our Poets use to be by at the Rehearsals, and so tell the Players every particular that they are to do; but besides the negligence of the Players in the execution of this, how shall any body do, that would act the Play without the Poet? how shall they know where the Scene lies? what Decorations belong to it, and what Clothes the Actors have, and so in any other Circumstances necessary to the understanding and Ornament of the Play? *Eschylus* his Tragedies have been often acted at *Athens*, after he was dead.

The same thing was done by *Plautus's* Comedies at *Rome*; and is done every day at *Paris* by our old Plays; all which could not well have been perform'd, if the Poet had not been careful to explain all things by the Actors. I know indeed that to help the dulness of some Readers, many of our Poets have made Marginal Notes in their printed works, which express that which is not said in the Play; As *here appears a Temple open, here a Palace adorn'd with divers Columns of noble Architecture, here the King whispers his Favourite,* and the like. But in all these Notes 'tis the Poet that speaks, which he is not allowed to do in this sort of Poems, and it cannot be done without interrupting the Reader in the midst of passions, and dividing his application, and so dissipating some of those Ideas which he had receiv'd already for the understanding and relishing the Play.

But I say more than all this, a Play ought to be made with so much Art, and the Actors are to speak so, that it shall not be necessary to marke the distinction of the Acts, nor Scenes, nor so much as to put the Names of those that speak, and to

prove

prove what I fay, we need only to confider, that when an Actor comes upon the Stage, the Poet does not come to tell his name, it muft be known by himfelf, or fome other of the Actors ; and the failing in this has made, that in fome Plays, that I have feen, three Acts were over, before the Audience knew the Name of the chief Actor, and that without any apparent neceffity of hiding either That or his Qualitie ; for fometimes it is neceffary he fhould be *Incognito*, but then 'tis as neceffary that it fhould be known he is fo.

In this particular the Ancients have been fo accurate, that I dare boldly fay, that let one have a Tragedy, either of *Sophocles*, or *Euripides*, or a Comedy of *Terence*, or *Plautus* without Title, Diftinction, Names of the Actors, or any Character particular, to make either Them, or the feparation of the Acts and Scenes known, I would prefently difcover both the Name, Quality, Equipage, Clothes, Gefture, and Interefts of all thofe who fpeak ; the place of the Scene, its decorations, and in a word, all that can make any part of the Theatral Action ; and all Plays, which cannot in the fame manner make all things known to the Reader, are certainly defective. But to do this well, there are many Ingenious Artifices to put fuch words in the mouth of an Actor, as may be a reafonable pretext for him to explain what is neceffary for the underftanding of the Subject ; and thefe following Contrivances may ferve for an Example.

Sometimes the furprize of an Actor is a very agreeable way of doing it ; fo in *Plautus*'s *Curculio*, *Palinurus*, is furprized to fee *Phædromus* come out of his Houfe before day with *Flambeaux* and

Servants

Servants loaden with Bottles of Wine.

Sometimes one employs the compaſſion which he ought to have of the miſerable ſtate of ſome other Actor, as *Electra* in *Euripides* does, to make it known that her Brother was before the Gates of his Palace, laid all along wrap'd up in his Cloke, and tormenting himſelf with his own diſquiets.

It may be done likewiſe by way of raillery; as in the *Trinummus* of *Plautus*, where *Charmides*, to deſcribe the great broad brimm'd Hat of a Cheat, diſguiz'd like a Souldier, ſays, *I believe this fellow is of the race of the Toadſtools, for he is all head.*

Or elſe it may be contriv'd, that two Actors ſhall ſhew one another ſome thing extraordinary; as in the firſt Act of the *Rudens* of *Plautus*, where by that Artifice one is inform'd, that there has been a Shipwrack, that there are ſome perſons yet alive ſwimming to the ſhore, that two women are alone in a ſmall Bark, and are by the Waves carried upon the Sands, where they fall into the Sea, and then getting up again with much ado gain the ſhore.

Sometimes by the Actions themſelves the Actors are ſufficiently known, as in *Euripides*, *Polyphemus* and the Satyrs drinking and growing drunk.

Very often an Actor by a cholerick word or action makes known what another Actor is doing; as in the *Caſina*, *Cleoſtrata* ſeeming angry, makes it appear that her Husband is chucking of her with his hand, to bring her into good humor again. Theſe may ſerve for Examples, many ſuch being obvious to an ingenious Fancy.

Not that a Poet need be very particular neither

ther, he is not bound to make an Exact defcrip-
tion of all the Columns, Portico's, or other Ornaments of Architecture in a Temple or Palace;
'tis enough that he mention in general terms, the
Decoration of his Theatre: And yet when any
Circumftance is to have an Effect in the Play,
then not only he may, but he muft ftay upon it
a little; as in the *Io* of *Euripides*, where it not
being permitted to the Women to go into the
Temple of *Apollo*, they ftay without and talk of
the painting, which made the Ornament of it on
the outfide; and in the *Moftellaria* of *Plautus*,
where *Tranio* defirous to perfwade his Mafter
Theuropides, that he had purchas'd the Houfe of
one of his Neighbours, onely to get fome Money
upon that pretext out of the old Man, he fhews
him the Avenue of it, and makes him obferve
it's Veftibule, Pillars, and other Singularities, which
muft be fuppos'd neceffary in the decoration of
the Stage, when the Play was acted.

There is no neceffity neither that many particulars fhould be explain'd, which are fufficiently underftood by natural Confequence; as when
a Poet fhall make *Horatius* a *Roman* fpeak, he
need not tell us what drefs he is in, nor endeavour to make us admire the Generofity of his
Sentiments; for 'tis of Neceffity, that he fhould
be drefs'd and fpeak like a *Roman*.

Two things, which muft never be forgot for the
underftanding of the Play, are the Time, which
the Poet gives to the Theatral Action, and the
Place where the Scene is laid. The Ancients have
Practis'd this with fo much Art, that often they
that read their Plays hardly take Notice of it at

I   firft;

firſt ; *Plautus* opens the Stage in his *Amphytrio*, at
the end of that long night which *Jupiter* had made
on purpoſe to come and viſit *Alcmena* in, before ſhe
was brought to bed ; which appears clearly by the
diſcourſe of *Soſias*, who complains in the very firſt
Scene of the length of the night, and ſays, *that he
believes Aurora has a Cup too much, and cannot wake
ſoon enough*; and the Play ends before Dinner, as it
appears again by the Order which *Jupiter*, under
the ſhape of *Amphytrio*, gives to *Soſias*, to go and
invite *Blepharo* to Dinner, as ſoon as he ſhall have
finiſh'd his Sacrifice ; for after this Order given, all
the Events are ſo quick, that 'tis plain that all the
Intrigues which perplex'd *Amphytrio* are firſt ſolv'd
and made open.

The ſame Author has been as carefull to expreſs
the place of his Scene, as has been already
ſhew'd in his *Rudens* and *Curculio*; and the ſame is
obſerv'd in the *Frogs* of *Ariſtophanes*, and the *Ajax*
of *Sophocles*.

Very often it happens, that things are not explain'd juſt as they are done, but a good while after ;
as the Poet thinks moſt convenient, and where he
can do it with the leaſt Affectation. I ſhall give no
other example, but that of *Corneille* in his *Andromeda*, where when the winds carry her away, *Phineas* is thrown to the ground by a Thunder-clap, of
which at that time no further notice is taken, but
'tis made known in the ſecond Act, where *Phineas*
complaining of the violence of the Gods againſt the
endeavours he made to ſave *Andromeda*, ſays, That
they were forc'd to ſtrike him to the ground, to
take that occaſion to cary her away.

And ſince I am faln upon this Play, which is a-
dorn'd

dorn'd with fo many Machines, I cannot but obferve, that all the Decorations and extraordinary Actions which are in the third and fifth Act, are very dexteroufly explain'd, and with an Art worthy of a *Grecian* Theatre; but for that great Palace, which makes the Decoration of the firft Act, and that Magnificent Temple, which does the fame in the 4th, I think there is not one word faid by which it may appear that they are there; and I was forc'd, when I read the Play, to have recourfe in thofe places, to the explanation which is before each Act, or elfe I had never known what the Decoration had been; and to fay truth, one may put the Temple in the firft Act, and the Palace in the 4th, and it will do altogether as well, without being oblig'd to any change in the Verfes, or order of the Subject; by which it appears, how requifite it is to explain the Decorations in the Play it felf, to joyn judicioufly the Subject with the Place, and Actions with Things, and fo make a Total full of fymmetry and ornament in all its parts.

The End of the Firft Book.

I 2 THE.

THE
Whole Art
OF THE
STAGE.

The Second BOOK.

CHAP. I.

Of the Subject of Dramatick Poems.

Upposing here what the Poet ought to know of that part of a *Drama*, which the Ancients call'd the *Fable*; we, the Story or Romance; and I in this place, the Subject: I will onely say that for Subjects meerly invented, and of which one may as well make a Trage-dy as a Comedy; if they do not take, 'tis perfectly

the

the Poets fault, and a fault without excufe or pretext, which he can never clear himfelf of; for being
Mafter as well of the Matter as of the Form, the
mifcarriage of the Play can be attributed to nothing,
but to his want of Conduct in the thing, and to the
Errors of his own Imagination. But as for Subjects drawn from Story, or from the Fables of the
Ancients, he is more excufable if he miffes of
fuccefs in the Reprefentation of them, for he
may be many ways conftrain'd; as if a great
man command him to preferve certain Circumftances, not fo fit for the Stage, or that he
does it himfelf out of fome confideration more important to him than the Glory of being a good
Poet would be. But if he be free in his choice, he
may be fure that he fhall be blam'd if his Play does
not take, it being certain, that Art out of an ill Story
may make an excellent *Drama*; as for Example,
if there be no Plot, the Poet muft make one; if it
be too intricate, he muft make it loofer and eafier;
if too open and weak, he muft ftrengthen it by Invention, and fo for the reft. On the other fide,
there is no Story fo rich in it felf, but an ill Poet
may fo fpoil the beauty of it, that it will hardly be
known to be the fame Story.

Befides, one is not to think, that all fine Stories
are fit to appear with fuccefs upon the Stage; for
very often the beautifulleft part of them depends
upon fome Circumftance, which the Theatre cannot fuffer; and it was for this, that I advis'd one
who had a mind to undertake the Loves of *Antiochus* and *Stratonica*, to let it alone; for the moft
confiderable incident in it, being the cunning of the
Phyfician in difcovering the Prince's Paffion, by
caufing

caufing all the Ladies in the Court to pafs one by
one before the Princes Bed, that fo by the emotion
of his Pulfe, he might judge which of them it was,
that caufed his Difeafe ; I thought it would be very
odd, to make a Play where the Hero of it fhould always be a bed, and that it would be hard to change
the Circumflance fo, as to preferve the Beauty of
it ; and that befides, the Time and Place of the
Scene would be difficult to bring together ; for if *Antiochus* be fuppos'd fick a bed in the morning, 'twould
be improbable to lay much action upon him all the
reft of that day ; and to place the Scene in a fick
mans Chamber, or at his door, would be as
unlikely.

'Twas for the fame Reafon, that the *Theodora* of
Corneille had not all the approbation it deferv'd :
'Tis in it felf a moft ingenious Play ; the Plot being
well carried, and full of variety ; where all the
hints of the true Story are made ufe of to advantage,
the Changes and Turns very judicious, and the Paffions and Verfe worthy the Name of fo great a man.
But becaufe the whole bufinefs turns upon the Profti-
tution of *Theodora* to the Publick Stews, it could
never pleafe ; not but that the Poet, in that too, has
taken care to expofe things with great modefty and
nicety ; but ftill one is forc'd to have the Idea of
that ugly Adventure fo often in ones Imagination,
particularly in the Narrations of the 4th Act, that
the Spectators cannot but have fome difguft
at it.

There are a hundred Stories like thefe, and harder yet to manage for the Stage ; and likewife on
the contrary there are lucky ones, which feem to
have

have happened on purpofe; as that of *Sophonisba*, who is a Widow, and married again, lofes her kingdom, and recovers it all in a day.

The way therefore of chufing a Subject, is to confider whether it be founded upon one of thefe three things ; either upon Noble Paffions, as *Mariamne* and the *Cid*; or upon an intricate and pleafing Plot, as *Cleomedon*, or the *Difguis'd Prince* ; or upon fome extraordinary Spectacle and Show, as *Cyminda*, or the *Two Victims* ; and if the Story will bear more Circumftances of this nature, or that the Poets imagination can fitly fupply the Play with them, it will be ftill the better ; provided, he obferve a juft moderation, for though a Poem ought not to be without a Plot, nor without Paffions, or noble Spectacles, yet to load a Subject with any of them, is a thing to be avoided. Violent Paffions, too often repeated, do as it were numm the Soul, and its Sympathy; the multitude of Incidents and Intrigues diftract the Mind, and confound the Memory ; and much Show takes up more time than can be allowed it, and is hard to bring on well. 'Tis for this reafon, that fome of our Poets who had contriv'd in every Act a memorable Incident, and a moving Paffion, did not find that the fuccefs anfwer'd their Expectation.

If I am ask'd, what is the meafure of employing thofe things ? I fhall anfwer, 'tis every ones natural judgment; and it may happen that a *Drama* may be fo luckily contriv'd, that the preparation of the Incidents, and the variety of the Paffions, fhall correct the defect of the abundance of them; and that the Art of the Machines fhall be fo well underftood, that they may eafily be made ufe of in

every

every Act, as I formerly propounded to Cardinal *Richelieu*, but hitherto they are little in use in our ordinary Theatres.

'Tis besides most commonly ask'd here, how far the Poet may venture in the alterations of a true Story, in order to the fitting of it for the Stage. Upon which we find different Opinions among both the Ancient and Modern Criticks; but my Opinion is, that he may do it not only in the Circumstances, but in the Principal Action it self; provided he make a very good Play of it: For as the Dramatick Poet does not much mind the time, because he is no Chronologist; no more does he, nor the Epick Poet, much mind the true Story, because they are no Historians; they take out of Story so much as serves their turn, and change the rest; not expecting that any body should be so ridiculous as to come to the Theatres to be instructed in the truth of History.

Arist. c. 15. Quis nescit omnibus Epicis Poëtis historiam esse pro argumento? quam illi aut adumbratam, aut illustratam, certè alia facie quam ostendunt, ex historia conficiunt Poëma. Nam quid aliud Homerus? quid tragicis ipsis faciemus? Scal. l. 1. c. 2.

The Stage therefore does not present things as they have been, but as they ought to be ; for the Poet must in the Subject he takes reform every thing that is not accommodated to the Rules of his Art ; as a Painter does when he works up on an imperfect Model.

'Twas for this Reason that the death of *Camilla* by the hands of her Brother *Horatius* was never lik'd of upon the Stage, though it be a true Adventure, and I for my part gave my Opinion, that to save in some measure the truth of the Story, and yet not to offend against the decency of the Stage, it would have been better that that Unfortunate Maid, seeing her Brother come towards her with his Sword drawn, had run upon it of her self; for by that

K   means

means she would still have dyed by the hand of *Horatius*, and yet she might have deserved some compassion, as unfortunate but innocent, and so the Story and the Stage would have been agreed.

In a word, The Historian ought to recite matter of Fact, and if he judges of it, he does more than he ought to do; the Epick Poet is to magnifie all Events by great Fictions, where truth is as it were sunk and lost; and the Dramatick Poet ought to shew all things in a state of decency, probability, and pleasingness. 'Tis true, that if Story is capable of all the Ornaments of Dramatick Poetry, the Poet ought to preserve all the true Events; but if not, he is well grounded to make any part of it yield to the Rules of his Art, and to the Design he has to please.

Hinc Horatius cum dixisset, Famam sequare, quod pertinent ad τὸ ὅμοιον. Voss. lib 1. c. 5. Many against this do alledge the Authority of *Horace*, who sayes, *that he ought in Story to follow the common receiv'd Opinion, or at least to invent things that may be as conformable to it as possible.* But I answer, that *Horace* in that place does not treat of the Subject of the Play, but of the Customs and Morals that ought to be given the Actors; who ought not to be represented different from what they were believed; as it would be to make *Cæsar* a Coward, or *Messalina* chaste; and this *Vossius* has well observ'd in his *Poetick Art*, and I wonder that people should be abus'd by Citations applyed quite contrary to the Sense of the Author; and yet I am not of opinion that a known Story, yet fresh in the minds of the People, can suffer to be considerably chang'd, without great caution: but in such a case I should advise the Poet rather to abandon such a subject, than to make an ill Play of
it,

it, out of a humour of following truth; or at leaſt to manage it ſo, as not to check directly the re-ceiv'd Opinion among the Vulgar. If we examine well the Senſe of *Ariſtotle*, I believe he will be found to be of this Opinion; and as for the Ancient Poets they have always taken that Liberty, the ſame Story having hardly ever been treated the ſame way by different Poets. As for example, The Adventures of *Polydorus* are very different in *Euripides* and *Virgil*. *Sophocles* kills *Emon* and *Antigone*, but *Euripides*, who has made the ſame Story in two Plays, marrys them together in one; contrary to what he himſelf had done before in the other call'd, The *Phænician* Ladies. The ſame *Sopho-cles* in *Oedipus* makes *Jocaſta* ſtrangle her ſelf, and *Euripides* makes her live 'till the combat of her Sons *Eteocles* and *Polynices*, and then kill her ſelf upon their dead bodies. *Oreſtes* and *Electra* are ve-ry different in many Circumſtances, though both Works of the ſame Poet. In a word, the four Tragick Poets of the *Greeks*, whoſe Works we have, are all different in the diſpoſition of the ſame Stories, and I believe that they were the cauſe of that grand diſorder and confuſion there is in Story and Chronology in thoſe old times, becauſe that they having chang'd both the Times and Events for their own ends, they have influenc'd ſome Hiſtorians, who thought to pick out of them the truth of Story, and ſo made all things uncer-tain; any body that will read the *Electra* of *Eu-ripides*, that of *Sophocles*, and the *Cœphores* of *Æſchi-lus*, will eaſily ſee that they made no difficulty of contradicting one another, and themſelves.

As for the different kinds of Subjects, letting

alone

alone thofe ordinary divifions of *Ariftotle*, and his Commentators, I here propofe three forts of Subjects

The firft confifts of Incidents, Intrigues, and new Events, when almoft from Act to Act there is fome fudden change upon the Stage, which alters all the Face of Affairs; when almoft all the Actors have different Defigns; and the means they take to make them fucceed come to crofs one another, and produce new and unforefeen Accidents, all which gives a marvellous fatisfaction to the Spectators, it being a continual diverfion, accompanied with an agreeable Expectation of what the Event will be.

The fecond fort of Subjects are of thofe rais'd out of Paffions; when out of a fmall Fund the Poet does ingenioufly draw great Sentiments and noble Paffions, to entertain the Auditory: and when out of Incidents that feem natural to his Subject, he takes occafion to tranfport his Actors into extraordinary and violent Sentiments, by which the Spectators are ravifh'd, and their Soul continually mov'd with fome new Impreffion.

The laft fort of Subjects are the mixt or compound of Incidents and Paffions, when by unexpected Events, but Noble ones, the Actors break out into different Paffions; and that infinitely delights the Auditory, to fee at the fame time furprizing Accidents, and noble and moving Sentiments, to which they cannot but yield with pleafure.

Now tis certain, that in all thefe three forts of Subjects the Poet may fucceed, provided the difpofition of his Play be ingenious; but yet I have
obferv'd

obferv'd fome difference, according to which they take more or lefs.

Subjeƈts full of Plot and Intrigue are extreme agreeable at firft, but being once known, they do not the fecond time pleafe us fo well, becaufe they want the graces of Novelty, which made them charm us at firft, all our delight confifting in being furpriz'd, which we cannot be twice.

The Subjeƈts full of Paffions laft longer, and affeƈt us more, becaufe the Soul which receives the impreffion of them, does not keep them fo long, nor fo ftrongly, as our Memory does the Events of things; nay, often it happens, that they pleafe us more at fecond feeing, becaufe that the firft time we are employed about the Event and Difpofition of the Play, and by confequent do lefs enter into the Sentiments of the Aƈtors; but having once no need of applying our thoughts to the Story, we bufie them about the things that are faid, and fo receive more Impreffions of grief or fear.

But it is out of doubt, that the mix'd or compound are the moft excellent fort, for in them the Incidents grow more pleafing by the Paffions which do as it were uphold them, and the Paffions feem to be renew'd, and fpring afrefh, by the variety of the unthought of Incidents; fo that they are both lafting, and require a great time to make them lofe their Graces.

We are not to forget here (and I think it one of the beft Obfervations that I have made upon this Subjeƈt) that if the Subjeƈt is not conformable to the Cuftoms and Manners, as well as Opinions of the Speƈtators, it will never take, what pains foever the Poet himfelf take, and whatfoever Ornaments he employs to fet his Play off. For all Dramatick Poems muſt be different, according to the People before whom they are reprefented; and from thence often proceeds that the fuccefs is different, though the Play be ſtill the fame. Thus the *Athenians* delighted to fee upon their Theatre the Cruelties of Kings, and the Misfortunes befalling them, the Calamities of Illuſtrious and Noble Families, and the Rebellion of the whole Nation for an ill Action of the Prince, becaufe the State in which they liv'd being Popular, they lov'd to be perfwaded that Monarchy was always Tyrannical, hoping thereby to difcourage the Noble Men of their own Commonwealth from the attempt of feizing the Soveraignty, out of fear of being expos'd to the the fury of a Commonalty, who would think it juſt to murther them. Whereas quite contrary among us, the refpect and love which we have for our Princes, cannot endure that we fhould entertain the Publick with fuch Spectacles of horrour; we are not willing to believe that Kings are wicked, nor that their Subjects, though with fome appearance of ill ufage, ought to Rebel againſt their Power; or touch their Perfons, no not in *Effigie*; and I do not believe that upon our Stage a Poet could caufe a Tyrant to be murder'd with any applaufe, except he had very cautioufly laid the thing. As for Example, that the Tyrant were an Ufurper, and the right Heir fhould appear, and be own'd by the People, who fhould take that occafion to revenge the injuries they had fuffer'd from the Tyrant; but Ufurpation alone, againſt the will of the People, would not juſtifie without horrour the death of the Soveraign by the hands of his rebellious Subjects. We have

seen

seen the tryal of it in a Play call'd *Timoleon,* whom no confideration of State or common Good, no love nor generofity towards his Country, could hinder from being confidered as the Murderer of his Brother and his Prince; and for my part I efteem that Author who avoided to have *Tarquin* kill'd upon the Stage, after the violence he had offer'd to *Lucretia.* The cruelty of *Alboin* infpir'd horrour into the whole *French* Court, though o-therwife it were a Tagedy full of noble Incidents and lofty Language.

We have had upon our Stage the *Efther* of Mr. *Du Ryer,* adorn'd with great Events, forti-fied with ftrong Paffions, and compos'd in the whole with great Art; but the fuccefs was much unluckier at *Paris,* than at *Roüen*; and when the Players at their teturn to *Paris* told us the good fortune they had had at *Roüen,* every body won-dred at it, without being able to guefs the caufe of it; but for my part I think that *Roüen,* being a Town of great Trade, is full of a great Num-ber of *Jews,* fome known, and fome conceal'd, and that by that reafon they making up a good part of the Audience, took more delight in a piece which feem'd entirely *Jewifh,* by the Conformity it had to their Manners and Cuftoms.

We may fay the fame thing of Comedies; for the *Greeks* and *Romans,* with whom the Debauches of young People with *Curtizans* was but a laughing matter, took pleafure to fee their Intrigues repre-fented, and to hear the difcourfes of thofe pub-lick Women, with the tricks of thofe Minifters of their Pleafures countenanc'd by the Laws. They were alfo delighted to fee old covetous men

over

over-reach'd, and cheated of their money, by the circumvention of their Slaves, in favour of their young Masters ; they were sensible to all these things, because they were subject to them one time or another; but amongst us all this would be ill received ; for as Christian Modesty does not permit persons of Quality to approve of those Examples of Vice, so neither do the Rules by which we govern our Families allow of those flights of our Servants, nor do we need to defend our selves against them. 'Tis for the same Reason that wee fee in the *French* Court, Tragedies take a great deal better than Comedies; and that on the contrary, the People are more affected with the latter, and particularly with the Farces and Buffooneries of the Stage; for in this Kingdom the persons of good Quality, and Education, have generous thoughts and designs, to which they are carrried either by the Motives of Vertue or Ambition, so that their life has a great Conformity with the Characters of Tragedy ; but the people, meanly born and durtily bred, have low Sentiments, and are thereby dispos'd to approve of the meaness and filthiness represented in Farces, as being the Image of those things which they both use to say and do ; and this ought to be taken notice of, not only in the principal part of the Poem, but in all its parts, and particularly in the Passions, as we shall say more amply in a Chapter about them ; for if there be any Act or Scene that has not that conformity of manners to the Spectators, you will suddenly see the applause cease, and in it's place a discontent succeed, though they themselves do not know the cause of it. For

the

the Stage and Eloquence are alike in this, that their Perfections and Faults are equally perceiv'd by the Ignorant and by the Learned, though the cause is not equally known to them.

L   CHAP.

C H A P. II.

Of Probability and Decency.

The French word is vray-semblance, *for which we have not an English word Expressive of all its Sense.*

HEre is the bottom and ground work of all Dramatick Poems; many talk of it, but few underftand it; but this is the general touchſtone, by which all that comes to paſs in a Play is to be tryed and examin'd, and it is the very Eſſence of the Poem, without which nothing rational can be done or ſaid upon the Stage.

Syneſ in Caluit. encom. p. 72. e-dit. Pariſ. an. 1612.

'Tis a general Maxim, that Truth alone is not the Subject of our Theatres, becauſe there are many Truths which ought not to be ſeen, and many that cannot be repreſented publickly; therefore *Syneſius* has ſaid very well, that Poetry and other Arts, founded in Imitation, follow not Truth but the common Opinion of men. It is very true, that *Nero* caus'd his Mother to be murder'd, and then had her cut up to ſee the place, where he had lain nine Months before he was born; but this Barbarity, though pleaſant to him that executed it, would yet be not only horrible to thoſe, to whom it ſhould be ſhew'd, but incredible becauſe ſuch a thing ought not to have come to paſs: I believe that amongſt the great number of Stories, from which the Poet may take Subjects,

Subjects, there is hardly any one which in all its true Circumftances is fitted for the Stage, fo as to be reprefented without altering fomething of the Event, the Time, the Perfons, and many other particulars.

That which is fimply poffible is left a Subject for Plays, for many things may come to pafs by the rencounter of Natural Caufes (or the adventures of humane Life) which yet would be ridiculous, and almoft incredible, to be reprefented. 'Tis poffible that a Man may dye fuddenly, and that happens often; but That Poet would be ftrangely laugh'd at, who to rid the Stage of a troublefome Rival, fhould make him dye of an Apoplexy, as of a common Difeafe; and it would need exceeding ingenious and artful preparations.

There is nothing therefore but *Probability*, that can truly found a Dramatick Poem, as well as adorn and finifh it; not that True and Poffible things are banifh'd off the Stage, but they are received upon it, only fo far as they are Probable; and therefore all the Circumftances, that want this Character, are to be alter'd fo as to attain it, if they hop'd to appear in publick.

Res effe oporct in ipfis etia Comœdijs adm dumverifimiles, ut tametfi fictā reprefentari magis quam fingi videantur Scal. lib.6. cap 3.

I fhall not here expatiate upon ordinary and extraordinary Probability, the Mafters of the Art have made ample Treatifes about it; and no body is ignorant, that things naturally impoffible become poffible, and even probable, by the Power of God Almighty, or That of the Devil; and that the Probability of the Stage does not oblige to reprefent only thofe things which happen according to the common courfe of Humane Life, but likewife gives leave to launch into the wonderful Accidents of it,

L 2   which

which makes the Events fo much the more furprifing, if they are (ftill probable ; but that which I have obferv'd in this matter) is , That few have underftood, how far this Probability ought to reach ; every body indeed believing that it ought to be obferv'd in the principal Action of the *Poem*, and likewife in the moft fenfible Incidents of it , but they went no further.   Now is it moft certain, that the leaft Actions, brought upon the Stage, ought to be probable, or elfe they are entirely faulty, and fhould not appear there.   There is no Action of Humane Life fo perfectly fingle, as not to be accompanied by many little Circumftances, which do make it up ; as are the Time, the Place, the Perfon, the Dignity, the Defigns, the Means, and the Reafons of the Action ; and fince the Stage ought to be a perfect Image of Action , it ought to reprefent it entire, and that Probabilty and Decency be obferv'd in all its parts.   When a King fpeaks upon the Stage , he muft fpeak like a King, and that is the Circumftance of his Dignity, againft which nothing ought to be done with Decency ; except there be fome other reafon to difpenfe with this laft, as that he were in difguife.   Befides, without doubt a King fpeaking according to his Dignity muft be fuppos'd to be fomewhere , and therefore the Stage muft carry the Image of the place where he then was, for there are things which in Probability ought not to be done or faid, but in certain places.   It ought alfo to appear, in what time he fpoke , for one ought to fpeak differently in different times, as a Prince before he gives Battel, will fpeak otherwife than after he has won it, or loft it.

Therefore

Therefore to preserve this Probability in the Circumstances of the Treatral Action, the Poet must be Master of the Rules of the Stage, and Practise them, for they teach nothing else, to make all the parts of an Action appear with Probability and Decency, and to represent a whole and entire Image of them.

To this some have said, That Reason and Common Sense are sufficient of themselves to Judge of all these things. I grant it, but it must be Reason and common Sense, instructed in the affairs of the Stage, and in what is design'd to be represented: For suppose, that a Man of good Sense should have never seen nor heard of a Play, and be brought to see one, without being told what it is he is carried to; 'tis certain that he will hardly know, whether the Players be true Kings and Princes, or only the Images of them; and when he does know, that all that is but a Fiction, yet will he scarce be able to judge of the Faults or Perfections of the Play, without making many Reflections to consider, whether what is represented be profitable or no? For to judg perfectly of a Dramatick Poem, our Natural Reason must be instructed and inured to that kind of Images, which are made use of by men to represent any Action, and know precisely, how Probability is to be preserved in all the strokes of this animated Picture; and that cannot be attained to, but by a great number of Observations made by length of time and different Persons. The Art of the Stage was by these Observations framed by the Ancients, and had so flow'd Progress, that from *Thespis*, who first added an Actor to the Chorus, who before that acted Tragedies alone, to the time of *Aristotle*, who reduced these Rules into an Art, there passed two
hundred

hundred years : He therefore that, on a fudden without ſtudy or reflection, will pronounce his Judgment of a Play, will often find himſelf miſtaken ; becauſe 'tis very hard he ſhould have before his Eyes on a fudden all thoſe Conſiderations, which are requiſite to examine the Probability of what has been repreſented ; and it has often happened, that People of very good underſtanding have at firſt commended ſome Actions of the Stage for well invented things, which upon being better informed, they have found contrary to all Probability and Ridiculous.

But it is a much ſtranger thing, and yet very true, that I have ſeen People, who had for many years compos'd Plays themſelves, read a Play of anothers, and that over and over again, and yet never find out the length of time, nor the place of the Scene, nor many of the Circumſtances of the moſt important Actions, ſo as to judge whether they were probable or not. *Heinſius* himſelf, though very Learned, and who has publiſhed the Art of compoſing Tragedies, is ſo far miſtaken in the *Amphitryon* of *Plautus*, as to think it contains nine Months, though it do not really contain above eight hours, and at leaſt is comprehended between Midnight and Noon the day following. *Voſſius*, one of the moſt Learned of our time, and very underſtanding in the Art of Poetry, writes as He does, that *Plautus* in his *Amphytrion* makes *Hercules* be conceived and born in one Night, though 'tis certain he ſuppoſes him Conceived ſeven Months before ; and *Mercury* ſays it twice expreſly in the Play ; therefore I think my ſelf bound to give my Readers warning, that of all that that excellent man has made,

there

Plautus novem menſes uno Dramate complexus eſt, ut vix maior ampliorque Homericæ Iliados quam Amphitryonis ſit periodus : Alcumena autem concipit & parit ; quod ſi fieret, iam nullo epiſodio opus eſſet, ideoque nec ars eſſet comœdiam ſcribere.
Heins. in Horat.
Voſſ. lib.2.c.3.

there is nothing to be so carefully avoided, as his Third Chapter of his First Book, where he treats of the Errors of Poets, and pretends to Correct the Ancients. for he himself falls into much greater. *Scaliger* has said in two places, that in *Æschylus*, *Prometheus* is kill'd by a Thunder-Bolt, and yet 'tis certain that he is only carried away in the storm , and that appears by the words of *Prometheus*, and those of *Mercury*, who both say it clearly enough. There are those who have read *Æschylus* over and over, and yet have been so negligent in observing of him, that they believe (and amongst them, the Author of the Argument of his *Agamemnon* is one) that he makes *Agamemnon* be murdered upon the Stage , though it be said by the Chorus, that they hear the Cries and Lamentations he makes in his Palace, and are ready to break in, to see whats the matter ; from which Resolution they are diverted by the Arrival of *Clytemnestra*, who comes and tells, how she had with her own hand committed that Cruel action. Many Learned Men have said, That the Third Comedy of *Terence* contained two days ; *Scaliger*, *Muretus*, *Vossius*, *F. Membrun*, and others have been of that Opinion ; but it does not contain above ten hours, as I have made it appear, in my Dissertation of *Terence Justified*. And Monsieur *Menage*, who writ upon this Subject, only to contradict Truth out of Malignity, has not dar'd to allow it above 14 or 15 hours, and to compass that, he has been fain, to pervert the Order of the *Athenian* Months, that he might shorten the day, and lengthen the night, and so overthrow the Oeconomy of Nature, to find some Fault with the Disposition of the Play.

Ridicule se dat Plautus, cum in Amphitryone fingat eadem die Alcumenam & concipere & parere.

Hodie illa pariet filios geminos duos, alter decumo post mense nascetur puer quam seminatus est ; alter mense septumo.

Amphitry. Act. 1. sc. 2.

Lib. 7. c. 4. Poet. & lib. 3. c. 97.

ἰδίως δὲ Αἰχύλ⟨Θ⟩ τὸν Ἀγα. μέμνονα ἐπὶ σκηνῆς ἀναιρεῖσθαι ποιεῖ.

Arg. Agam. Æschyl.

I

I have feen fome others, whom I had much diffi-culty to perfwade, that in the *Phœnicians* of *Euri-pides*, the *Electra* of *Sophocles* , and the *Clouds* of *Ariftophanes*, the Unity of place was obferved ; fo much do old Errors fometimes blind us : And fo true it is, that in this Art, as well as in all others, our natural Reafon needs the knowledge of the Rules of the Art, to judge well of the Perfection or Faults of the product of the Art, and I dare boldly fay, that whoever fhall read this Treatife, fhall condemn ma-ny things which they formerly thought very Ratio-nal.

C H A P.

C H A P. III.

Of the Unity *of* Action.

'TIS one of *Ariftotle*'s Rules, and without doub-
a very Rational one , that a Dramatick Po
em ought to comprehend but one Action ; and he
does very pertinently condemn thofe, who make a
Play of the whole Story, or Life of a Hero.┐ For
though we fpeak but of one principal Part , on
which all the other Events, bad and good, do depend; yet there are divers fubordinate Actions. But
to explain this more particularly , I will here give
the Reafon of this Rule, as I apprehend it ; and how
likewife one may comprehend upon the Stage divers Incidents in one Action.

'Tis certain, that the Stage is but a Picture or I-
mage of Humane Life; and as a Picture cannot
fhew us at the fame time two Originals, and be an
accomplifhed Picture : ⟦It is likewife impoffible that
two Actions, I mean principal ones , fhould be reprefented reafonably by one Play.⟧ Let us confider
what the Painter does, who is to make a Picture of
fome Story ; he has no other defign, but to give the
Image of fome Action, and that Action is fo limit-
ted, that it cannot reprefent two parts of a Story together , and lefs all the Story upon which he has
fix'd ; becaufe it would be neceffary that the fame
Perfon fhould be Painted , and appear in different
M   places,

places, which would make a ſtrange Confuſion
in the whole Picture, and it would be hard to diſtinguiſh any Order amongſt ſo many different Actions; and by conſequent, the Story would be very obſcure and confuſed: Therefore inſtead of that, the
Painter would chuſe, amongſt All the Actions which
made up the Story, the moſt important One, and
the fitteſt for the Excellency of his Art, and which
in ſome meaſure ſhould contain all the others; ſo
that with one look one might have a ſufficient knowledge of all that he deſigned to expreſs; and if he
deſired to expreſs two parts of the ſame Story, he
would make in ſome corner of the Picture a Lontananza, where he would paint that other Action,
which he had a mind to repreſent, that he might
make it be underſtood, that he deſign'd the painting
of two different Actions, and that it was two Pictures, and not one.

As for Example, Suppoſe he deſigned to draw
the Story of *Iphigenia*, it would be hard for him to
comprehend in one Picture, all the Adventures of
that Princeſs; [therefore he would chuſe that of the
Sacrifice,] which the *Greeks* were going to make of
her to *Diana*, to appeaſe her Anger, and the ſtorms
of the Sea; for in this Action her whole Story
would in ſome meaſure be comprehended. The
ſtorms of the Sea, which kept the Fleet in the Port
of *Aulide*, would be conſidered as the Cauſe; the
Grief of her Father, and the Compaſſion of the other *Grecian* Princes, would be the Circumſtances;
and her being carried away by that Goddeſs her ſelf,
as an extraordinary Favour, by which ſhe was to be
ſav'd; and the if he had a mind to expreſs that
Diana carried her to *Tauris*, where ſhe was upon
the

the point of Sacrificing her Brother *Orestes*, he would put her in one of the Corners of his Picture, in the particular dress of *Diana's* Priestess, with some other marks of this second Adventure, and so make two Pictures of two different Actions of the same Story.

The Dramatick Poet must imitate the Painter, and when he undertakes the Composition of a Play, he must reckon that he undertakes to make a living speaking Picture, and that therefore he cannot comprehend in it a whole History, or the Life of an *Hero*, because he would be necessitated to represent an infinite number of Events, and employ a vast number of Actors, and mingle so many things, that he would make up a work of perfect Confusion, and would be forc'd in most places to offend against Probability and Decency, and to go beyond the time and extent, ordinarily allowed to Dramatick Poems; or if he would keep within the limits of the *Rules* of his Art, he would be forced to hasten all the Incidents, and as it were heap them one upon another, without either Graces or Distinction, and so be obliged to stifle and suppress all the Passionate strokes; and in a word, shew such a Monstrous Extravagant Image, as They have done, who have represented in the First Act of a Tragedy, the Marriage of a Princess; in the Second, the Birth of her Son; in the Third, the Amours of that young Prince; in the Fourth, his Victories; and in the Fifth, his Death; in all which there was matter enough for above twenty Plays. Our Poet therefore, amidst this vast extent, shall pitch upon some one remarkable Action; and as one may say, a point of Story, notable by the Happiness or Misfortune of

some

some Illustrious Person, in which point he may comprehend, as Circumstances, all the rest of the Story, and (by representing one chief part make the whole known by some sleight to the Spectators, without multiplying the principal Action) and without retrenching any of the necessary Beauties to the perfection of his Work; and if by chance he should meet in the same Story with two or more Actions, so considerable, that they each of them deserved a Play, and so independent or opposite to each other, as not to be reconciled; he ought to make Two or More plays of them, or chuse the most Important, and particularly, the most Pathetick for his Subject.

Thus the *Suppliants* of *Euripides* do not contain the whole War of *Thebes*, but only the Burial of the two Princes of *Argos*. *Hecuba* contains not the taking of *Troy*, but the last misfortunes of that Queen in her Captivity. The *Ajax* of *Sophocles*, shews not all the Exploits of War of that Hero, nor his Disputes with *Ulysses* for the Arms of *Achilles*, but only represents his madness, which was the cause of his Death; and so we may say of most of the ancient Plays. But in all these the Poets have shewed so much Art, as to instruct the Spectators, either by Narrations, Discourses, Complaints, or other sleights of the Art, in all the Circumstances of those Stories which they treated.

As likewise, when the Subjects, that fell into their Hands, were of too great an Extent to be comprehended in one Play, and having in them many Actions of equal importance, they have made different Pictures of that, which could not be comprehended under one Image.

Euripides

Euripides has not confounded the Sacrifice of *Iphigenia* in *Aulis*, with the Adventures of the fame Princefs in *Scythia*. *Æfchylus* in one Play caufes *Agamemnon* to be murdered by *Clytemneftra*; and in another brings her to punifhment for it ; and from thence it comes amongft the Ancients, many Plays have the fame Name, and often many Events of the fame Story are reprefented in different Plays, which indeed was fome ways neceffary in *Athens* ; for as their Poets were to work for the Solemnity of the four great Feafts or Holy-days, and to have four Plays for each of them ; of which there were three to be Serious, and the fourth Satyrical or Comical, which made up the *Tetralogy*. I am of Opinion, they took all their Subjects from the fame Story, as I have fhewed more at length in my *Terence Jufti-fied.*

Now, as to the manner of bringing many diffe-rent Incidents into one Action, and to make a Po-em of them, which fhall naturally contain many Acts, and different Scenes ; to explain this well, I return to the comparifon of Painting, which I have fo often us'd already.

We have faid that a Picture can reprefent but one Action, [but it ought to be underftood one principal Action, for the Painter may very well place in the fame Picture many Actions, which depend upon that chief Action, which he pretends principally to re-prefent.] And indeed there is no one action of Life fo fingle, but it was preceeded, accompanied, and followed by many others, all which do compofe it, and give it its Being : Therefore the Painter muft, whether he will or no, draw thefe fubordinate Acti-ons, or elfe his principal one is imperfect. If he

paints

paints the Sacrifice of *Iphigenia*, he cannot place her
all alone at the foot of *Diana's* Altar, or without
any body, but *Chalchas* who is to facrifice her ; but
rather, following the Example of the Painter *Ti-
mantes*, he will place there all the *Grecian* Princes
with fad Countenances ; *Menelaus* her Uncle fhall
be extreamly afflicted ; *Clytemneftra*, her Mother,
fhall be expreffed all in Tears and defpair ; and *A-
gamemnon*, her Father, with a Vail upon his Face,
to hide the weaknefs of his Nature to the chief of
the *Greeks*, and yet allow fomething by this flight
to the excefs of his Grief; he will not forget to
make *Diana* appear in the Sky, ready to ftop the
Arm and Sword of *Chalchas*, becaufe all thefe Actions do as it were wait upon, and make up this dole-
ful Religious Action, which elfe would be weak
and naked of all its Ornaments, without all thefe
ingenious Circumftances.

'Tis in the fame manner, that a Dramatick Poem ought not to contain above one Action, but it
muft be brought upon the Stage entire, with all its
Dependencies, and nothing muft be forgot of thofe
Circumftances, which naturally are appropriated
to it. And of this I think I need not propofe any Example ; but it will not be amifs to give our
Poet one Advertifement, which is, That if the
principal Action be in the Story loaded with too
many Incidents, he muft reject the leaft important, and leaft pathetick ones ; and on the contrary, if the Story want thofe Incidents, he muft
fupply that want by his own Fancy, which he may
do two ways.

Firft, either by inventing fome Intrigues,
which naturally might make a part of the principal

pal Action : Thus the Author of the Tragedy of
the *Horatius*'s has very well invented the
Marriage of *Sabina*, Sister to the *Curiatius*'s,
with the Eldest of their Enemies, that so he
might introduce the Passions of a Wife, to mingle with those of *Camilla*, who was a Maid, and
in love with one of the *Curiatius*'s.

Secondly, He may seek out in Story, things
that have happened before or after the Action,
which makes the Subject of his Play, and with
Art joyn them to his Plot, saving still the differences of times and places, according as we shall
shew in the following Chapters. This has been
observed by the Author of *Cleopatra*, who makes
Octavia, *Antony*'s Wife, come privately to *Alexandria*, and so has the pleasure of shewing so great
a Lady with all her generous Sentiments.

But we are to observe here, that the Poet, as
near as he can, ought to take his Action as single as possible, because he will still be so much
the more Master of the Passions, and other Ornaments of his Play, which by that means he can
shew to the best advantage; whereas, if he meets
with them in Story, they will still be clogg'd with
some Circumstances, which will constrain the
whole Design, and give him a great deal of trouble; and in short, little and single Subjects in the
hands of an ingenious Poet, who knows how to
work them, cannot miscarry. 'Tis *Scaliger*'s advice, and we have seen the proof of it in *Alcionea*,
a Play of Mr. *Du Ryers*, which though it had no fund
in Story, nevertheless ravished the Audience, by
the force of the Passions, and richness of the Style.
And on the contrary, all those, who in the same

Argumentum brevissimum sumendum, idque maxime varium multiplexque faciendum. l. 3. c. 97. Scal.

Poem

Poem, have brought in divers illuſtrious important Actions, have ſtifled the Beauty of them all, in not giving room enough to the Paſſions, as we have experienced in ſome Plays, where all the Actions, though in ſome meaſure depending on a principal one, yet were ſo ſtrong in themſelves, that they hindred each other, and were every one of them capable of being the ſubject of a Play.

CHAP

CHAP. IV.

Of the Continuity of the Action.

AFter the Poet has chofen the Subject or Story, which he thinks capable of the Ornaments of Dramatick Poetry, and that he has fix'd upon the point, in which he will make the Unity of his Theatral Action confift ; he muft remember, that his Action ought to be not only one, but continued, that is, That from the opening of the Stage, to the very clofing of the Cataftrophe, from the firft Actor, that appears upon the Scene, to the laft that goes off ; the principal Perfons of the Play muft be always in Action ; and the Theatre muft carry continually, and without any interruption the face of fome Defignes , Expectations, Paffions, Troubles, Difquiets, and other fuch like Agitations , which may keep the Spectators in a belief, that the Action of the Theatre is not ceafed, but ftill going on. This is one of the Precepts of *Ariftotle* , as well as of Reafon ; and his Interpreters have always obferved the Ceffation of Action for one of the greateft Faults of the Drama ; 'tis of this fault, that fome People, but impertinently, do accufe *Terence* in his Third Comedy, call'd *Heautontimoreumenos* ;

συνεχῶς ϗ μιας. *Arift. Poet. cap. 11. Gcuean in Terent. Heaut. Scalig. lib. 6. cap. 3. Poet.*

N   but

but I have fufficiently juftified him elfe-where. The Ancient Tragedians could hardly fail in the obfervation of this Rule, becaufe they had Chorufes, and the bufinefs of thofe Chorufes being to reprefent thofe who were prefent upon the Scene at the time of the Action, 'tis probable they would have gone off as foon as they fhould have feen the Action ceafe, as having no pretext to ftay there any longer. 'Tis befides certain, that if upon our Stages the Action fhould ceafe in the middle of the Play, or about the Second or Third Act, all the Intrigues being finifhed, nor no preparation for any new Incident or Paffion to come, the Spectators would be in the right to rife and be gone, fince they would have reafon to believe the Play done, and if they ftayed any longer, knowing there were two or three Acts to come, it would be only by the knowledge they had of what the Poet ought to do, and not by any hint of his, to prepare them for it; as if a man hapned to be there, who had never feen a Play, 'tis certain he would believe it at an end as foon as he had nothing new to expect ; and in this cafe, I have feen fometimes Ladies ask, if the Play were done, though they had often been at Plays, and knew they were generally of greater length ; fo much does the Ceffation of the Action upon the Stage furprize the Spectators, and perfwades them that there is nothing more to come. If we feek the reafon of it, it is becaufe the Action would not be one, if it were not continued ; for Moral Actions, fuch as are thofe of the Theatre, come to be divided and multiplied , whenever they break off ; and are interrupted for then, if they begin again, they are two Theatral Actions , both of them Imperfect. 'Tis for this that the beft Dramatick

tick Poets always ufe to make their Actors fay, where they are going, and what is their Defign, when they go off of the Stage, that one may know, that they are not idle while they are abfent, but are acting fomething of their part, though one fees them not.]

But when we fay, that the chief Perfons in the Play are always to be in Action, we do not mean by that, the Hero or Heroine of the Play, for they often Act the leaft, and yet fuffer the moft in the whole Bufinefs; for in regard to the Continuity of the Action, the Principal Actors are thofe who carry on the Intrigue or bufinefs of the Play, it may be a Slave, a waiting Woman, a Cheat, or fome fuch Perfon; and for the Continuity, 'tis enough if the leaft Actor is but doing, provided it be neceffarily, and that the Spectator from his working may naturally expect fome important change or adventure in the Subject.]

'Tis worth obferving too, that often in appearance the Action of the Stage ceafes, though it be not really fo; which happens when the Poet prepares an Incident, which is to appear afterwards, and of which one of the Actors fpeaks flightly, and *en paffant*, which is an Artifice of the Poets.]

The Example is very ingenious in the *Ajax* of *Sophocles*, where the Action feems entirely to ceafe in the beginning of the Third Act, but is continued by a Meffenger, who comes and tells of *Teucers* Arrival in the Camp, and of all that had been done there fince his coming, concerning his Brothers Fury, and the Cure of it, by which means the Action is not only well renewed, but continued; becaufe in the precedent Acts, *Ajax* often fpeaks, and complains of the length of his Brothers abfence, which makes all

the

the Spectators wish his return, as a means to save *Ajax* himself, so that when the news of his Arrival is brought, it appears that the Action had not ceased at all, for *Teucer* was acting in the Camp for his Brother according to the expectation of the Audience ; of all which neverthelefs there comes nothing to pass of what they hop'd, and 'tis in that that consists the Poets chief Art, to promise that which never comes to pass, and to bring that to pass which he does not promise.

'Tis necessary to observe here befides, that the Theatral Action does not always cease, though all the Actors be in Repose, and as it were without Action ; because that fometimes 'tis a necessary Action of the Play, that they all should be so ; and the Spectator expects some Event from the Actors doing of nothing. This we shall make clear by Examples, and particularly by the *Plutus* of *Aristophanes*, where we fee that after the Second Act, the Actors carry *Plutus* to the Temple of *Æsculapius*, to cure him of his Blindnefs, where they go to Bed to sleep, and remain without Action ; for this Sleep and Repose was the Natural state, in which they were to be, to receive from that God, the favour of being cured, and is by consequent a necessary Action to the Stage. By

Resp. au dis-cours sur l'Heautont. p. 7. ed. 2. p. 102.

which it appears, how much Monsieur *Menage* has been miltaken, to believe that the Action of the Stage ceased as to those who were asleep, and was only continued in the Person of *Carion* who was awake ; for 'tis quite contrary, he that is awake is a Slave, who eats and steals the remainder of the Sacrifice without any regard to the Subject of the Play ; and they who sleep do that which Custom prescribed to those, who were to expect a Cure from *Æsculapius*, and as *Plutus* and
his

his Companions did : One might fay, perhaps, that the Action of *Æfculapius*, who cures *Plutus* and what *Carion* faw, as he tells it afterwards, are enough to continue the Action ; but ftill there would be a breach and fome time loft in it, from that in which the Actors lye down to the time of *Æfculapius*'s coming, if it were not true, that their very lying down and going to fleep, continues the Action of the Comedy.

This Chapter may receive fome more light by the Treatife I have made upon the third Comedy of *Terence*, where I have touch'd this matter, and by what I have done upon that Author, it will be eafie to find, how to examine the Ancients, if one would difcover the Artifices, which they ufe to obferve in this Continuity of the Action of the Theatre.

CHAP.

C H A P. V.

Of the Subjects with two Walks, whereof one is by Modern Authors called Episode.

OUR Modern Authors do now by an Episode mean a Second Story, which comes as it were cross the principal Subject of the Play, and some for this Reason call it a Play with two Walks ; but the Ancient Poets have not known, or at least have not practis'd this Multiplicity of Subjects : *Aristotle* makes no mention of it, and I know no Example of it, except some will say that the *Orestes* of *Euripides* is of this kind, because there are two Marriages concluded in the Catastrophe ; but there is not in the Body Body of the Play any mixture of Intrigues, to carry on those two Amours, and bring them to this Conclusion.

Comedy has been otherwise managed, for having received many more Changes than Tragedy, from what they Both were at first ; it has admitted of this mixture of two Stories in the same Play : And we have yet some in *Plautus*, and a
great

great many in *Terence,* who may afford an Inftruction how to compofe with Art and Grace
that fort of Plays better than *Plautus.*

But however, not ftanding here upon the word
Epifode, which amongft the Ancients fignified
quite another thing. I am content the fignification of the Word fhould be according to our
Modern Authors ; and do allow that Tragedy
may have fome Epifodes, as well as the Epick
Poems , and not unlike them ; but in Tragedy
there are two things to be obferved. Firft, That
thefe Epifodes, or Second Stories be fo incorporated into the chief Subject, that they cannot be
feparated from it, without fpoiling the whole
Play ; for elfe the Epifode would be looked upon
as a fuperfluous and troublefome part, which
would but hinder the Union of the chief Adventures, and flacken the motion of the Incidents, which tend to a Conclufion ; as indeed
in the Play, of our time the moft applauded, the
Epifode of the Princeffes love has been condem- *The Cid.*
ned by all , becaufe it was abfolutely ufelefs.
Therefore to avoid that Inconvenience, 'tis neceffary that the Perfon ingaged in the Epifode,
be not only concern'd in the Succefs of the Affairs of the Stage ; but befides, the Adventures of
the Hero or Heroine ought to be of that concern to the Perfons of the Epifode , as that the
Audience may rationally apprehend fome mifchief,
or hope fome good out of thofe Perfons for the
whole concern of the Stage ; and for the intereft
of thofe who feem ftrangers, and are not then unufe-
fully fo.

The other Obfervation to be made about thefe E-
pifodes,

pifodes, is, That the fecond Story muft not be equal in its Subject, nor in its Neceffity, to that which is the foundation of the Play, but it muft be fubordinate to it, and fo depend upon it, that the Events of the principal Subject caufe the Paffions of the Epifode ; and that the Cataftrophe of the firft produce naturally and of its felf the Cataftrophe of the fecond, or elfe the principal Action would be no longer fo. Thefe are the two Reflections, which I have made upon the Epifodes of our Modern Poets, which may give hints to better underftandings than mine, to make fome more confiderable ones.

C H A P.

CHAP. VI.

Of the Unity *of* Place.

AFter the Poet has order'd his Subject according to the Rules we have given, or it may be Better, which his own Induſtry and Study may furniſh him with; ſe muſt reflect, that the beſt part of it muſt be repreſented by Actors, which muſt be upon a Stage fix'd and determinated ; for to make his Actors appear in different places, would render his Play ridiculous, by the want of Probability, which is to be the foundation of it.]
   This Rule of Unity of Place begins now to be look'd upon as certain; but yet the ignorant, and ſome others of weak judgment, do ſtill imagine that it cannot but be repugnant to the Beauty of the Incidents of a Play ; becauſe that they, happening often in great diſtance of place, cannot but loſe by this conſtraint; and therefore whatſoever Reaſon you oppoſe againſt their imaginations, they fancy a falſe impoſſibility in the Execution, and reject ſtubbornly all that's ſaid to convince them ; on the other ſide, thoſe that are but half read in Antiquity, do well perceive the ſtrength of what it alledg'd for this Rule, but yet they make Objections ſo unbecom-
                  O   ing

ing a literate thinking man, that they have often mov'd pity in me, though I had more mind to laugh at them. 'Tis the property of little Genius's not to be able to comprehend many things at the fame time, fo as to reduce them to a point ; their judgment not being able to affemble fo many images as they muft have prefent all at once ; and therefore they make fo many difficulties, that 'tis eafie to fee, they would be glad that there were Reafons wanting to convince them.

As for the truely Learned, they are thoroughly convinc'd of the neceffity of this Rule, becaufe they fee clearly that Probability can no ways be preferv'd without it ; but I may boldly fay, that hitherto no one of them has explain'd this Rule, and made it intelligible, either becaufe we do not take the Pains of making all the neceffary reflexions upon the Works of the Ancients, to difcover the Art which is moft commonly hid in them, and which always ought to be fo, without an apparent neceffity of the Subject or the Intereft of the Actors ; or elfe becaufe no body ftrives to go beyond the firft great Mafters, and what They have neglected is given over moft commonly by their Followers.

Ariftotle has faid nothing of it, and I believe he omitted it, becaufe that this Rule was in his time too well known ; the Chorus's, which ordinarily remain'd upon the Stage from one end of the Play to the other, marking the unity of the *Scene* too vifibly to need a Rule for it ; and indeed, would it not have been ridiculous, that in the Play call'd the *Seven before Thebes*, the young Women who make the Chorus, fhould have found themfelves fometimes before the Palace of the King, and fometimes
times

times in the Camp of the Enemies, without ever
ftirring from the fame place ; and the Three famous
Tragedians of the *Greeks*, whofe Works we have,
are fo punctual in the Obfervation of this Rule,
and do fo often make their Actors fay, where they
are, and whence they come ; that *Ariftotle* muft
have fuppos'd too much Ignorance in his Age, and
in thofe who fhould read thefe Poets, if he had
gone about to Explain fo fettled a Rule.   But fince
the Ignorance and Barbarity of fome paft Ages have
brought fuch diforder upon the Stage, to make
people in the Play appear in different parts of the
World on the fame Stage, it will not be amifs to give
here at length the Reafon of this Rule, fo well
practis'd by the Ancients, and that in honour of
fome of our Modern Poets, who have very handfom-
ly imitated them.

To underftand it then, we muft have recourfe
to our ordinary Principle, which is, that the Stage
is but a Reprefentation of things ; and yet we are
not to imagine, that there is any thing of what we
really fee, but we muft think the things themfelves
are there of which the Images are before us.   So
Floridor is much lefs *Floridor*, than the *Horatius* of
whom he acts the Part, for his drefs is *Roman*, he
fpeaks, acts, and thinks as that *Roman* did at that
time ; but as that *Roman* could not but be in fome
place acting and fpeaking, the place where *Floridor*
appears does reprefent that where *Horatius* was, or
elfe the Reprefentation would be imperfect in that
Circumftance.

Loci ficti vera Loca imitantur. Scal. l. 1. cap. 13.

This Truth, well underftood, makes us to know
that the place cannot change in the reft of the Play,
fince it cannot change in the Reprefentation, for one

and the fame Image remaining in the fame ſtate,
cannot repreſent two different things ; now it is
highly improbable, that the fame ſpace, and the fame
floor; which receive no change at all, ſhould repreſent two different places;] as for Example, *France*
and *Denmark*; or within *Paris* it ſelf, the *Tueilleries*
and the *Exchange* ; at leaſt to do it with ſome ſort
of colour, one ſhould have of that ſort of Theatres
which turn quite round and entire, that ſo the
Place might change as well as the Perſons acting ;
and to do this, the Subject of the Play ought to furniſh ſome Reaſon for this change, and as that cannot
well happen, but by the Power of God Almighty,
who changes as he pleaſes the Face of Nature, I
doubt it would be hard to make a reaſonable
Play without a dozen Miracles at leaſt.

Let it then be allowed for a certain truth, that
the Place, where the firſt Actor, who opens the Play,
is ſuppos'd to be, ought to be the ſame place to the
end of the Play ;[and that, it not being in the ordinary courſe of Nature, that the place can receive
any change, there can be none likewiſe in the Repreſentation ; and by conſequent, that all your o-
ther Actors cannot rationally appear in any other
place.]
But we muſt remember,that this Place,which cannot be ſuppos'd to change, is the *Area* or floor of the
Stage, upon which the Actors walk, and which the
Ancients call'd by the name of *Proſcenium* ; for as that
repreſents that ſpot of ground,upon which the perſons
repreſented did actually walk and diſcourſe, which
could not turn about or change on a ſudden, or without a Miracle,ſo when you have once choſen the place
where

where you intend your Action to be begun, you
muſt ſuppoſe it immovable in all the reſt of the
Play, as it was in effect and really.

'Tis not the ſame with the ſides and end of the
Theatre, for as they do but repreſent thoſe things
which did actually environ the Perſons acting, and
which might receive ſome change, they may likewiſe receive ſome in the Repreſentation, and 'tis in
that that conſiſts the changing of Scenes, and other
Ornaments of Decoration, which always raviſh
the People, and pleaſe the beſt Judges, when they are
well done ; ſo we have ſeen upon our Stage a Temple adorn'd with a Noble Front of Architecture,
which coming to be ſet open ſhew'd the inſide of
it, where in Perſpective were deſcryed Pillars and
an Altar, and all the other Ornaments of a Church
extremly well done; ſo that the place did not
change, and yet had a fine Decoration.

We are not nevertheleſs to imagine, that the Poets *Capricio* is to ru'e theſe Decorations ; for he muſt
find ſome colour and appearance for it in his
Subject.

So for Example, he might feign a Palace upon
the Sea ſide, forſaken, and left to be inhabited by
poor Fiſhermen ; a Prince landing, or being caſt a-
way there, might adorn it with all the rich Furni-
ture fit for it ; after this by ſome Accident it might
be ſet on fire ; and then behind it the Sea might
appear, upon which one might repreſent a Sea
Fight ; ſo that in all the five changes of the Stage,
the unity of Place would ſtill be ingeniouſly pre-
ſerv'd ; not but that the very floor or *Proſcenium*
may change too, provided it be ſuperficially, as if
ſome River ſhould overflow it, as the *Tyber* did in
                                                    the

the time of *Augustus*; or if Flames came out of the Earth and cover'd the face of it, in all these cases the unity of place would not be broke. But as I have said already, the Subject of the Play must furnish probable Reasons for these changes, which I repeat the oftner, because I am still afraid, that it will not make Impression enough in the Reader.

'Tis not enough neither to say, that the Floor or Stage should reprefent a place immoveable; it must befides be a place suppos'd open in the reality, as it appears in the Reprefentation; for fince the Actors are suppos'd to go and come from one end of it to the other, there cannot be any solid body between, to hinder either their fight or motion; therefore the Ancients did ufe to chufe for the place of their Scene in Tragedies fome publick place, as that before the gate of a Palace; and in their Comedies fome part of a Town, where different Streets met, and where the Houfes of the principal Actors were suppos'd to be; becaufe thefe places were moft fitly reprefented by the empty Stage, adorn'd with the Figures of thofe Houfes. Not that they always followed this, for in the *Suppliants*, and in the *Ion* of *Euripides*, the Scene is before a Temple; and in the *Ajax* of *Sophocles*, the Scene is before his Tent, pitch'd in the Corner of a Forreft; in the *Rudens* of *Plautus*, it is before the Temple, and fome fcatter'd Houfes, from whence one fees the Sea. And indeed all this depends upon the Poets Invention, who according to his Subject chufes the place, the moft convenient for all that he has a mind to reprefent, and adorns it with fome agreeable Appearance.

One may judge from all this, how ridiculous was the Wall in the *Thisbe* of Poet *Theophile*, it being plac'd

plac'd upon the Stage; and *Pyramus* and *She* whifpe-
ring through it, and when they went out, the Wall
funk, that the other Actors might fee one another:
For befides that the two places on each fide of
the Wall reprefented the two Chambers of *Pyramus*
and *Thisbe*; and that it was contrary to all appearance of Reafon, that in the fame place the King
fhould come and talk with his Confidents, and
much lefs that a Lion fhould come and fright
Thisbe there; I would fain know, by what fuppos'd means in the action it felf, this Wall could
become vifible and invifible? and by what enchantment it was fometimes in being, and then ceas'd quite
to be again? The fault is not lefs in thofe, who fuppofe things done upon the Stage, which have not
been feen by the Spectators, it not being probable
they could have been done without being feen, or
elfe things muft be fuppos'd to have been invifible
in the reality of the action; upon which I think
one of our Modern Poets fell into a great Errour of
this kind, having plac'd a Baftion upon the Stage,
and having afterwards caus'd the Town to be taken
by that Baftion, which was never feen to be either
attack'd or defended.

As for the Extent which the Poet may allow to
the Scene he chufes, when it is not in a Houfe
but open, I believe it may be as far as a man can fee
another Walk, and yet not know perfectly that 'tis
he; for to take a larger fpace would be ridiculous,
it being improbable that two people being each of
them at one end of the Stage, without any Object
between, fhould look at one another, and yet not fee
one another; whereas this diftance, which we allow often, contributes to the working of the Play
by

by the miſtakes and doubts which a man may make by ſeeing another at a diſtance ; to which the Theatres of the Ancients do very well agree ; for being, as they were, threeſcore yards in front among the *Romans*, and little leſs among the *Græcians*, it was pretty near the proportion we allow them.

I deſire the Reader beſides to conſider, that if the Poet did repreſent by his Stage all the Places and Rooms of a Palace, or all the Streets of a Town, he ſhould make the Spectators ſee not onely all that happened in his Story, but all that was done beſides in that Palace, or in the Town ; for there is no Reaſon to hinder the Spectators from ſeeing all that, nor why they ſhould ſee one thing ſooner than another, particularly conſidering, that ſince they can ſee at the ſame time into the Garden of the Palace, and into the Kings Cabinet, according to the Subject of the Play, they muſt likewiſe hear and ſee all that is done there, beſides the Theatral Action ; except there were an Enchantment to ſhew onely that which the Poet had a mind to, and to hide all that was not of his Subject ; beſides the Stage would never be empty of any of the Actors, except they went out of the Palace or Town, for ſince the place repreſents the Palace with its Garden, Court, and other Appartments, one cannot forbear ſeeing any one who ſhould go from any of thoſe Appartments into the Court or Garden ; and by conſequent, as long as any of the Actors were in the Extent repreſented by the Stage, they cannot avoid being ſeen. To which it cannot be anſwer'd, that to mark the different Appartments, there may be Curtains to ſhut and draw ; for theſe Curtains
are

are fit for nothing, but to tofs their Inventors in them, like Dogs in a Blanket.

I have fpoken fo clearly of this in my *Terence Juftified*, that I have nothing more to fay againft this grofs Piece of Ignorance.

If it be faid befides, that the Poet has the liberty of fhewing and hiding what he pleafes ; I grant it, provided there be a probability that one thing be feen, and another not ; but there would need a fin-gular Invention to contrive, that ever and anon the fame Perfons, acting and fpeaking in a Palace, fhould be feen, and not be feen ; for that would be making of the Walls to fink and rife, go backwards and forwards every moment.   This may be enough to fhew the error of thofe, who upon the fame Scene reprefent *Spain* and *France*, making their Stage, not onely almoft as big as the Earth, but likewife cau-fing the fame Floor to reprefent at the fame time things fo far diftant from one another, and that without any apparent caufe of fo prodigious a change.

We may likewife obferve, how they are miftaken, that fuppofe in one fide of the Stage one part of the Town, as for example, the *Louvre*, and on the other fide another part, as the *Place Royal;* thinking by this fine Invention to preferve the unity of Place. Indeed if two Parts or Quarters of a Town, thus fuppos'd, were not far from one another, and the fpace between were really empty of Houfes, fuch a thing were not improper ; but if between the two places, there are many Houfes and folid bodies, I would then ask, how it comes to pafs that thofe Houfes do not fill up the empty place of the Stage ; and how, if they do, an Actor can fee another

P   place

Place at the other end of the Stage, beyond all these Houses; and in a word, how this Stage, which is but an Image, represents a thing of which it has no resemblance?

Let it then be setled for a constant Maxim, That the *Proscenium*, or floor of the Stage, can represent nothing but some open place of an ordinary extent, where those, that are represented by the Actors, might naturally be in the truth of the Action ; and when we see it written, The Scene is at *Aulis*, *Eleusis*, or *Argos*, 'tis not that the place, where the Actors appear, is all that Town or Province, but onely that all the Intrigues of the Play, as well what passes out of the sight of the Spectators, as what they see, are treated in that Town, of which the Stage takes up but the least part.

Thus in the Prologue of the last Comedy of *Plautus*, the Poet, explaining the Place of the Scene, says, that he begs of the *Romans* a little space in the middle of their noble Buildings to transport thither the Town of *Athens*, without the help of Architects; upon which *Samuel Petit* observes, that we ought not to imagine that *Plautus* pretends to place all the City of *Athens* in that of *Rome*, but onely a small part of it, where the things represented in the Play did come to pass, to wit, the Quarter of the *Plotæans*, and of all that Quarter only the place, where *Phronesion* liv'd, and he confirms this by the mending of two *Greek* words, of which he pretends one *Latin* one was made by a mistake, and by a Verse, which he mends by some Manuscripts which he had seen, making the Prologue then speak thus; *I abridge here the Town of Athens, upon this Stage, during this Play, and in this House lives Phronesion.*

Thefe

Perparvam partem postulat Plautus loci de nostris magnis atque amœnis manibus, Athenas quoque Ar. chitectis conseret. Prolog Truc ul.

Ibi Samuel Petit. Non totas Athenas sed Athenarum regionem illam deformabat hæc Plauti scena , in qua res istæ quæ hoc Dramate repræsentabantur gestæ dicebantur ,&c. Et en suite id est Plotheensium regionem, eamque non totam, sed extremam illius partem in qua habitare fingitur Phronesion meretrix.

Athenas arcto, ita ut hoc est proscenium tantisper dum transigimus hanc Comediam, hic habitat mulier nomine quæ est Phronesion &c. Prolog. Truc.

These are the only Authorities of any either Ancient or Modern Authors, that I have found concerning the place of the Scene. *Castelvetro* indeed says, that Tragedy requires but a small space; but since he has not explain'd himself better, we are not bound to guess in his favour.

These things then once setled for the Doctrine or Theory; I have thought of what follows for the Practical part The Poet does not desire to represent to his Spectators all the particulars of his story, but the principal and most moving circumstances, and thus he is oblig'd to some part out of the sight of the Spectators; and indeed he ought not to do it, there being many things fitter to be hid then shewed, he must then first of all consider exactly, what persons he most wants and cannot well be without, then let him chuse a place where they may probably meet; for as there are places which certain persons cannot leave without extroardinary motives; so there are others, where they cannot be without great Reason. A Nun cannot leave the place of her retreat but upon some pressing motive, and a woman of Honour cannot accompany *Messalina* to the place of her infamous debauches.

Paralipsis est, cùm res omittitur, quæ adeò necessaria est, ut etiam non relata intelligatur: & per annos decem quot partes quot arma mente restituenda sint: sic non semper legimus quoties cibum capiant aliique naturæ necessaria expediant. Id quod sanè figura est, nam plebeia oratio, nihil omittere. Scal. lib. 3. c. 77.

Besides, he must observe, whether or no in his Subject there be not some Circumstances or notable Incident, which it will be necessary to preserve for the beauty of his Play, and which cannot happen but in a certain place, for then he must accommodate to that the rest of his parts; so he that would shew *Celadon* half dead upon the Shore and found there by *Galatea*, must of necessity place his Scene upon the bank of a River, and accommodate to it the rest of the Theatral Action. *Plautus* followed

P 2   lowed

lowed this method in his *Rudens*, where he defir'd to fhew the relicks of a Shipwrack, and therefore was forc'd to place his Scene on the Sea fide, where all the reft of his Adventures are very dexteroufly brought to pafs.

The Poet, having chofen the place, muft examine next, what things are fitteft to be fhewed with delight to the Spectators, and be fure to reprefent them; as for the others not fo fit to be feen, they muft be told fome way, that they may be fuppos'd done, and that in places fo near the Stage, that the Actor who tells them, may be fuppos'd to have been there and back again, from the time he has been abfent from the Stage, or elfe he muft be fuppos'd gone before the Play began, for then he may come as far off as you will. All which *Terence* hath obferv'd in his third Comedy, where the two Slaves, *Syrus*, and *Dromo*, had been fent a great while before for *Clitophon's* Miftrefs; and by confequent, all that *Syrus* tells of their Negotiation is very credible, what time fo ever there needed for the dreffing of the Lady, and the doing of all the reft.

And if the things or places to be fpoke of in the Play, have been done too far from the Scene, or are in themfelves too remote, one muft bring them nearer in the Reprefentation; which may be done two ways; either by fuppofing that they happened in other places nearer, when 'tis all one to the Story, as *Donatus* obferves, that in Plays, Country Houfes are alwayes fuppos'd to be in the Suburbs : Or elfe by fuppofing the places nearer than they really are, when 'tis impoffible to change them, but in this laft, one muft obferve not to bring known places fo near, that the Spectator cannot follow the Poet in his be-

Nunc adif ubi opus eft Pottæ: & vide hanc caufam fuiffe cur non ad villam diverterit, omnes villas comicus fuburbanas effe, commoditatem ipfam nunc explicat & oftendit. Donat. in Euuuch. Terent.

belief: As for example, if a man fhould bring the
Alps, or *Pyrenæan* Mountains in the place of Mount
Valerian, that fo he might bring an Incident to Play,
which elfe he could not; the Scene being at *Paris;*
truly the rigour of the Rule would be followed, as
to the Unity of the Scene and its Decencies, but
the Beauty of the Art, which is to pleafe and perfwade, would be loft : 'Tis therefore that I cannot
approve of this force upon Nature, as to the diftance
of places, which we fee done in the *Suppliants,* and
the *Andromache* of *Euripides,* in the *Captives* of *Plautus* and fome other pieces of Antiquity. I fpeak not
here of our Modern Poets, for all the World knows,
there never was any thing fo monftrous in this
point, as the Plays we have feen in *Italy, Spain,* and
France, and indeed except the *Horatius* of *Corneille,* I
doubt whether we have one Play, where the unity of
the Scene is rigoroufly obferv'd, at leaft, I am fure I
have not feen any.

It is neceffary to give one advertifement more to
the Poet in this place, which is, that none of his
Actors ought to come upon the Scene without fome
apparent Reafon, fince elfe it is not probable they
fhould be there; and he muft avoid to follow the Example of a Poet, who made a Princefs come a purpofe
out of her Tent upon the Stage which was before it,
to fay fome paffionate complaints of a fecret Misfortune of hers, for it was much more probable that fhe
fhould make them in her Tent: Therefore he ought
to have feign'd either that the Company of fome people in the Tent, was importunate and troublefome
to her, and that to avoid them fhe came out, or elfe
he ought to have given her fome fudden impatience
to look out, and then, as naturally upon reflexions
of our Misfortunes we are carried to expreffions of
them,

them, he might have put in her mouth what words he had thought neceſſary for his Subject. Thus when the paſſion of ſome perſon upon the Scene is to be ſhew'd by ſome Narration, which the Spectator has had already, and which cannot be repeated without diſguſt, one muſt ſuppoſe the thing to have been told that Perſon in ſome place near the Scene, and make him come in near towards the end of it with words in his mouth, expreſſing the knowledg of the thing, and cauſing the paſſion he is to ſhew afterwards upon the Stage. The Examples of this are frequent among the Ancients, and the imitation of them cannot but ſucceed well.

CHAP.

C H A P. VII.

The Extent of the Theatral Action, or of the time fit to be allowed a Dramatick Poem.

THERE is no queſtion more debated than This, which I am now treating. The Poets make it their diſcourſe, and the Players ſcarce talk of any thing elſe, as well as thoſe who frequent the Theatres; nay, the Ladies in their *Ruelles* undertake to decide it, and all this while the thing is ſo little underſtood, that I have a great deal of Reaſon to endeavour to explain it carefully. To talk with ſome knowledge then of this Matter, one muſt conſider that a Dramatick Poem has two ſorts of Time, each of which has a different and proper laſting.

The firſt is the true Time of the Repreſentation; for though this ſort of Poem be but an Image and ſo ought to be conſider'd as having a repreſentative Being; neverthelesſ one ought to conſider, that there is a reality in the very Repreſentation, for realy the Actors are ſeen and heard, the Verſes are really pronounc'd, and one ſuffers really either pleaſure or pain in aſſiſting at theſe Repreſentations, and there is a real time ſpent in amuſing the Audience,

dience, that is from the opening of the Stage to the
end of the Play: This time is call'd the lasting of
the Representation.

Of this time the measure can be no other, but so
much time as will reasonably spend the patience of
the Audience, for this fort of Poem being made for
pleasure, it ought not to weary and fatigate the
mind; and it must not likewise be so short, as that the
Spectators go away with an opinion of not having been well nor enough diverted. In all this, Experience is the faithfullest Guide, and tells us most
commonly, that a Play cannot last above three hours
without wearying of us, nor less without coming
short of pleasing us. I have seen a very learned
Gentleman, who was present at the Representation
of the *Pastor Fido* in *Italy*, who told me, that never
was any thing so tedious, it having lasted too long,
and that this Play, which ravishes the Reader, because
he can lay it by when he will, had most horridly dif-
gusted the Spectators.

There is another observation to be made here,
which is, that the time, which we allow the Representation, may be spent many other wayes.

The Ancients had in their Tragedies many different mixtures, as *Mimes*, *Pantomimes*, and other Buffoons. These Diversions pleas'd the people, and
yet I do not believe they made the Representations
longer than those of our time; for besides that these
Interludes were short, their Tragedies themselves
were not of above a thousand Verses, and those
Verses much shorter than our Heroick ones. Therefore the Poet must take great care, that if his
Play be of the ordinary length, his Interludes be not
too long, for let them be never so pleasing they will
dif-

difquiet the Spectator in the Impatience, which he
will naturally have to know the Event and Succefs
of the Story.

The other Time of the Dramatick Poem is
that of the Action reprefented, fo ar as it is
confidered as a true Action, and containing all
that fpace which is neceffary to the performing of
thofe things, which are to be expos'd to the
knowledge of the Spectators, from the firft to the
laft Act of the Play.

Now this Time is the chief Time, not only becaufe 'tis natural to the Poem, but becaufe alfo
it all depends on the Poets Invention, and is made
known by the Mouth of his Actors, according
as his Ingenuity can fuggeft him the means of doing it, and this is the Time fo much talk'd of in
our days. The three *Greek* Tragicks, *Æfchylus*,
Euripides, and *Sophocles* allow but a few houres
to the lafting of the Theatral Action in their Poems; but their Example was not followed by
the Poets who fucceeded them; for *Ariftotle*
blames thofe of his time, for giving too long an
Extent to the lafting of their Plays, which makes
him fet down the Rule, or rather renew it from
the Model of the Ancients, faying, That Tragedy ought to be comprehended in the Revolution
of one Sun. I do not know, whether this Rule
was obferv'd by thofe that came after him, as
by the Authors of thofe Tragedies which carry
the Name of *Seneca*, which are regular enough
in this Circumftance: But for all thofe that I
have feen, which were made at the re-eftablifh-
ment of Learning in *Spain* and *France*, they are
not only irregular in this point, but in all the o-

Q   ther

ther moſt ſenſible Rules, inſomuch that one would admire, that Men of Learning ſhould be the Authors of them : When I firſt had the Honour to be near Cardinal *Richelieu*, I found the Stage in great eſteem, but loaded with all theſe Errors, and particularly with that, of exceeding the Time, fit to be allowed in Tragedy ; I ſpoke of it in thoſe Plays which were acted at Court ; but I was generally oppos'd, and moſt commonly turned into Ridicule both by the Poets, the Actors, and the Spectators ; and when I, to defend my ſelf, began to alledge the Ancients, I was paid with this Anſwer, That what they had done was well for their time, but now a days they would be laugh'd at, if they were here : As if the general Reaſon of Mankind could grow old with time ; and accordingly we ſee, that at laſt it has prevailed over Prejudice and Ignorance, to make all the World confeſs, that the Time of a Tragedy ought to be ſhort and limited : But becauſe, even in this, there are different Interpretations given to *Ariſtotle*, and that ſome Poets do believe, to circumſcribe too narrowly the laſting of the Theatral Action would be to ſpoil moſt of the Incidents ; I will here give the true Explanation of the Rule, and ways of practiſing it with Succeſs. *Ariſtotle* has ſaid, that one of the principal differences, which is between an Epick Poem and a Tragedy, is, That the Firſt is not limited in any time, and that the Second is comprehended in the Revolution of one Sun. Now, though *Ariſtotle* does expreſs himſelf in few words, yet I cannot underſtand, how there was ground for ſo much Diſpute : For ſince he ſays, the Revolution of one Sun, it cannot be meant, the Annual Revolution, for that is the time generally allowed

to

to an Epick Poem, and there is none of the moſt
Indulgent, that have offer'd to extend the Rule to
that excels in Tragedy. It remains then to ſay,
he means the Diurnal Revolution ; but as the day
is conſidered two ways, the one with regard to the
Primum mobile, which is call'd the Natural day, and
is of twenty four Hours, and the other by the Suns
preſence upon the Horizon, between his riſing and
ſetting, which is call'd the Artificial Day. It is neceſſary to obſerve, that *Ariſtotle* means only the Artificial Day, in the extent of which, he makes the
Theatral Action to be comprehended. *Caſtelvetro*
and *Picolomini*, upon *Ariſtotles* Poetick, are of this
Opinion againſt *Seigni*, who extends the Rule to the
Natural day of 24 hours.

The Reaſon of this is certain, and founded upon
the Nature of Dramatick Poems ; for this ſort of
Poem ought to carry a ſenſible Image of the Actions
of Humane Life ; now we do not ſee, that regularly men are buſie before day, nor much after
night, and accordingly, in all well governed places,
there are Magiſtrates to watch thoſe, who employ
the night naturally deſign'd for reſt, in the Actions
of the day.

Beſides, we have ſaid, and it cannot be called in
queſtion ; that the Theatral Action ought to be one,
and not comprehend any other Actions, which are
not neceſſary to the Intrigue of the Stage. Now
how can that be obſerved in a Play of 24 hours ?
would it not be a neceſſity, that the Perſons Acting
ſhould ſleep, and eat, and buſie themſelves in many
things, which would not be of the Subject of the Play,
and though the Poet ſhould ſay nothing of it, yet
the Spectators muſt needs conceive it ſo.

Q 2

But

But befides, the Action of the Stage is to be continued, and not interrupted or broken. Now that could not be in a Play of twenty four hours ; Nature could not, without fome reft, endure fo long an Action ; fince all that Men can commonly do, is to be in Action for the day time.

Moreover, we cannot omit a Reafon of the Ancients, which originally is Effential to Tragedy, which is, that the Chorufes, which they ufed, did not regularly ufe to ftir off the Stage for the whole Play, or at leaft from the time they firft came on ; and I do not know with what appearance of Probability, the Spectators could have been perfwaded, that People, who were never out of their fight, fhould have ftaid twenty four hours in that place ; nor how in the truth of the Action, they could imagine, that thofe, whom they reprefented, had pafs'd all that time without fatisfying fome neceffities of Nature.

After all, we can never better underftand *Ariftotle*, than by thofe three Excellent Tragick Poets, whom he always propofes for Examples, who have regularly obferv'd , not to give above 12 hours to their Plays : And I do not think, that there are any of their Works which do comprehend the whole fpace between the rifing and fetting of the Sun.

It being moft certain, that their Stage geneally opens after Sun-rife, and is fhut up before Sun-fet , as one may obferve in the Comedies of *Plautus* and *Terence.* 'Tis therefore that *Roffi*, an *Italian* , allows but eight or ten hours . And *Scaliger*, more rigoroufly but more reafonably, would have the whole Action performed in fix hours.

Scenicum go-tium totum fx cellare horis per agitur l. 3. c. 97. Poet.

hours. It were even to be wiſh'd, that the Action of the Poem did not take up more time , than that of the Repreſentation, but that being hard, and almoſt impoſſible, in certain occaſions the Poet has the Liberty to ſuppoſe a longer time by ſome hours, in which the Muſick that marks the Intervals of the Acts, and the Relations of the Actors upon the Stage, while the others are buſie off of it , with the natural deſire of the Spectators to ſee the Event, do all contribute very much, and help to deceive the Audience , ſo as to make them think, there has paſſed time enough for the performance of the things repreſented.

What we have ſaid hitherto of *Ariſtotle's* Rule might ſuffer ſome difficulty in thoſe Plays , which repreſent Actions that happened in the Night, if we did not own, that he has foreſeen the Objection, when he ſays, That *Tragedy endeavours to comprehend its Action in the Revolution of one Sun*, or in *changing that time a little*; for by that means he lets us know, that the Poet is not always bound to place his Action between Sun-riſing and Sun-ſetting, but may take a like time out of 24 hours, and place his Action in the night, as in the *Rheſus* of *Euripides*, and ſome other Plays of the Ancients, of which we have nothing but Fragments in *Athenæus*. Nay, he may take ſome of his time in the day , and the reſt in the night, as *Euripides* has done in his *Electra,* and *Plautus* in his *Amphitryon ;* they that, upon this of *Ariſtotle,* have ſaid, that he gave leave to exceed the Revolution of a Sun , and go ſome hours beyond, did not well underſtand him, having taken the word Changing for Exceeding.

ἢ μικρὸν ἐξαλλάττειν. Poet. c. 5. aut parum variare. Vict. p. 52. Aut pauliſper variare. Ricco- boni in Poët Ariſt.

But

But without ftanding upon this fcrupulous nicenefs, I muft tell the Poet, that he need not fear to fpoil his Play, by ftraitning his Incidents in fo fmall a compafs of time ; for quite contrary, 'tis that, which fhall make his Play agreeable and wonderful; 'tis that, which will afford him the means of introducing extraordinary furprizes and paffions , which he may carry, as far as he will ; let him confider well *Horatius, Cinna, Polyeuct,* and *Nicomedes* , the latter works of Mounfieur *Corneille* , and I believe, he cannot but agree to it.

Now to contribute for my fhare to the neceffary means of practifing this Rule , I here deliver my thoughts.

Firft, Let the Poet be very careful in chufing the day, in which he will comprehend all the Intrigues of his Play, and that choice ought generally to be made from the moft Noble Incident of the whole Story, that is, from that Incident, which is to make the Cataftrophe, and to which all others do tend, like Lines to their Center ; and if he be free to take what day he will, his beft will be to pitch upon that, which will moft eafily bear the Affemblage and Concurrence of all the Incidents of the Stage. So *Corneille*, being to reprefent the Death of *Pompey*, took the laft day of his Life, becaufe he could not do otherwife ; but when he was to make his *Cinna*, he chofe what day he pleas'd for to facilitate the bringing in of the Confpiration of *Cinna*, with the deliberation of *Augu-*
'us, whether he fhould forfake the Empire or no.

The choice being thus made, the next flight is, to open your Stage, as near, as 'tis poffible, to the Cataftrophe, that you may employ lefs time in the negotiation part, and have more Liberty in extending the Paffions and Difcourfes which may pleafe ; but

to

to Execute this luckily, the Incidents muſt be prepar'd by ingenious Contrivances, and that muſt appear upon occaſion in the whole Conduct of the
Action.

This we may obſerve in the *Jon* of *Euripides,* the
Amphytrion of *Plautus,* and the *Andria* of *Terence.* *Corneille* practiſes it likewiſe well in *Horatius* and *Cinna.* The Stage in *Horatius* is opened
but a moment before the Combat of the three *Horatius's* againſt the three *Curiatius's,* who are told of
their being choſen to fight againſt each other, as
ſoon as they come upon the Stage. And *Cinna* had
already made his Conſpiracy, before the opening of
the Stage, which opens juſt before the Sacrifice, which
was to be the pretext of the Execution of it.

Things being thus diſpos'd, the Poet muſt next ſtudy to bring together the Incidents all in one day, ſo
Artfully, that there appear no Force nor Conſtraint
in the effecting of it : And to ſucceed in this, he muſt
rectify the time of thoſe things, that happened before
the opening of the Stage ; and ſuppoſe, ſome of
them to come to paſs that day, though they really
happened before ; but he muſt joyn them with ſo
much Art, as they may ſeem to be naturally con-
nexed, and not put together by the Poets Invention.

Thus *Sophocles* makes, that *Creon,* who was ſent to
Delphos to conſult the Oracle, comes back juſt at
the ſame time that the news comes to *Thebes,* of the
Death of *Polybius* King of *Corinth,* though theſe two
things did not happen on the ſame day. So *Plautus*
makes *Amphitryon* return victorious that very night
that *Alcmena* is brought to Bed of *Hercules.* But that
which one muſt particularly have a ſ   n   to
conjoyn the time of the Incidents a   ,   :

cipitation, that Probability be deftroyed by it , as in the *Suppliants* of *Euripides*, the *Captiv's* of *Plautus* and fome other pieces of the Ancients, which I cannot approve of, though for fome other Confiderations they are not unexcufable.   They are indeed according to the Rule of time , but without any of the Graces of the Art.   In a word, we muft ftill remember, that *Ariftotle* in giving his Rule of the confining Tragedy to the Revolution of one Sun, means, that the Poet ought fo to prefs his imagination, as to order all the Events of his Theatre in that time, but fo, as not to offend Probability, which is always the principal Rule , and without which all the others become no Rules at all.

C H A P.

CHAP. VIII.

Of the Preparation of the Incidents.

IT may be some may Imagine, that the Instruction we are going to give the Poet in this Discourse,
will be injurious to him, and, contrary to our promise, destroy all the Graces of the Stage: for say
they, if the Incidents must be prepar'd some time
before they happen, without doubt they will likewise be prevented, and so be no longer surprizing,
in which consists all their beauty, and without which
the Spectator has no pleasure, nor can the Poet
pretend to any glory in his Art.

To this I answer, That there is a great deal of
difference between preparing an Incident, and preventing it, for an Incident is then prevented, when
it is foreseen, but it ought not to be foreseen though
it be prepar'd.

To explain our selves better upon this matter,
we are to understand that there are some things in
the Composition of a Theatral Action, which do
carry the minds of the Spectators naturally and almost necessarily, to the knowledge of some others;
so that as soon as the first are either said or done,
one may conclude easily those that depend upon

R them,

them, and that is call'd an Incident prevented; and we do allow all thefe Preventions to be faulty in a Dramatick Poem, becaufe they fpoil the Events, and make them of no effect in the Imagination of the Spectators, who moft commonly expect things contrary to what they fee, and feem to be promis'd.

But there are another fort of things, which are to be laid as a foundation to build others upon, according to the Rules of Probability, and yet neverthelefs do not at all difcover thefe fecond ones, which they are to produce; not only becaufe there is no neceffity they fhould come to pafs in confequence of the firft; but alfo becaufe the firft are fhew'd with colours and pretexts fo probable, according to the ftate of the Affairs of the Stage, that the Minds of the Spectators pafs them over, not thinking that from thence there can fpring any new Incident, fo that the preparation of an Incident, is not to tell or do any thing that can difcover it, but rather that may give occafion to it without difcovering it; and all the Art of the Poet confifts in finding Colours and Pretexts to fettle thefe Preparations, fo, that the Spectator may be convinc'd, that that is not thrown into the Body of the Play for any other defign, than what appears to him. *Scaliger* has own'd this to be neceffary, even in the Epick Poems, and calls it, *The Seeds of a future Harveft*: as if he would fay, that juft as the Grain or Seed contains in it felf the force and virtue of producing in its time Flowers and Fruit; and yet Nature is fo fram'd it, as that one cannot difcover any li'hood of fuch a Production, by the fight of the Seed; fo muft the Difcourfes and other confiderations to
prepare

Arift. c. x. poet. In multis a- conomia Co- micorum Poeta- rum ita fe habet, ut cafu putet Spectater v. nif- fe quod confilio Scriptorum fa- ctum fit. Donat. in Terent. Andr. & in Eunuch. Idem aliis ver- fis.

Vbique verò aliquid jacit fe- minum ad fu- turam meffem, ut auditorem quafi pregufta- tione allisiat ad epulas. Similis preparatio in primo, cum enim recipiendus eft Æneas proponit boc intelligen- dum ex pictura, in ea namque ip- fe quoque pictus erat. lib. 4. c. 25.

prepare an Incident, enclose it so secretly, and hide it so well, as nothing can be guess'd of the Event from them. This Excellent Man brings divers Examples of this, and particularly, that taken from the *Æneid* of *Virgil:* For he observes, that to make way for the kind reception, which *Dido* gives to *Æneas* and his *Trojans*, *Virgil* tells us, how Queen *Dido* had caus'd the Story of the War of *Troy* to be painted in a Temple, where *Æneas* himself was represented, fighting in the midst of the *Greeks*; for then this painting seems only an Object for the admiration of *Æneas*, to see that the *Trojans* misfortunes were already known all the World over; but the secret is, that it serves to give a foundation in the Mind of *Dido* to the kind welcome she makes to those, to whose ill fortune in all probability she had already given some compassion.

As for the Dramatick Poem, I have not met with any Examples in all the Authors that I have seen, except in one *Victorius* in his Commentaries upon *Aristotles* Poetick; and neither there does he do it by way of Instruction, but simply by way of Remark upon the Tragedy of *Medea*, made by *Euripides*, of which he says, that the Catastrophe is defective, because the Poet unfolds the Plot by the flight of *Medea* in an Enchanted Chariot, of which before hand he had not given the least hint or preparation, the preceding Events contributing no ways to this last. These two passages of *Scaliger* and *Victorius* came not to my knowledge, till after I had made all the necessary Observations upon this Subject; but as I never affected to be thought the Inventor of any thing, so am I never better pleas'd, than when having by my Meditations

Reprehensus est Poeta, quia semina nulla hujus fabulæ exitus antea iacta erant, nec unquam is sum diuuart superio. res partes Tragædiæ. Victer. in Arist. p. 149.

attain'd

attain'd to a certain knowledge, I difcover that o-
thers more able, and of greater reputation, had
faid the fame things before I thought them ; and
for that very reafon I have not diffembled thefe
two paffages which make to our Subject, and if
the efteem due to thefe Excellent Authors deprives
me of the honour of having faid the firft thing, of
which I thought I was the only Inventor, I fhall
draw that advantage at leaft from them, that they
give Authority to my thoughts ; and the Poet cannot refufe the Counfel I give him, of preparing ingenioufly his Incidents, when *Scaliger* efteems *Virgil* for having done it with prudence, and *Victorius*
condemns *Euripides* for having fail'd in it.   I fhall
give two Examples of both thefe out of Monfieur
Corneille, the firft is in *Rhodogune*, and the other in
his *Theodora*.

In the firft Example, he kills *Cleopatra* by the
violence of a Poyfon, fo ftrong, that *Rhodogune* difcovers the effect of it, before *Antiochus* has pronounc'd ten Verfes.   Indeed, that *Cleopatra* was
wicked and enrag'd enough to poifon her felf, that
fhe might poifon her Son and *Rhodogune*, That is
very well prepar'd in all the precedent Acts, where
her hatred, ambition, and fury appear to the height,
having kill'd her husband with her own hand,
and deftroyed one of her Sons to preferve her felf
upon the Throne ; but that the effect of the poyfon
fhould be fo fudden, as to be difcover'd in fo fmall a
fpace of time, That is not prepar'd enough, becaufe,
the thing being rare in it felf, *Cleopatra* fhould
have faid, when fhe hopes by it to deftroy *Antiochus*
and *Rhodogune*, how ftrong a Poyfon fhe had prepar'd, and how fudden its Effect would be, and
                                                    fhould

should have exprefs'd joy at it; by which means, fhe would have prepar'd the Incident, without preventing it.   The Event, I fay, would have been prepar'd ; for fo fudden a Poifon, as fhe had mention'd, would have been expected to work that Effect it did upon her felf ; but withall it would not have been prevented, becaufe the Audience would have thought, that fhe had faid it as defigning it for the deftruction of the Innocent, and fo there would not have been any means of forefeeing, that fhe fhould have fuffer'd by it her felf.

The other Example is in all the Exactnefs that a Dramatick Poem can wifh, which muft needs make us confefs, that when *Monfieur Corneille* has well meditated upon the conduct of an Incident, there is no Author, either among the Ancient or Modern Poets, that executes it better.

In his *Theodora*, there are five notable Incidents, to wit the death of *Flavia* ; the deliverance of *Theodora* from that infamous place, to which fhe had been condemn'd ; the death of *Didymus* and *Theodora* by the hands of *Marcella* ; the death of *Marcella* by her own hand ; and the wound of *Placidus* endeavouring to kill himfelf ; all thefe Incidents are fo well prepar'd, that there is not one, which might not probably come to pafs in confequence of thofe things which preceded it.

That *Flavia* fhould dye that day, is not ftrange; fince 'tis often faid that fhe is defperately ill ; but when that is faid, 'tis onely to give a pretext to the fury of *Marcella*, and to thofe violent means fhe ufes of being reveng'd of *Theodora*, without giving an Impreffion that her Daughter fhould really dye fo foon,

That

That *Didymus* should expose himself to save *Theodora*, in giving her his Clothes; that might well be, since he appears very passionately in love with her, and that *Theodora* did not reject his love but only out of Religion; but when this passion is talk'd of upon the Stage, it seems in appearance to be, to foment the Jealousie of *Placidus*, without any likely-hood of foreseeing so Extraordinary an Action.

That *Marcella* should with her own hands kill *Didymus* and *Theodora*, that is probable, she knew the love of *Placidus*, and the refolution he had taken to save the two Lovers, she saw him arm'd, and followed by a great number of his Friends, all these are preparations enough to make that Woman revenge the death of her Daughter, and all the injuries she had receiv'd by one furious transport in an occasion so precipitated; and nevertheless, though one could not from all these things expect this Event, yet they have all their necessary Colours, when they appear upon the Stage.

The same happens in the death of *Marcella*; she had persecuted *Placidus*, and injur'd him in the person he most tenderly lov'd; she sees him with his Sword drawn, and being animated with nothing but furious Sentiments, she was resolv'd not to fall under the power of her Enemy, from these Circumstances it follows, that probably she might kill her self, and that she was pref'sd to make that desperate end.

As for *Placidius*, who endeavours to kill himself, after having seen his Mistress murder'd by the hand of his Enemy, 'tis an Incident well prepar'd, because of the Excessive love he bore her, and

and by the difpofition he appears to be in, to forfake all the Grandeur of the World to poffefs
her, who was his Soveraign felicity ; and neverthelefs, of all thefe Confiderations one could pre-
fume naturally nothing more, than that he would
do all he could to fave her. Thus fo many different Events arife from one another, and without any precipitation in the Body of the Story.
I know not how Mr. *Corneille* may value this
Play, but I fay that in my mind it is his Mafter-
piece, for though in the Subject, the punifhment,
to which *Theodora* is condemn'd, does fomething
offend the modefty of the Spectators ; yet all the
reft is in fo much regularity, and there is fo much
Art and Conduct fhewed by the Poet, that if the
choice of the Subject had anfwer'd the skill of the
Author, I believe we might propofe this Play as
a moft perfect Model.

He that would cite here all the Plays of the
Ancients, where the Incidents are well prepar'd,
would be oblig'd to copy whole Poems, for they
have always done it with great Art and Judgment.
See the *Curculion* of *Plautus*, there is a Ring, which
ferves to find out *Planafion*, to be a freeborn Woman and the Sifter of *Terapontigonus*, when 'twas
no ways poffible to forefee this Event ; but it is
fo well prepar'd in all the Play, where this Ring
is employed in a great many other Intrigues,
that it is not at all forc'd, though much againft
the Expectation of the Spectators : And when this
Ring is ftol'n from the Souldier, and that from
thence it runs through a great many hands, 'tis for
fome prefent action, which has no regard to the
Cataftrophe, the event of which could not thence
be forefeen.   And

And when in the 4th Act, *Cappadore* fays, that he had paid but ten Mines of Silver for that Maid, 'tis probably, onely to explain the profit he makes by felling her for thirty; but 'tis in effect to prepare the Narration which *Planefion* makes her felf of her own Adventure.

So in his *Trinummus*, *Carmides* arrives at a nick of time, from a long Voyage, for a very diverting Incident, meeting with a Cheat which was fuppos'd to come from him, but That is very well prepar'd by the difcourfe of *Calicles* in the firft Act, and by that of his Slave in the fecond. And neverthelefs when *Calicles* fpeaks of the abfence of his Friend, 'tis onely to make known the fidelity he owes him; and that which the Slave fays of his return, is onely to make his Son *Telesbonicus* be afraid of his Fathers juft feverity.

In a word, I deliver here all that I can fay of this matter, which is, that the Events are always precipitated, when there has been nothing faid before, from whence they might probably proceed, as when a man appears exprefly in the end of the Play, of whom there has not been one word faid all along, and yet this man comes to make the winding up of the Plot. Or when towards the end, there is fome important Action done, which has no coherence with all that pafs'd before; for though the Spectators love to be furpriz'd, yet 'tis ftill with probability; and they are not bound to fuppofe any thing, but what follows naturally thefe things which the Poet fhews. The Theatre is a world by it felf, where all is comprehended in the notions and extent of the Action reprefented, and has no communication with the great World, onely fo far as the Poet him-

felf

felf extends it, by the knowledge which with Art he difpenfes abroad. But the main thing to be remembred, is, that all that is faid or done as a Preparative or Seed for things to come, muft have fo apparent a Reafon, and fo powerful a Colour to be faid and done in that place, that it may feem to have been introduc'd only for that, and that it never give a hint to prevent thofe Incidents, which it is to prepare.

S   CHAP.

CHAP. IX.

Of the Cataſtrophe or Iſſue of the Dramatick Poem.

I Do not think it neceſſary here to trouble my ſelf much about the explication of this word *Cataſtrophe.* 'Tis taken ordinarily, I know, for ſome ſad calamitous diſaſter, which terminates ſome great deſign, for my part I underſtand by this word a ſudden change of the firſt Diſpoſitions of the Stage, and the return of Events, which change all the Appearances of the former Intrigues, quite contrary to the expectation of the Audience. Comedies have generally happy *Cataſtrophes*, or at leaſt they end in ſome buffoonry or fooling, as the *Stichus* of *Plautus* ; but as for ſerious Tragedies, they alwayes end either by the Misfortune of the Principal Actors, or by a Proſperity ſuch as they could wiſh for ; we have Examples of both in the Poems of the Ancients, though that latter way, of terminating their Tragedies, was not ſo common with them, as it has been in our time. But now, I come to the Obſervations, which may be uſeful in all ſorts of Poems, as they are common to all ſorts of *Cataſtrophes.*

Cataſtrophe converſio negoti exagitati in tranquillitatem non expectatam. Scal. l. 1. c. 9.

S 2   The

The principal Obfervation has a dependance on what has been faid in the laft Chapter, which was, *that Incidents, not prepar'd, offended againft Probability, by being too much baftned at laft:* For this fault appears no where fo much as in the *Cataftrophe.* Firft, the *Cataftrophe* is the term of all the Affairs of the Stage, by confequent they muft be difpos'd by times, that they may arrive there eafily. Secondly, 'tis the Center of the Poem, therefore all the other parts, like lines, cannot be drawn ftraight to any other point. Thirdly, 'tis the laft expeCtation of the Audience therefore all things ought to be fo well order'd, that when they fall out, it may not be ask'd, by which way they came to pafs, and therefore there needs for it, as for the moft confiderable Event, the greateft and moft judicious Preparations. *Ariftotle*, and all his Followers, would have the *Cataftrophe* drawn from the very middle of all the bufinefs of the Stage, and that the very knots, which feem to embarrafs the whole SubjeCt, fhould at laft ferve for the opening of it, as if they were laid for that purpofe. Therefore they always valued this way of ending a Tragedy, much more than That which was founded upon the prefence or favour of fome God; and when they did make ufe of Gods in Machines, they always defir'd, that in the Body of the Play, there fhould be reafonable Difpofitions for it, either by the particular care that That God took of that Hero, or by the intereft the God might take in the Theatral ACtion, or by a natural and rational expeCtation of the affiftance of fome God, or fome fuch Inventions.

Yet this firft Rule may feem ufelefs in thofe Plays, where the *Cataftrophe* is known either by the Story

ry

ry or Title, as the *Death of Cæfar*, and fuch like,
Therefore in this Cafe, without omitting any of
the neceffary preparations we have mention'd, one
may do thus.

The Poet muft fo manage all the Affairs of the
Stage, that the Spectators may be inwardly perfwaded, that That perfon, whofe life and fortune
are threatned, ought not to die: For by this Art
he keeps them in fentiments of pity and commi-
feration, which encreafe and become very tender
at the laft point of his Misfortune, and the more
one finds motives to believe, he fhould not die, the
more one is concern'd, when one knows he muft,
the injuftice of his Enemies raifes a ftronger averfion in us for them, and his difgrace is pitied even
with tears.   We have feen the Examples of this
in *Mariamne*, and the Earl of *Effex*, though, in many other things, they were very defective Plays.

But if the *Cataftrophe* be not known, and that
the Poet defigns, that, for the greater Ornament of
his Play, it fhould unfold all the Intrigues of it
by a fuprizing Novelty ; he muft be very careful not
to difcover it too foon, and particularly order it fo,
that none of his preparations do prevent it, for not
only then it would become ufelefs and difagreeable,
but as foon as ever it fhould be known, the Theatre
would grow dull, and be without Charms for the Audience : And we are not in this Circumftance to govern our felves by what happens in a Play, that we
have feen, or of which the *Cataftrophe* is known ;
for they do ftill pleafe, becaufe the Spectators in that
cafe confider things only as they pafs, and give
them no greater extent, than the Poet would have
them.   They confine all their underftanding to
                                        the

the pretexts and colours, which he advances, without going any further, and being all along fatisfied of the Motives of the chief Actions, they do not prevent thofe, which are not made known to them, fo that, their imagination being deceiv'd by the art of the Poet, their pleafure lafts ftill. Whereas in the other Cafe, when the *Cataftrophe* is prevented by the want of Art in the Poet, the Spectators are difgufted, not fo much that they know the thing, as becaufe they are perfwaded, that they ought not to know it, and their difcontent in thefe occafions proceeds lefs from their knowledge, though certain, than from the imprudence and ill conduct of the Poet.

The laft Rule is, that the *Cataftrophe* do entirely finifh the *Dramatick* Poem, that is, that there be nothing left of what the Spectators ought to know, for if they have reafon to ask, *What became of fuch a one concern'd in the Intrigues of the Stage?* or if they have juft Subject to enquire, *What are the Sentiments of one of the chief Actors, after the laft event which makes the Cataftrophe?* Then, I fay, the Play is not well finifh'd, and wanted yet a ftroke or two, and if the Spectators are not yet fully fatisfied, the Poet certainly has not done his duty. 'Twas a confiderable fault in *Panthea*, who by her death leaves a reafonable defire to the Spectators, to know what became of *Arafpes*, who was fo paffionately in love with her: Whereas on the contrary, in the Earl of *Effex*, Queen *Elizabeth* fpeaks as fhe ought, after the death of the Earl, and fo finifhes the *Cataftrophe* perfectly.

But to avoid this inconvenience, the Poet muft not fall into another, that is, to add to the *Cataftrophe* fuperfluous Difcourfes and Actions, of no ufe as

to

to the concluding the Play, which the Spectators neither look for, nor are willing to hear; such is the Complaint of the Wife of *Alexander*, Son of *Herod*, after the death of her Husband, of which I shall speak in the Chapter of Pathetick Discourses; and such is likewise the Explication of the Oracle in *Horatius*, for that having had nothing to do with the Plot, the Spectators never think on't, nor care to have it interpreted.

I might lengthen this Discourse with many more Remarks, as well upon the Tragedies as the Comedies of the Ancients; but since all *Catastrophes* turn upon these Principles, which I have laid down, it will be easie in reading their Works to see which are well or ill finish'd. The Tragick Poets have generally taken more care than the Comick, and amongst the Comick, *Terence* is the most exact; for *Aristophanes* and *Plautus* have left the best part of theirs unfinish'd. I leave our Modern Authors to themselves, they generally are willing to be believ'd infallible, and when any body shews them that they might have done better, they are so much the more angry, as they find themselves convinc'd, and not able to oppose the strength of reason.

The End of the second Book.

THE
ART
OF THE
STAGE.

Book the Third.

Chapter the First.

Of the Actors or Persons to be brought upon the Stage, and what the Poet is to observe about them.

I Do not design here to instruct the Players, but the Poet, who will find in this Chapter some Observations for the better disposing of the Drammatick Poem, as to the persons that are to appear upon the Stage.

But before we begin them, it will not be amiss to

[A]   observe

obferve to the Reader a thing which will make us make a wifh in favour of our Stage, when we reflect upon the Magnificency of the Reprefentations of the Antients, which is, that in many places of their Poems, where we fee but one Actor nam'd, he did not appear alone upon the Stage; but on the contrary, when it was a Prince, or Princefs, or fome Perfon of Eminent Quality, he was followed by a very great Retinue, fuitable to his Dignity; fometimes of Courtiers, fometimes of Souldiers, and always of Perfons proper to the Subject of the Play : Nay, a rich Citizen appear'd with a great many Servants, and a publick Curtizan, if fhe were of free condition, and Miftrefs of her own actions, had always a great many Maids and Servants about her; and in fhort, Perfons of Quality were always well accompanied, except fome particular reafon requir'd they fhould be alone, which may be eafily perceiv'd by the Verfes, or the Nature of the Action. So *Ajax* in *Sophocles* is alone when he kills himfelf; and this the Antients did for two Reafons; firft to fill their Stage, which was much bigger than ours, and the other to make their Reprefentation more magnificent; whereas now five or fix People fill our Stage, and befides, the Players cannot be at the charge of more for pure Ornament fake.

The truth of this appears in moft of the Antients Plays, but particularly in the feven before *Thebes*, where *Eteocles*, who opens the Scene, feems to be alone, becaufe there is no body fpeaks but he, but it is clear that he was followed by a very great number of Perfons, to whom he addreffes himfelf, and gives them different Orders for the Defence of the Town.

Oreftes

Orestes seems to be alone in the *Electra* of *Euri-pides*, and yet one may see that he *speaks* to a great many Servants who followed him, whom he commands to enter his Sisters house, who did not know him, and is angry with her Husband for letting so many People of Quality come into his house. I cannot omit here the mistake that some Authors have made in interpreting *Euripides*; for having not observ'd that *Hyppolitus* is followed by a company of Hunters, with whom he comes back singing a Hymn in the honour of *Diana*, they have taken him to be alone, and that they who sung were the *Chorus* of the Tragedy; whereas the *Chorus* in that Play is compos'd of Women, followers of *Phædra*, who only come upon the Stage after *Hyppolitus* and his Company have sung their Hymn, and one of them Entertains him some time about the respect due to *Venus*; after which Dialogue *Hyppolitus* commands his People to go and prepare his Dinner at his own house, out of which they follow him again, when by his Fathers command he is forc'd to withdraw.

But *Plutarch* affords us a proof of the state with which the chief Actors us'd to appear upon the Stage, in a pleasant Story he tells in the life of *Phocion*;for a Player being to represent a Queen and his Attendance, which was to be numerous, not being ready, he refused to come upon the Stage, whereupon *Melanthius Choragus*, whose Office it was to see all things well in order, thrust him by force upon the Stage, with these words, *Doest not thou see that* Phocion's *Wife, whose Husband governs us all, is seen every day in the Street attended but with one Maid :* At which all the People fell a laughing, and by that Railery he excus'd the defect of the Representation; which by the by may ferve our Poets for an Advertifement, to Read carefully the Works of the Antients, and not truft to the Printed Gloffes or Interpreters; but now let us come to our other more neceffary Obfervations.

And to begin, it has been often ask'd how many Actors may be brought on at once, fpeaking and acting upon the Stage, in the fame Scene. Some have confin'd us to Three, taking their Rule from *Horace*'s Art of Poetry; but Experience is the beft Judg in thefe Cafes; and *Horace*, I believe, is not fo well underftood as he fhould be. 'Tis true, that the Stage having attain'd to have Three Actors in the time of *Sophocles*, who brought Drammatick Poetry to its perfection; the *Greeks* feldom bring any more than Three Actors at a time upon the Stage, if there be a Fourth, he generally is filent; and indeed a Scene is not ill fill'd when Three chief Actors are difcourfing at once upon the Scene. But the Anfwer to this Queftion depends not fo much upon the number of Perfons, as upon the order or confufion that would follow if too many were fpeaking in the fame Scene; and therefore I am of Opinion, that the Poet may bring on as many as he pleafes, provided neither their number, nor their difcourfes do confound the Spectators Attention; and there will be no confufion if the Actors Names, and their Concerns be fo known as to give a true underftanding of what is in Action: Three Actors indeed feldom bring any confufion, becaufe there is no Spectator fo fimple, but he can eafily diftinguifh their words and defigns; but ftill the Poet muft confider what neceffity he lies under; for if his Subject requires that Four or Five fhould appear and difcourfe in the fame Scene, if he performs it with diftinction,
and

and without obfcurity, I don't believe any body will fay he goes againft the Rules, there being nothing there againft probability. The Examples of this are frequent in the Comick Poets, both Greek and Latine; and as for *Horace*, his Advice is only that the Poet do not bring a Fourth Perfon upon the Stage *Ne quarta laboret.* fo as to embarafs or confound the bufinefs in hand, or perplex the Difcourfe of the other Three.

Our fecond Obfervation is, that the Poet muft bring no Actor upon the Stage that is not known to the Spectators as foon as he appears, and that not only as to his Name and Perfon, but alfo as to the Sentiments he brings upon the Stage, elfe the Spectator will be puzzled, and the Poets fine Difcourfes will be loft, becaufe the Audience will not know how to apply them; and I have feen often 20 or 30 noble Verfes thrown away becaufe the Spectator knew not him that fpoke them, nor how to apply them. The Antients never fail'd in this, to which the *Chorufes* were a great help to them; for they never leaving the Stage, generally as foon as a new Actor came on, they nam'd him with fome expreffions of fear, aftonifhment or joy, according as the Subject requir'd; but if he were a ftranger, and unknown to the *Chorus*, then he nam'd himfelf, giving fome account of his good or bad Fortune, or fome confident of his, declar'd it without affectation, either by pitying him, or feeming to be concern'd for the doubtful fuccefs of his Enterprize.

As for us who have no *Chorufes*, we muft, inftead of them, make fome of thofe Actors fpeak who are already upon the Stage, and known; and if we open an Act with Perfons unknown, they muft themfelves declare their condition, or fome of their Followers muft.

muſt by the by, and without affectation inſinuate it: But if it be neceſſary that an Actor ſhould be *incognito* both as to his Name and Quality, in order to his being known with more pleaſure towards the end of the Play, then the Spectators muſt at leaſt know that he is *incognito*; and in a word all confuſion muſt be avoided, and it will be well if the Spectators conceive ſomething in general concerning the Inteterefts of this new Actor; not indeed ſo far as to diſcover or prevent an Incident, but ſo much as is neceſſary to facilitate their eaſier comprehending all that is to be ſaid afterwards.

The Third Obſervation is, That the Actors do always come on, and go off of the Scene with ſome probable reaſon, which makes it more proper for them to do ſo than otherwiſe, and yet that muſt not be done groſly, but by nice and natural pretexts. For any Art that diſcovers it ſelf too much, loſes its grace; and yet it is not neceſſary that the reaſon which makes the Actors go on and off ſhould always take effect; quite contrary, the leſs things ſucceed according to their firſt appearance, the more pleaſing and ſurpriſing they are. 'Tis one of the beauties of the Stage, that things croſs one another, and ſo produce unforeſeen Events; and when an Actor is upon the Stage, his good or bad Fortune is in the Poets hands, though the reaſon that brought him on be not at all conformable to what he meets with there.

As for the Practice of this Rule, I muſt deſire our Poets to have recourſe to the Antients, and to obſerve with what Art they govern themſelves; for the Reading of one Poem of theirs, particularly of *Sophocles*, will give them more light in this matter,
than

than all the Allegations with which I might fwell this Treatife.

The Fourth Obfervation is about a Difpute which I have often been witnefs to, which is, Whether or no in the fame Act the fame Actor may appear more than once ? Firft, To anfwer this Queftion right, it is neceffary to diftinguifh the Plays ; for in a Comedy, the Subject whereof is taken from the meaner fort of People, it would not be amifs that the Perfons concern'd fhould appear more than once in an Act, becaufe they are People whofe bufinefs is not weighty, their actions quick, and the manner of their life unquiet, and their Intrigues, moft of them happening in the Neighbourhood, fo that they need but a little time to go and come; but in a Tragedy, where they are moft commonly Kings and Princes, where their manner of living is very different, their actions all full of gravity and weight, it does not appear eafie nor reafonable to make them appear more than once in an Act; for their Intrigues are generally with Perfons remote, their Defigns great, and which are not to be brought to pafs but by flow means, and with great circumfpection , fo that more time is regularly requir'd to move all the Springs of their Affairs.

Secondly, In both thefe forts of Poems, one muft confider the condition of the Perfon; for in a Slave or Servant it would be nothing to fee him often in an Act, but it would be fomething ftrange in a Man or Woman of Quality, if fome very extraordinary reafon did not oblige them to precipitate their Actions.

Thirdly, We are to confider how far an Actor went, and if the thing he went about requir'd much time ; or if he had fome reafon to return fo foon ;

for

for the place he went to being near, and having but a fhort bufinefs, and being obliged to return immediately, all thefe are circumftances which may bring an Actor upon the *Stage* twice in an Act, without offending againft the Rules. *Plautus* does it very ingenioufly in many of his Comedys, but I know no Example of it in any Tragedys of the Antients. *Monfieur Corneille* indeed in his *Horatius* brings his *Hero* twice on in the fame Act, becaufe he went but from the Hall of his Pallace to his Fathers Chamber, to take his leave of him before he engaged in the Combate between the Six Brothers. But for my part, I fhould counfel the Poet to do it as little as poffible, and with great circumfpection; for, methinks, it is a little undecent to fee a Perfon of Quality go and come fo fuddenly, and Act with fo much appearance of precipitation.

The Fifth Obfervation is about a thing which the Antients never fail'd in, and the Modern Writers often have, which is, to bring their Principal Actors on, upon the opening of the Stage, and indeed with a great deal of reafon, becaufe their Perfons being confidered as the Principal Subject of all the Adventures of the Play, and as the Center to which all the other Lines are to be drawn, the Spectators defire to fee them at firft, and all that is faid or done before their Arrival gives them more impatience than pleafure, and is often reckoned for nothing : And befides, they often take the firft Actor of Quality for the *Hero* of the Play, and when they are undeceiv'd, find themfelves in confufion and perplexed; therefore thofe Authors who bring not on their Chief Actor till the Third or Fourth Act, are much to blame, for that caufes in the Audience fo
much

much impatience and uncertainty, that it is afterwards very hard to fatisfie them; not but that in
fome occafions one may luckily defer the bringing
on a chief Actor for a while, but then that muft give
fome extraordinary grace to the Play, and be order'd fo, as not to confound the Spectators Application.

The Sixth Obfervation is, That the chief Actors
ought to appear as often, and ftay as long as poffible upon the Stage; Firft, becaufe they are always
the beft Actors, and fo fatisfie moft; then they are
the beft cloth'd, and fo pleafe the Spectators, who
are taken with their Drefs: And laftly, becaufe they
have the fineft things to fay, and the nobleft paffions
to fhew; in which, to fay truth, confifts the greateft
charm of the Stage; and befides, the whole Event
being to turn upon them, the Spectator rejoyces
and grieves with them, fears and hopes as they do,
and always has fome inward concern according to
the prefent ftate of their Affairs.   This makes me
not approve of *Seneca*, who in a Play where *Agamemnon* is the chief *Hero*, and is kill'd, makes him
fay not above two and twenty Verfes in all.   The
beft Advice I can give the Poet in this matter, is not
to have any thing told by way of Narrative, which
may be any ways decently perform'd by the chief
Actors themfelves; but if the Subject cannot fuffer
that the chief Actors fhould appear every Act, he
muft endeavour that that Act where they do not
appear, be fill'd with fome great circumftance of the
Story, and that the fecond Parts may repair the
want of the firft by fome noble and majeftick Adventure, elfe it is certain the Play will pall and lan-
guifh.

[B]   The

The Seventh and laſt Obſervation of this Chapter is particular enough, and it may be at firſt will not be relliſhed by all our Poets; but I deſire them to examine it in the practice, before they judg of it hereupon the Paper. To explain my ſelf rightly, we muſt obſerve, that where an Actor appears firſt upon the Stage, he may come on in one of theſe Three Diſpoſitions, either in a moderate, calm temper, or in a violent paſſion, or in a diſpoſition ſomething moved, but not rais'd to the high pitch of Tranſport; and that may be call'd a half-paſſion. Now in the firſt caſe an Actor may eaſily acquit himſelf, for it comes ſo near our natural temper, that few fail to perſonate it well. In the ſecond caſe likewiſe of violent Tranſport, good Actors ſeldom fail to repreſent it well, becauſe Experience has taught them how far their Voice and Action is to be ſtrain'd in ſuch a caſe; but as it is much eaſier to go from one Extremity to another, than to ſtop with diſcretion in the middle; ſo the Actors, though they can eaſily repreſent theſe two Sentiments directy oppoſite, they do not always ſucceed when they are to come upon the Stage with the Sentiment of a *half-paſſion,* which paſſes a little our natural Tranquillity, and yet riſes not to the extremeſt violence; and the reaſon is, that not being ſtirr'd of themſelves, and yet not daring to riſe to the higheſt pitch of violence, 'tis hard for them to find that juſt temper to enter into this half paſſion; from hence it comes, that they often provoke the laughter of the Audience, by delivering with an ill grace, and unconcernedly, that which requires ſome Emotion, or appearing over-allarm'd at that which does not in its nature ſo highly affect the Spectators. Therefore my Obſervation

tion to the Poet is, that he firſt put ſome more moderate words in his Actors mouth, before he raiſes him to that half-paſſion, that he may grow warm by little and little, and that his Voice may riſe by degrees, and all his geſtures acquire more and more motion with his Diſcourſe ; and as for the Actor, I will tell him what in this caſe I have ſeen *Mondory*, the beſt Actor of our days do, which was, that in theſe occaſions having taken a turn or two upon the Stage, and with ſome poſture ſuitable to his Part, as lifting up his Hands and Eyes, or the like; having begun to move himſelf, he brought himſelf to the true point of a half-paſſion, and ſo came ſenſibly out of the natural ſtate of Indifferency in which he came on upon the Stage ; withal, retaining his motions ſo as they ſhould not go too far. All this will be better underſtood by both Poets and Actors, if they pleaſe to make ſome Reflections at Reheaſals, and have the Comedians own Opinions who are beſt Judges, having often experienced this, and other Methods of performing a half-paſſion.

Chapter the Second.

Of Diſcourſes in general.

IF we conſider Tragedy in its own nature, it implies ſo much Action, that it ſeems not to have any room left for Diſcourſe : 'Tis called a *Dramma*, which ſignifies an Action, and the Perſons concern'd are called Actors, as thoſe that are preſent are nam'd Spectators, or Lookers on, not Hearers. And indeed

all

all the Difcourfes of Tragedy ought to be as the Actions of thofe that appear upon the Stage; for there to fpeak, is to act, there being not there any Speeches invented by the Poet to fhew his Eloquence. So we fee that the Narration of the Death of *Hyppolitus* in *Seneca*, is rather the action of a Man frightned at the Monfter that he faw come out of the Sea, and at the fad Adventure which befel *Hyppolitus*. In a word, all Difcourfes upon the Stage are but the Acceffaries of Action, though the whole Play in its Reprefentation confifts in Difcourfes. 'Tis they that are the chief work of the Poet, and in which he Employs all the ftrength of his wit; all that he invents, is in order to have it well deliver'd upon the Stage, and he fuppofes many actions that they may ferve for Subject of thofe Difcourfes. Thus he feeks all ways to make love, joy, hatred, grief, and the reft of our paffions fpeak upon the Stage; and yet if we examine rightly this Poem, the beft part of the actions are but in the imagination of the Spectator, to whom the Poet by his Art makes them as it were vifible, though there be nothing fenfible but the Difcourfes. And we may obferve in two of the Greek Poets, that though *Euripides*'s Tragedys are fill'd with more Incidents and Actions than thofe of *Sophocles*, yet they had not fo good fuccefs upon the Stage of *Athens*; neither are they now fo pleafant to read; the reafon whereof is, that the Difcourfes of *Sophocles* are more Eloquent, and more Judicious than thofe of *Euripides*. Nay, thofe *Dramma's* which carry the name of *Seneca*, howfoever irregular and defective they are in other things, do neverthelefs pafs very well, by reafon of the fenfe and force of fome Difcourfes that are in them.

them. And we have ftill a greater proof of this in the Works of our *Corneille* ; for that which has fo clearly fet him above all the Poets of his time has not been the Plot, or Regularity of his Plays, but the Difcourfes, and the noble ways of Exprefling thofe violent paffions which he introduces, even fo far, that we fee very irregular actions in them fo accompanied with ingenious and pathetick Expreffions, that the fault could not be perceiv'd but by the Learned Obfervers, the beauty of the Thoughts and Language dazling the underftanding of all the reft of the Audience, and taking away from them the liberty of judging of any thing elfe. For Example, it was not very probable that *Rodrigues*, all bloody with the Murder of his Miftrefs's Father, fhould go and make her a Vifit, nor that fhe fhould receive it, and yet their converfation is fo pleafing and full of fuch noble Sentiments, that few have obferv'd that Indecency, and they that did were willing to fuffer it. Again, when *Don Sanche* brings his Sword to *Chimene*, he ought not to let her run on in thofe miftaken Complaints, fince with one word he could undeceive her; but that which fhe fays is fo agreeable, that the Spectator cannot wifh *Don Sanche* had been more prudent.

All the Learned men in the Drammatick Art tell us, that thofe Plays which they call *Polymythes*, that is, loaded with many Incidents, either are bad, or at leaft none of the beft; but they have not given the reafon, which in my judgment is, becaufe they are all taken up in action, and fo leaving no room for Difcourfes, the Subject is as it were ftif'd for want of Air; and on the contrary, a Play which has but few Incidents, and a fmall Intrigue, but fill'd with

Excellent

Excellent Language, and thought, can feldom fail of pleafing.

We muft neverthelefs obferve fome difference in this Point between *Comedy* and *Tragedy* ; for *Comedy*, whofe bufinefs lies among the common fort of People, not fo capable of gravity and thought, as the Tragick Actors, is much more in action than in Difcourfes ; there is required there little Eloquence, and much Intrigue. *Terence* is pleafanter to read than *Plautus*, becaufe he is more Elegant, but *Plautus* took better with the *Romans*, becaufe he is fuller of action. *Terence* has many ferious Moral fayings, which is not the proper work of *Comedy*, where the Spectators defign is to laugh. *Plautus* is full of Intrigues, from which many Jefts, and ingenious Raileries are created, and that's the thing we wifh for in Comedy.

I could wifh therefore that our Poets would excel in the Art of Rhetorick, and ftudy Oratory and Eloquence to the bottom ; for we are not to imagine, that it confifts in fome puns and quibbles, to make the Citizens and Country Gentlemen laugh, nor in fome *Antithefes*, or other Figures often ill employ'd ; no, the Poet ought to know all the paffions, the fprings, that bring them on, and the way of expreffing them with Order, Energy, and Judgment.

He may fee many Examples of this amongft the Antient Poets, who beft can fhew him the way of pleafing, and acquiring Reputation. I, for my part, pretend to nothing here, but to give him my particular Obfervations, which at leaft may ferve him to make better of his own. But to do this with order, I confider there are generally in a Play Four forts of Difcourfes, *Narrations, Deliberations, Didactick*
Difcourfes

Difcourfes or *Inftructions*, and *Pathetick Difcourfes*, or the motions of paffions. This is the Method which I eftablifh to explain my felf, to which any body may add what they think neceffary, and take away all that they fhall judg fuperfluous ; and in a word, change all that fhall not pleafe them, and have my free confent to do it.

Chapter the Third.

Of Narrations.

THefe Narrations which happen in a Dramma-tick Poem, do generally regard two forts of things ; either thofe which have happened before the opening of the Stage, wherefoever they came to pafs ; nay, though it be long before ; or elfe they regard thofe things which happen off of the Scene in the Contexture of the Theatral action, after once the Stage is open, and within the Extent of time that it requires. As to the firft fort which are brought into the body of the Poem, for the better under-ftanding of things which happened before the open-ing of the Stage, they may regularly be us'd in the beginning of the Play, that they may give a Foun-dation to the whole Action, and prepare the Inci-dents, and by that means facilitate to the Spectator the underftanding of all the reft ; or elfe they may be made ufe of toward the end of the Poem, and ferve to the *Cataftrophe*, or the untying and opening of all the Plot.

Not but that they may be made in other parts of
the

the Play, as we fee it done in a Play call'd *Virginia*, where the chiefeft Narration is in the Fourth Act, and is perform'd with great grace, and equal fuccefs ; but in that part of the Play 'tis very dangerous to ufe them ; for they run a hazard of either difcovering the *Cataftrophe*, which is near at hand, or elfe they leave the Stage in fome obfcurity, and the Specta-tors ill inform'd of many circumftances, for having too long delay'd the opening of them; fo that to avoid both thefe Inconveniences, the Poet muft have a very fteddy hand, fince he muft order it fo as his Narration do not in the leaft prevent the beauty of the *Cataftrophe*; nor his firft acts be lefs intelligible for having kept back his Narration.

As for thofe things which happen in the courfe of the Action, the recital of them is to be made as they happen; or if it be thought neceffary, or more pleafing to delay them, there muft be us'd fome Art to feed the Spectators defire of knowing them with-out impatience; or elfe you muft quite ftifle his Ex-pectation, that he may be the better furpriz'd when they come to pafs. But we muft remember befides, that thefe Recitals or Narrations are introduced only to inftruct the Spectator about what paffes off of the Scene ; for to relate either thofe things that have been feen, or might have been feen, as being fuppos'd to have been done upon the Stage, would certainly be very ridiculous ; and befides, thofe things that give ground to thefe Incident Narrations, ought to be very confiderable, or elfe they are to be avoid-ed, and the thing to be infinuated into the Audience by fome words fcattered here and there either before or after.

Now all thefe Narrations do enter into the Composition

polition of the Drammatick Poem, for two ends, either to make it clear and intelligible, or to adorn and fet it out ; but againft both thefe ends the Poet often falls into Errours, which deftroy his firft Intention.

The firft is, when his Narration is obfcure, and loaded with circumftances hard for the Audience to retain diftinctly ; fuch are *Genealogical* ones (which *Scaliger* blames in *Homer* ; or a great number of Names, with a Chain of actions embroyl'd one in in another; for the Spectator will not give himfelf the trouble to obferve and retain all thefe different *Idæa's*, he coming to the Stage only for his pleafure, and in the mean time for want of remembring all this, he remains in the dark as to the reft of the Play, and is difgufted for all the time he ftays. Such a Story might be that of the three Brothers, and three Sifters, which is defcrib'd in *Aftræa*, and that of the two Children born of two Women, who had each of them married one anothers Sons ; if any body fhould upon fuch Stories found the whole Intrigue of a Play, he might be fure no body would underftand it, and by confequent it would have few Spectators.

The Second fault of Narrations is when they are tædious, and they are always tædious when they do not contain things neceffary or agreeable; as alfo when they are made with weak and faint Expreffions, fuch as do not captivate the Spectators favour or attention, which by confequent muft pall, and make him give over minding the Play ; and this happens likewife when they are too long; for variety being the life of the Stage, and that being wanting, the beft things grow dull, and weigh upon the Spectator, who takes it ill to be fix'd to one Subject with-

[C] our

out diverſity for ſo long a time ; and though it may
be the capacity of ſome would carry them thorow
to comprehend it all, yet being come for diverſion,
they will not take the pains to do it, which joyn'd
with the incapacity of others to hearken to ſo long a
Story, cauſes at laſt a general diſguſt in the whole
Audience.

We may moreover make this diſtinction upon the
length of Narrations, for they may be ſo either for
the matter, when they are fill'd with too great a
number of Incidents, and Perſons, of Names and Places ; or they may be ſo out of the form for the
many words they contain, as when the circumſtances of an Action are too much exaggerated and parti-
culariz'd in minute and inſignificant things;and when
the Expreſſions are too full of *Epithets,* Adverbs, or
other unneceſſary terms, with Repetitions of the
ſame thing, though in a different way.

And indeed, to examine the difference of theſe
two ſorts of lengths in Narrations, we may ſay, that
the firſt is vicious in any place of the Play whereſo-
ever it is plac'd :   For firſt, at the opening of the
Stage, the Spectator, who thinks all that Recital
neceſſary for the underſtanding of the Play, endeavours to retain it all in his memory ; but finding
his Imagination confounded, and his Memory di-
ſtracted with ſo many things, he is firſt vex'd with
himſelf, and then with the Poet, and at laſt gives
out, without minding any more of the whole Poem.

Theſe long Narrations are not better plac'd in the
courſe of the Action, for thoſe things which come
to paſs after the opening of the Stage, becauſe it
will never be thought probable that ſo many things
ſhould have come to paſs in ſo little a time; (as for
Example,

Example, the Interval of an Act feems to be) not
but that it is ordinary to fuppofe in that time a
Battle, a Confpiracy, or fome fuch other Event ; but
to do it with probability, the Poet deceives the Spectator, and bufies him with fomething elfe that is
agreeable, that fo he may be infenfibly perfuaded
that there has been time enough for all the reft ; but
that which is particularly to be heeded in that place
is, that at that time the Stage is in all the hurry of
Action, and in the turns of Incidents, which thefe
long Narrations do cool and pall, whereas a true
Narration ought to quicken the Stage, and lay the
foundation of fome new paffion, which to obtain,
it muft be fhort, pithy, and full of life and warmth.
The contrary of this appears in that Narration,
which the Rich in Imagination makes in the Play
call'd the *Vifionaires.*

When thefe long Narrations happen towards the
Cataftrophe, they are then abfolutely infupportable ;
for the Spectator, who is impatient to fee which way
the Intrigue turns, has all his pleafure fpoil'd juft
in the time when he ought to receive the moft,
which is fo much the more dangerous for the fuccefs of the Play, becaufe the Audience is already
tir'd and difpos'd to give out.

In a word, I think it may be a kind of General
Rule, that Narrations may be longer at the opening
of the Stage than any where elfe, becaufe the Spectator is frefh, and willing to give attention, and his
memory receives agreeably all thofe new *Idæa's*, in
hopes they are to contribute to the pleafure which is
prepar'd for him ; and alfo that they are as much to
be avoided at the *Cataftrophe*, where they do fo
chock the Audience, who is then impatient to know

the

the Event, that no Figures of Rhetorick can make him amends. See, amongſt others, how dexterous *Plautus* is in the Narration of the knowing of *la-neſia*, at the end of the *Curculio* ; 'tis one of the moſt regular Narrations that he has.

Beſides theſe Cautions, it will not be amiſs to ob-ſerve, that theſe Narrations may be made in two manners ; either all of a piece, where a Story is told that is to give a foundation to all the Plot of the Play ; (though they that among the Poets do it beſt, have ſome Pathetick or other ingenious Inter-ruptions) as the *Oreſtes* of *Euripides*, and in the Comical kind, the *Hecyra* of *Terence*, and the *Pſeu-dolus* of *Plautus* in the firſt Acts do ſufficiently il-luſtrate : Or elſe, theſe Narrations are made by piece-meals, according as the Poet thinks fit to hide or diſcover any part of his Subject, to frame the dif-ferent Acts with more Ornament, as one may ſee in the *Sphigenia* of *Euripides*, and in the *Oedipus Ty-rannus* of *Sophocles*, where the Story is told by dif-ferent Perſons, and at different times ; which may be perform'd, when he that makes part of a Narra-tion knows not all the Story, or when for ſome other neceſſary reaſon which muſt appear ſo to the Audi-ence, he will not tell all he knows ; or when he is interrupted by ſome body elſe (which muſt be done with great Art, and not by bringing on a purpoſe a man who has nothing elſe to do in the reſt of the Play, but to interrupt that Actor ;) Or laſtly, when thoſe things that are neceſſary to be known, are not yet come to paſs, as *Corneille* has moſt ingeniouſly practiſed in his *Horatius* ; for by opening his Stage after the Truce concluded, he has found a way to bring *Curiatius* to *Rome*, and there has reſerv'd to
himſelf

himſelf to make different Narrations of the Combate of the three Brothers in ſuch places of his Play
as he thinks the fitteſt to change the ſtate of Affairs
upon his Stage.

I may aſſure our Poets, that a Narration thus ingeniouſly divided, requires great Art and Medita-
tation to conſider how far one may carry each part
of it, and to give all the neceſſary grounds and colours to the Audience, for leaving off in ſuch a place,
and beginning again in ſuch another ; and indeed
ſuch a Narration well managed, produces an admirable Effect ; for leaving the Spectator always in the
expectation of ſome Novelty, it warms his deſire,
and entertains his impatience ; and then the new
diſcoveries that are made in the reſt of the Narration furniſh the Stage with Subjects to vary all the
Motions and Paſſions of the Actors.

Narrations may beſides be conſidered as ſimply
and plainly telling the Tale, or as exaggerating pa-
thetically the circumſtances of the Adventure. In
the firſt caſe they ought to be ſhort, becauſe they are
without motion or ornament, and yet they are often neceſſary, as when ſome important Advice is to
be given to obviate ſome preſſing miſchief.

Pathetick Narrations are always the fineſt, and the
only indeed fit to come upon the Stage, when they
are contain'd within the bounds of a reaſonable Ex-
aggeration ; then the mixture of fear, aſtoniſhment,
imprecations, and the like, according to the circumſtances of the Story is fit, and produces a good Effect. But particularly, theſe paſſions ought to be
mingled in the Narration, when the perſon to whom
it is made is not at all ignorant of the whole Story,
and yet there is a neceſſity of informing the Audience
by

by him; and I believe that I firſt found out this
ſleight, to avoid abſurdity in doing of it; for in this
caſe it would be ridiculous to make to him a plain
Story which he knows already; therefore to avoid
that one muſt bring in natural paſſions growing from
the Story it ſelf, and the preſent ſtate of the Affairs
of the Stage, either by Complaints, or Sentiments of
joy, or fear; for by this means the Story is told, and
yet no affected cold Narration brought on againſt
all the Rules of probability.   Such is the Narration
of the Death of *Clitemneſtra* in the *Electra* of *Euripides*, and ſuch is the diſcourſe of *Tecmeſſa* in *Sophocles* in his *Ajax*, where the Poet makes her make
an ingenious Narration of all that the Spectators were
ignorant of under pretext of complaining of her own
misfortunes, and the Narration of *Soſias*.   In *Amphytrio* is one of the moſt ingenious ones, where the
Poet, that he may inſtruct the Audience about *Amphytrio*'s Voyage, and the War, makes that Slave meditate to himſelf what News he ſhall tell his Miſtreſs,
for by that means, though the Narration be made to
himſelf, and very pleaſant things in it, fit for a Slaves
wit to ſay, yet at the ſame time the Spectator is informed of every thing, without any apparent affectation.   But in theſe Narrations the Poet muſt be
very careful to keep up the humour, ſo as nothing of
a ſtudied Recital do appear, for then 'tis faulty, as
done on purpoſe for the Spectators. Therefore I can
never adviſe him to uſe a certain way, common
enough now adays, which is when an Actor knows
ſome part of the Story, though the Spectators are
not informed of any part of it; in this caſe I ſay Poets
do often make another Repeat that which the Actor
knows already, ſaying only, *You know ſuch a thing,*
                                                      and

☞ p. 393. middle.

and then adding, *Now here is the reft which you do not know.* To fay truth, this appears to me ver grofs, and it were better to let that which the Acto, knows already, be expreffed to the Audience by fome motions of paffion, and then find fome ingenious pretext to tell the reft in an ordinary Narration.

That which remains now to be done upon this Subject, is to explain fome Rules, from which, without abfurdity the Poet cannot depart.

The firft is, that he who makes the Narration be rationally fuppos'd to know perfectly the thing he tells, or elfe he cannot be thought to tell it with any probability.

Secondly, That on his fide, there be fome apparent and powerful reafon for him to tell it, either by the neceffity of giving notice to fome other perfon, or by fome well-grounded curiofity, or by the Authority he has over the perfon that fpeaks with him, or fome fuch confiderations.

Thirdly, He that hears him muft have fome juft Subject to be inform'd of the thing that is told him, and I for my part cannot bear that a *Varlet* fhould out of fimple curiofity be entertain'd with the Adventures of a great Prince, as the Poet has done in *Rhodogune*; for Narrations are always flat that are not made to a perfon concern'd for want of paffions to animate both the Audience, and the Man that makes the Recital.

Befides, a Narration ought to be made in a fit place, where probably both he that hears, and he that fpeaks, might be fuppos'd to meet; wherefore I cannot approve that in the Hall of a Pallace, where probably People go and come continua'.y, there fhould be a long Narration made of fecret Adventures,

tures which ought not to be difcover'd without great
precaution for the danger that attends their being re-
vealed ; and therefore I never could conceive how
Mr. *Corneille* can bring to pafs with decency that.
In the fame place *Cinna* tells *Æmilia* all the circumftances of a great Confpiracy againft *Auguftus*, and
yet in that very place *Auguftus* holds a fecret counfel
of his two intimate Favourites ; for if it be a publick
place, as it feems to be, fince *Auguftus* fends away all
his Courtiers and Attendance to talk alone with his
friends, what probability is there that *Cinna* fhould
there vifit *Æmilia*, with a Difcourfe of about 130
Verfes, and a difcovery of the moft dangerous Affairs in the World, which might be over-heard by
fome body going or coming ; and if the place be pri-
vate, and fuppos'd the Emperor's Clofet, who dif-
miffes thofe he would not have participant of his
fecret, how is it poffible that *Cinna* fhould come
there to talk all that to *Æmilia* ? And how is it probable that *Æmilia* fhould break out into outragious
Complaints and Invectives againft *Auguftus* ? This
is my Objection, to which *Monfieur Corneille* may
be pleas'd to give an Anfwer when he thinks fit.

    'Tis not lefs neceffary to chufe a fit time to make
a Narration probable ; for there are fome times
which will not bear a long Difcourfe : 'Tis a fault
which *Scaliger* does not fcruple to charge *Homer*
himfelf with, when he makes his *Hero's* make long
Narrations in the middle of a Battel or Engagement.
A Poet of ours has committed the fame fault in the
Scipio, while in the midft of the ftorming of a
Town, a victorious Army is abandoned to all Licence,
and the People in the diforder of a place taken by
affault. A young Maid difguis'd, makes a long
Narration

☞ p. 398.

Narration to difcover her felf, whereas in fuch a time fhe ought not at moft to have fpoke above four Verfes.

But I do not take heed that infenfibly I am difcovering the faults of our Modern Writers, who, it may be, will no: allow them to be fo, or at leaft will not be pleas'd with the difcovery; let the Poet then feek out of himfelf Examples of ill Narrations, and not expect from me that I fhould difcredit the beft part of our Plays, many of which have been fo favourably receiv'd either by the too much complaifance, or the ignorance of thofe who did not underftand their faults.

Chapter the Fourth.

Of Deliberations.

MY defign is not here to teach that part of Rhetorick which they call the *genus deliberativum*, by which is fhew'd the Art of faying ones Opinion floridly in all matters, in which counfel is askt. Our Poet ought not to ftay till he be upon the Stage to be inftructed in thofe Principles which are all comprehended under the name of the *Theory of the Stage*.

Drammatick Poetry is a kind of Quinteffence of all the Precepts of Eloquence that are found in Authors, becaufe they muft be us'd in it, but with fo much Judgment and Art, and fo nicely, that it muft often feem that one has quite laid them afide, the genius of the Stage being fuch, that a thing that does

[D]   not

not appear, contains in it very often the greateſt Artifice, and a Sentiment that ſhall imperceptibly have been conveyed into the mind of the Audience, an imperfect Narration, an Adventure, begun in appearance without deſign, are capable alone of making a Play take, by giving a foundation ſecretly to the ſtrongeſt paſſions, and by that means prepäring a noble *Cataſtrophe* ; and without doubt there is much skill requir'd for any body to perform this, without which one cannot pretend to true glory in the Art.

I begin therefore with this Advertiſement, which I think very conſiderable in matter of Deliberations, which is, that they in their own nature are not fit for the Stage, becauſe the *Theatre* being a place of Action, all things ought to be in agitation, either by Events which croſs one another, or by Paſſions born out of thoſe Incidents, as Lightning and Thunder from the Clouds. In a word, 'tis a place where every body is diſquieted and in diſorder ; and as ſoon as ever the calm and quiet ſucceed, the Play is at an end, or grows very dull all the while that the Action is ſuſpended ; how is it poſſible then that Deliberations ſhould have any part in the buſineſs? They are ſedate and quiet things where Moderation and Temper ought chiefly to appear. He that asks counſel does it with tranquillity, at leaſt in appearance, and they that are called to counſel ought leſs to be troubled either with Paſſion or Intereſt, they muſt ſpeak with all the clearneſs of Reaſon, and argue upon the diſcovery, and not in the Clouds, and darkneſs of Paſſion ; and if they grow but warm, they are preſently ſuſpected of ſome ſecret Intereſt ; ſo that without very great Art, it will be hard to reconcile them to the Scene, without making the Stage loſe its grace, and grow dull.   It

It may be anſwered, that the Stage abounds in Deliberations, and that the Antients have them in moſt Acts of their Plays ; and for the Moderns, *Monſieur Corneille* excels in them, and has ſcarce any thing in his Poems ſo moving, and ſo much admir'd, witneſs his *Stanzas* in the mouth of *Rodrigues* in the *Cid.* *Æmilia* in *Cinna* deliberates pleaſingly be-tween the danger ſhe expoſes *Cinna* to, and the re-venge ſhe covets. *Cinna* deliberates between the Ob-ligations he has to *Auguſtus,* and the love he bears his Miſtreſs ; and *Auguſtus* deliberates what to do in this laſt Conjuration, in which his Favourite was the chief man to murder him.

To all this I anſwer, That theſe are not the true ſort of Deliberations which I am treating of, though they do ſhew Irreſolution, and a diſpute between op-poſite Conſiderations ; they are rather to be plac'd in the rank of Pathetick Diſcourſes, which make the beſt Actions of the Stage. You ſee minds agitated by different Paſſions, and ſtill carryed into extremes, of which the Spectator cannot foreſee the Event ; all their Diſcourſes have the true Theatral Character, they are impetuous and figurative, and ſhew you rather the Image of a Soul tormented in the midſt of his Executioners, than one conſulting in the midſt of his Friends.

'Tis not therefore this ſort of Deliberations that I exclude ; on the contrary, I exhort all our Poets to bring them upon the Stage, as much as the Subject will afford, and to examine carefully with what va-riety and Art they are managed by the Antients, and in the Works of *Monſieur Corneille*, for if he be well conſider'd, 'twill be found that 'tis in that principal-ly that conſiſts that which in him is called *Admi-*

rable,

rable, and the thing which has made him so famous.

I only speak then of those Deliberations which are made designedly, and are Representations of the like Consults made in Courts upon some important Affair. We have two Examples remarkable in *Corneille,* that in the Play called *Cinna,* where *Augustus* deliberates whether he shall leave the Empire or no; and the other in a Play called *The Death of* Pompey, where King *Ptolomeus* deliberates what he shall do with so great a Man, newly arrived in his Country; and these two Deliberations have succeeded likewise very differently, for that of *Augustus* pleas'd the Audience to a wonder, and the other of *Ptolomæus* passes for a very common, ordinary Discourse; and that very difference of the success of these two Deliberations, confirms me in my Opinion, that they are dangerous upon the Stage, and have afforded me likewise the occasion of making some Reflections which may contribute to make them please.

The first is, That the Subject of the Deliberation ought to be great, noble, and extraordinary, and not of such things as fall every day in debate in Princes Councils, and 'tis in this for one, that the Deliberation of *Augustus* carrys it from that of *Ptolomæus,* for it is not ordinary that a Monarch should have the thought of laying down the Soveraignty, and bring so important a Point to be debated by two Friends. There was but one Example of such a thing before *Augustus's* time, and we have had but three since, of which the Queen of *Sweden* makes still an Illustrious Remembrance. But it was not a thing so rare to see *Ptolomæus* deliberate about the Life and Liberty of *Pompey;* 'twas an important Affair, but no extraordinary

becaufe then there has not been any paffion agitated which might produce fuch a Deliberation; but I would place them in the beginning of the fecond or third Act, that they may have fome foundation upon what is already done, and fome influence upon what remains to do.

They ought likewife not to be made all of a breath, without interruption from fome of the Counfellors, for that gives at leaft a little warmth to the coolnefs of the Stage. But above all, I think they ought to be as fhort as pofiible, for they cannot be long without being tedious in prolix reafonings void of figures, which neverthelefs I would have the Poet ftrive to bring in as *Apoftrophes*, *Profopopœas*, *Hypotypofes*, and fuch like ; in which much Art muft be ufed, becaufe regularly thefe figures do not enter into Deliberations.

But that which above all things I think neceffary is, that the Perfons advis'd with, be concern'd in the thing propos'd, becaufe then 'tis not a plain Advice, but it has fomething of the Theatral Action ; then the Spectator too is much more concern'd, as appears very well in the cafe of *Auguftus*, who being made to advife about the moft important thing of his Life, with two treacherous Friends, and the Audience being already inform'd of the hatred of *Æmilia*, and the love of *Cinna*, they are all attentive to what they fay, every Spectator having a curiofity to know how they will come off, fo that all that they fay is hearkened to, and not a word of it loft ; and when after all the Emperour is yet kind to both thefe Traitors, the Spectators begin to think they will relent of their Treafon, and particularly when they fee *Maximus* and *Cinna* afterwards a little in fufpenfe,

and

and then when at laſt they ſee them perſevere in
their deſign, they cannot imagine how the thing will
turn, nor what will be the Event; ſo that this Deliberation is upheld by the Intereſt of thoſe who adviſe,
and does it ſelf influence all the other Affairs of the
Stage.

I have nothing more upon this Subject, but one
general Obſervation, which is, That few People that
go to Plays do approve of the Examining and Condemning of Criminals upon the Stage, which nevertheleſs we ſee frequently repreſented there, and the
reaſon is, becauſe that when it comes to that forma-
lity, 'tis generally perform'd by the worſt Actors,
who being ſeated and out of action, and having a
few ſcurvy Verſes (which in ſuch an occaſion can
hardly be made better) to recite. The Audience can
hardly forbear laughing, ſo far are they from being
concern'd. I know no remedy for this but to endeavour to order the Story ſo, as it ſhall not require
ſuch a dull piece of Pageantry, ſo little capable of
deſerving any applauſe from the Audience.

Chapter the Fifth.

Of Didactick Diſcourſes or Inſtructions.

THis is a new Subject in our Drammatick Art,
I not having found any thing in thoſe Authors
who have compos'd great Volumes about it; and I
am the firſt that have made obſervations upon it, ſuch
as I may boldly ſay ought not to be deſpiſed by our
Poets.

I under-

I underſtand then by Didactick Diſcourſes thoſe
Maxims and general Propoſitions which contain
known Truths, and are only apply'd in the Play,
according as the Subject will allow, tending more
to inſtruct the Audience in the Rules of Morality,
than to explain any part of the Intrigue a foot. An
Example may illuſtrate the thing better. Suppoſe
then the Poet had a mind to treat this Propoſition.

*The Gods are juſt, and were they not ſo, they would
ceaſe to be Gods.*
Or this ;
A general Inſtinct cannot be ſuſpected of Errour.
Or this ;
A Subject that Rebels againſt his Prince is Criminal.

I ſay, That a Poet often endeavours to ſet out
ſome of theſe Maxims by a great number of Verſes,
upon which he demurs a great while, leaving all that
time his Subject, and the Intrigue of the Stage, and
keeping himſelf ſtill upon general Notions.

Now as to theſe Didactick Diſcourſes, I diſtinguiſh
them into two ſorts, ſome I call Phyſical, and the
others Moral ones.

I call thoſe Phyſical or Natural, which make a deduction or deſcription of the Nature, Qualities, or
Effects of any thing without diſtinction, whether it
be in the rank of natural or ſupernatural things ; or
of the number of Artificial Compounds.

Under the notion of Moral Diſcourſes, I comprehend all thoſe Inſtructions which contain any Maxim
of Religion, or Politicks, or Oeconomicks, or that
any ways regard humane Life

To come after this to my Obſervations, we muſt
lay

lay it down as a Maxim, That all thefe Didactick Difcourfes are of their own nature unfit for the Stage, becaufe they are cold, and without motion, being general things which only tend to Inftruct the mind, but not to move the heart, fo that the action of the Stage, which ought to warm our affections, becomes by them dull and indifferent. Young People who come to read *Euripides* and *Sophocles*, admire the firft much more than the latter, and yet *Sophocles* almoft always carry'd the prize from *Euripides* upon the Stage, and that by the Judgment of all the *Athenians*. This miftake of the young Reader proceeds from this, that they being themfelves not throughly inftructed in thofe Maxims, and finding a great many of them in *Euripides*, as well about Religion, as Politicks and Moral ones, they are charm'd to fee fuch Truths fo nobly expreffed, and the things themfelves being new to them, pleafe them beyond meafure. 'Tis for this that *Quintilian* in his Precepts of Rhetorick advifes young People to the Lecture of *Euripides* before *Sophocles*. In all which they do not obferve that *Sophocles* makes the groundwork of his Plays, of thofe very Truths. as well as *Euripides*; but he does it with fo much Art, that he utters them in a Pathetick manner, as well as in a Didactick one, whereby the People of *Athens* departed almoft always pleafed and charm'd by the high paffions which *Sophocles* fills his Stage with, but were more us'd to *Euripides*'s Maxims, which he fo often beats over to them, and by that means did not confider them as any thing rare and extraordinary: And from thence it proceeds, that in our Modern Plays, thofe very places in which the Poets have labour'd by noble Verfes, and high words to exprefs, some great Maxim, have least succeeded, because that falling into the Didactick way, they forsake the business of the Stage, and let the action cool. From thence it comes likewise that all Actors that appear with the Pedantick Character of teaching, such as are the Governour of a young Prince, a Doctor, a Governess, or the like, are still ill receiv'd by the Audience; the very presence of them displeases and imprints the Character of *Ridicule* upon the most serious Piece. I am confident that if the *Linco in Pastor fido* appear'd upon our Stage, he would be hiss'd off of it, notwithstanding all the good counsel he gives *Sylvio*; and that which makes me believe it the sooner, is that one of our best Modern Plays lost half its due applause, by there being a Governour to a young Prince, who was giving him Advice in the midst of most violent passions, with which he was tormented, that being neither the Time, nor the Stage the Place for such Instructions.

We do not see neither that either Astrologers, Conjurers, High Priests, or any of that Character, do much take, for the very reason that they can hardly speak without pretending to teach, or else talk in generals of the power of the Gods, the wonderful Effects of Nature, and such things which cannot fail of being tedious, when they are prolixely expressed. *Scaliger* will not allow them in the very *Epick* Poems, much less can they be receiv'd in the *Drammatick*, but ought to be quite banish'd the Stage.

We must observe besides, that Physical Instructions about Nature, and its Effects, are yet less welcom than Moral ones, because that 'tis hard an Actor should speak so long as to explain the nature of a thing,

thing, without diſguſting the Audience, which ſoon
grows weary of being ill taught the thing the Poet
would have him learn; which, together with the
little concern the no paſſion o: the Stage raiſes in
him, makes the whole very diſagreeable.   We have
a notable Example of this in *Mariamne*, where a long
Diſcourſe is made of the Nature of Dreams, the thing
is very fine, and the nature of them well explain'd ;
but it interrupts an agitation of the Stage, begun by
Herode s trouble at his waking; the Audience would
fain know the cauſe of his diſturbance, and the particulars of his Dream: But inſtead of that, there is a
long Diſcourſe of the Nature of Dreams in general,
to which the Spectator gives but little attention, as
being thereby diſappoined of his chief expectation.

   To all this it may be objected, That the Stage is
a place of publick Inſtruction, and that the Drammatick Poet is to inſtruct, as well as pleaſe; and
therefore that Didactick Diſcourſes may be proper
enough, or at leaſt ought not to be condemned.

   I confeſs that the Stage is a place of Inſtruction,
but we muſt well underſtand how that is meant. The
Poet ought to bring his whole Action before the
Spectator, which ought to be ſo repreſented with all
its circumſtances, that the Audience be fully Inſtruct-
ed ; for as Drammatick Poetry does but imitate humane actions, it does it only to inſtruct us by them,
and that it does directly, and properly: But for
Moral Maxims, which may incite us either to the
love of Virtue, or ſtir us up to hate Vice; it does it
indirectly, and by the *Entermiſe* of the Actions themſelves; of which Sentiment *Scaliger* is ſo much, as
I dare quote him for my Warrantee in this Opinion.
Now this may be done two ways ; the firſt, when

the Action of the Stage is fo judicioufly managed, that it fhews the force of Vertue triumphing in the midft of Perfecutions, after which it is often happily rewarded ; but if it is totally overwhelmed by them, it remains glorious even in its death. By this all the deformities of Vice are difcovered; it is often punifh'd,but when even it triumphs and overcomes, it is in abomination with the Audience, who thereupon are apt to conclude with themfelves, *That 'tis better to embrace Vertue through the hazard of Perfecution, than to follow Vice even with hopes of Impunity*

'Tis thus principally that the Stage ought to be Inftructive to the Publick by the knowledg of things reprefented; and I have always obferv'd, that it is not agreeable to the Audience, that a Man who fwerves from the way of Vertue, fhould be fet right, and repent, by the ftrength of Precepts and Sentences : We rather defire it fhould be by fome Adventure that preffes him, and forces him to take up reafonable and vertuous Sentiments. We fhould hardly endure that *Herode* fhould recal his Sentence againft *Mariamne*, upon a Remonftrance of one of the feven Wife Men of *Greece*; but we are pleas'd to fee, that after the Death of the Queen, his Love becomes his Tormentor ; and having opened his Eyes, drives him into fo fincere a Repentance, that he is ready to facrifice his Life to the regret he has for his Crime.

As for the other way of Teaching Morality, it depends much on the ingenioufnefs of the Poet, when he ftrengthens his Theatral Action with divers pithy and bold Truths, which being imperceptibly work'd into his Play, are as it were the nerves and ftrength of it. For, in a word, that which I condemn in

common

common *Didacticks*, is their ftile and manner of ex-
preffion, not the things themfelves, fince thofe great
Truths which are as it were the foundation of the
conduct of humane actions, I am fo far from banifh-
ing them off the Stage, that quite contrary, I think
them very neceffary and ornamental, which to attain,
I give thefe following Obfervations.

First, Thefe general Maxims muft be fo faftened to
the Subject, and link'd by many circumftances with
the Perfons acting, that the Actor may feem to think
more of that concern of his, he is about, than of faying fine things, that is, to fpeak in terms of Rhetorick,
he muft reduce the *Thefis* to the *Hypothefis*, and of
univerfal Propofitions, make particular Applications;
for by this means the Poet avoids the fufpicion of
aiming to Inftruct pedantickly, fince his Actors do
not leave their bufinefs which they are about.   For
Example, I would not have an Actor fpend many
words to prove that,

Vertue is always perfecuted; but he may fay to the
Party concern'd,

*Do you think to have better meafure than Vertue has
always had ? and can you expect to be priviledg'd from
Perfecution more than* Socrates *or* Cato *?*

And fo continue a little fpeaking ftill to the Party
prefent, and upon the Subject in hand, by which
means thefe Difcourfes feem a little to keep off from
being too general Precepts, and fo difguft the lefs.

Secondly. In all thefe occafions the Poet muft ufe
figurative Speech, either by Interrogation, Irony, or
others that his fancy fhall fuggeft; for thefe Figures,
by not circumftancing minutely the general Propofitions, make them more florid, and fo by ornaments
free them from the Didactick Character.   As for ex-

ample,

ample, if there be a defign of advifing a young Woman to obey her Parents; inftead of Preaching down-
right obedience to her, I think an Irony would do
better. As thus ;

*That's a fine way indeed, for a vertuous young Lady
to attain the reputation of a good Daughter, to be carryed away by her own paffions, and neglect not only the
cenfure of the beft fort of People, but break through all
the fences of duty and honour.*

My third Obfervation is, That when any of thefe
great Maxims are to be propos'd bluntly and in plain
words, it be done in as few as may be ; by that
means they do not cool the Stage, but add fomething
to the variety of it; but there muft be care taken
that this do not happen in the midft of a violent
paffion ; for befides that in thofe cafes men do not
naturally fpeak fentences, the Actour cannot then
appear with that moderation which thofe reflections
require. *Seneca* is very guilty of this fault in all
his tragedies where moft commonly in the heat of
paffion all his fine Common places are beftowed upon the Audience.

We have neverthelefs fome Examples of Didactick,
Propofitions made in direct terms, and at length not
without fome fuccefs in *Corneille*, which to attain as
well as he, requires the fame Ingenuity and Art. The
Expreffions muft be ftrong, and feem to have been
faid only for that particular Subject to which they
are applyed, and that requires a particular genius,
and much ftudy to accomplifh.

I have obferv'd befides, that common Truths,
though in a Didactick ftile, yet do very well upon
the Stage in the mouth of a Rogue or a Cheat when
his character is known ; for the Spectator is delighted

lighted to fee him cunningly ufe all the Maxims and Difcourfes of a good man to intents and purpofes quite contrary, fo that by that means 'tis all figurative, and moves the Attention of the Audience.

One may likewife fuccefsfully enough *burlesk* all thefe common Truths, but that can be perform'd no where but in Comedy, where by that means they forfake their natural ftate, and are difguiz d under a new appearance, which caufes both variety and ornament. But Tragedy in its own nature is too grave to admit of any thing fo low and bufloon as this would be; neither do I remember to have met with any thing of that kind in any ferious Tragedy; I fay *ferious Tragedy*, becaufe that in *Satyrical Tragedy* there was admitted a mixture of Heroick Actions, and low Buffooneries; and therefore this difguizing of ferious Precepts might have room among the reft in them.

Chapter the Sixth.

Of Pathetick Difcourfes; or of the Paſſions and Motions of the Mind.

I Do not undertake in this Chapter to teach the Nature of Paffions, nor their different Species, nor their extraordinary Effects; all Moral Authors do that fufficiently. I do not think neither that it is neceffary to fhew here the Art of ufing them in order to perfuade, after all that *Ariſtotle* has faid upon that Subject in his fecond Book of Rhetorick; fo that I will avoid all Repetitions of that nature, and

and not fo much as touch upon any thing that is contain'd in his Poeticks, or his Interpreters Commentaries, where may be feen which are the Paffions fitteft for the Stage, and how they are to be manag'd. *Monfieur de la Menardiere* has made two Chapters in his Poeticks on this Subject, fo learned and fo proper, that they alone would filence me, if I offer d at this matter, they being able to fatisfie the moft curious in that Subject.

I confider therefore here the Paffions, as they are plac'd in Difcourfe, and thereupon I bring my Obfervations towards employing of them with conduct upon the Stage. In a word, I only intend to fhew with what Art a Pathetick or Moving Difcourfe ought to be regulated fo as to make it agreeable to the Spectators, by the impreffion it is to make on them.

Firft then, The Caufe which is to produce a Motion in the Actors themfelves, and then in the Audience, ought to be fomething true, or believ'd to be fo, not only by the Actor who fpeaks (who would be ridiculous to make a great Difcourfe of Grief or Joy for a thing he fhould know to be falfe) but alfo by the Spectators, who probably would not be concern'd if they knew that the Subject he had to complain or rejoyce were fictitious; and if it fo fall out, that by the reft of the Story, the Spectator muft know a thing contrary to the belief of the Actor: As for Example, that a Princefs is alive, though a Lover believe her dead : I fay, if in that cafe one would have the Paffion take with the Audience, there muft not be a long Complaint mingled with Sentiments of kindnefs and grief ; but the Actor muft be prefently tranfported into Rage, that the Spectators may

be

be touched by his violent defpair, and feel a great
deal of compaffion, if in that Errour he happens to
kill himfelf, as we fee it falls out in *Pyramus* and
Thisbe in both kinds ; for the long Difcourfe he
makes upon the fufpicion he is in, that a Lion has
kill'd his Miftrefs, does not much affect the Audience; but when he draws his Sword to facrifice his
Life to the *Manes* of his dead Miftrefs, and fo expiate
his negligence in his own blood, there is hardly one
of the Audience that does not fhake with horrour ;
and upon this occafion I remember I faw a young
Lady, who had never been at a Play before, cry out
to her Mother, that *Pyramus* ought to be told
that his Miftrefs was not dead, which made me make
this Judgment, that the Poet ought not to have de-
ferr'd fo long bringing his Actor to the moving part ;
three or four Lines had been enough to have explain'd his belief of her death, and then all the reft
ought to have been pronounc'd, his Sword drawn,
and in the neareft difpofition to death, which would
certainly have produc'd immediate horrour and
compafsion in the Audience.

Not but that it happens often that the Actor may
lament or rejoyce at fomething he thinks true, while
the Audience neverthelefs muft know that it is falfe.
As for Example, if the Story requires that in the Perfon of that Actor there be feigned a Pafsion, of which
the Caufe is falfe, with a defign to have it believ'd
true by another, and by that means difcover fome
fecret ; 'tis good that the Spectators fhould be inform'd that he who feigns the Pafsion has no true
Subject for it, becaufe then they have the pleafure
of the Contrivance, to fee the Difguife well acted;
but he that is deceiv'd, ought not to make any long

[F]   Pathetick

Pathetick Difcourfes, becaufe that would not move the Spectators. It will fuffice that in few words he fhew the impreffion the fiction has made upon him, and what Event may be from thence expected. In a word, in all fuch cafes the Poet is to examine which of the two will beft pleafe the Audience to fee a circumventing defign well Executed, or to be concern'd for the Complaint made by an innocent, unwary perfon; for if they are pleas'd in the Cheat, they muft be inform'd of it, if in the Complaint, the falfenefs of the Grief muft be conceal'd from him, that they may believe as well as the Party grieved, that he has reafon to be afflicted.

Secondly, 'Tis not enough that the Caufe of fome extraordinary Motion of the Mind be true, but it muft alfo (to be agreeably reprefented upon the Stage) be reafonable and probable, according to the receiv'd Opinions of Mankind; for if any Actor fhould fly into a paffion of Anger, without reafon, he would be look'd upon as a Mad-man, inftead of being pitied; not but that there are fome paffions whofe Subject is falfe, which neverthelefs are very agreeable, though they are not reafonable in their grounds, for Example Jealoufie; but the nature of this paffion is to be without any foundation in truth or reafon, for elfe it would not be Jealoufie, but a juft Indignation which would infpire the Spectators with hatred againft the Woman, and compaffion for the Husband; whereas quite contrary, we have naturally averfion for a jealous Man, and compafsion for a poor Woman innocently perfecuted by him. The fame may be faid of Covetoufnefs, which will ftill be fo much the more diverting, if the cares and fears in keeping of a Treafure, with diftruft of all forts of People, be without grounds;

grounds; or rather, we may fay that the Difcourfes which are made to exprefs thefe pafsions, do not fo much pleafe the Spectator,by making him concern'd for thofe that fpeak, as they do it by giving him a fort of compafsion mingled with Sentiments of fcorn and derifion for the mifery and folly of thofe that are tyranniz'd over by them; at leaft thofe are the thoughts which I had in reading the fecond Comedy of *Plautus*, called *Aulularia*.

Thirdly, To make a Complaint that fhall touch and concern the Audience, the caufe of it muft be juft, for elfe no body will enter into the Sentiments of the grieved Perfon. For Example, if an Actor fhould exprefs great affliction for not having been able to Execute a Confpiracy againft a good Prince, or fome great piece of Treachery againft his Country, he would be look'd upon as a wicked, and not an unhappy Perfon, and all that he could fay would but encreafe the Peoples averfion to him.

Befides all thefe Confiderations, if the Pathetick Difcourfe be not neceffary, that is to fay, expected and defired by the Spectators,it will be very naufeous to them, let the Poets Art be what it will. That a Husband fhould be griev'd for the lofs of his Wife, is fo natural, that we need not be brought to the Stage to fee Examples of it; but that *Herode* fhould firft condemn his Wife in a tranfport of Rage, in fpight of all the tender thoughts infpir'd by his love;it excites our curiofity to know what his thoughts are after fuch an Action. That *Mafiniffa*, forced by the *Romans*, fhould fend his Wife Poifon, though paffionately in love with her, and fhe die of it, one cannot but defire to know what that unfortunate Prince can fay or do after fo defperate an Adventure. But

that

that for Example. The Wife of *Alexander*, Son to
Mariamne, fhould come and make great lamentations upon the Body of her Husband, whom *Herode*
had put to death without any other motive, than becaufe fhe was his Wife, that was very fuperfluous,
and did not prove very agreeable to the Audience,
who knew well enough that fhe had reafon to grieve,
but not upon the Stage, the Spectators knowing already all that fhe could fay upon that Subject ; and
from thence we muft likewife infer, that all Confidents and Attendants of Princes, though they are
very neceffary Perfons upon the Stage, for the union
of all the Intrigues, yet they cannot be fuppos'd to
carry their lamentations and reflections on their
Mafters misfortunes very far, becaufe every body
knows that they are things of courfe in true Friends,
and faithful Servants, and fo not extraordinary enough
for the Stage.

The fame thing may be faid of the chief Actors,
when their Interefts are not grounded upon fenfible
Motives.   For Example ; If a Rival having fought
his Miftrefs only for her Fortune, and not out of any
Inclination from his heart, fhould complain of having loft her, it would produce no Effect in the
Minds of the Audience, his lamentations having no
ground in nature or reafon.

But one of the chiefeft Obfervations of all is this,
That all pafsions that are not founded upon Opinions and Cuftoms conformable to thofe of the
Spectators, are fure to be cold, and of no effect, becaufe they being already poffeffed with an Opinion
contrary to the Action of the Player, cannot approve
of any thing he fays or does in another fenfe.   For
Example; The grief of one who had undertaken to kill
a Tyrant,

a Tyrant, and fail'd in his defign, would not move us in *France*, fo much as it would have done the People at *Athens*, becaufe we living in a Monarchy, look upon the Perfons of Kings as Sacred, be they never fo unjuft ; whereas the *Athenians*, bred up in a popular State, hated all Monarchs, and could not endure the name of them.

Thus, for the fame reafon, thofe Pathetick Difcourfes, which we read in the Greek and Latine Comedys, will never take with us, as they did upon the Stages of the Antients, becaufe we have but little Conformity to the Rules of their Lives, in many things more abominably licentious than ours ; and in others, their Cuftoms were fo various ; as that which was a Jeft and a Concern to them, can be none to us, who have not fo much as the fame things, to wit, the Cheats of their Slaves, nor the Hunger of their Parafites ; which made *Rotron*, one of our Poets, mifcarry in a Play of *Plautus's*, where his Parafite talks of nothing but eating, and is fo horrible a Glutton, that we could not bear him, having no fuch People among't us ; all our *Debauche* lying rather in drinking than eating ; and in that too we mingle Songs and Catches.

'Tis for this reafon too I imagine that Tragedys taken out of the Stories of Scripture, are not fo agreeable, for all the Pathetick Motions are founded upon Vertues that have not much Conformity with the Rules of our Life, to which may be added, that being fcarce pious enough to fufferDevotion in the Churches themfelves, it cannot be expected we fhould love it upon the Stage ; and none do but thofe who are touch'd with a true Chriftian Piety, and they are infinitely pleas'd at fuch Reprefentations.

Having

Having thus obferv'd what concerns the Caufe and Motive of Theatral Paffions, I have likewife made fome Reflections upon the manner of managing of them in a Pathetick Difcourfe.

The firft Obfervation is, That it is not enough to raife a pafsion upon a good Incident, and to begin with ftrong Lines, but it muft be carry'd to the point of its fulnefs. 'Tis not enough to have fhaken the Minds of the Audience, you muft ravifh them; and to do it, you muft feek matter, either in the greatnefs of your Subject, or in the different Motives and Colours which environ it; but particularly in the ftrength and richnefs of your own Imagination, which ought to be warm'd, and elevated, and as it were, be in labour to bring forth fomething worthy of admiration. In this particularly *Monfieur Corneille* does excel, for he has a moft difcerning Judgment to diftinguifh between rich pafsions, and the common ones, and then he drives them to their juft period, with the greateft felicity imaginable, but which cannot be but the Effect of ftrong and lafting Meditations. The difficulty here lies in the exactnefs of meafure; for as you are not to ftarve your Hearers appetite, fo you muft have as great a care not to cloy him; you muft give him the height of fatisfaction, without over-powering him with fatiety. He that in this cafe will do more than he can, does often lefs than he fhould.

This is a fault obferv'd not only in *Lucan's Pharfalia*, but in moft of *Seneca's* Tragedys, and particularly in his *Hercules Oeteus*, where the Author has given up himfelf to the fecundity of his own wit, not confidering that the excefs of it might fometimes be infupportable; and yet I could wifh our Poets rather

guilty

guilty of this noble fault, than of that mean one of fterility : For we have feen often upon our Stages, pafsions begun and forfaken half way, or at leaft purfued with fo little Art and warmth, that they had been lefs defectuous if they had ftop'd in the beginning of their career.   To give this meafure exactly, is impofsible; the Poet muft examine what his Subject, the force of his Difcourfe, and the beauty of the Pafsion will afford ; let him confult his Friends, and ufe all his Judgment in fo nice a point.

But he muft be very careful not to fpend all the ftrength of a pafsion at firft ; he muft referve fome thoughts for the continuation of it ; for the fame pafsion continued and held up by divers Incidents, with a change of appearances, muft certainly be much more agreeable than a new pafsion in every Scene ; and 'tis in that *Monfieur Corneille* is admirable in the *Cid*, for being to fhew the ftate of a generous Mind diftracted by the Sentiments of Honour, and the tendernefles of a violent Love, he produces the Monuments of thefe pafsions by degrees, keeping ftill, till the end many of his nobleft Thoughts and Exprefsions,which if he had not been very judicious,he might have us'd at firft ; he has done the fame thing in *Horatius*, and moft of his Plays.   'Tis true, that to imitate him requires a great deal of felicity and conduct: but whofoever fhall carefully ftudy the Antient Drammaticks,and apply himfelf to a diligent underftanding of the Morals of Life, will always be rich enough to anfwer thefe Intellectual Expences.

Secondly, To guide thefe Pathetick Motions to the point of their true Extent, it muft be done with order, and by following the Motions of Nature, with a regard to the quality of the things that are faid.

The

The order of Nature is very different, for sometimes the Mind breaks out into violent Transports, which not being able to hold, it returns to some Moderation, or rather some Relaxation of its own Excess, the passion remaining still very sensible at other times, the Soul moves slowly, and agitating it self by degrees, arrives to the highest Transport, even to sounding away. Now to regulate a Pathetick Discourse upon these different orders, there is no Advice can be given, the Poets prudence must guide him according to the Characters of the persons, and the present state of the Stage.

Yet he must always remember that Pathetick Discourses are not to end just as they begin; but after the greatest violence he may bring the passion to some moderation, so far as to doubt and debate; and as those who understand suiting of Colours, never place two Extremes together, because that would be too harsh. One must not likewise in the passions of the Stage fall from one extremity to another; nor of a sudden calm into some great agitation, without some precedent reason to arrive at that Tranquillity. Yet it may happen that even in those Extremes some very ornamental passage may be plac'd, but great circumspection is requisite. As to the order of the nature of the things that are to be said, the Mind is not to be hurried from one Motion to another, without connexion or dependance upon what has been said; nor is it to leap from one consideration to another, and then back again to the first; the Subject of which the Actor is to speak, ought to be carefully considered; the place, time, and other particulars, which may contribute to the passion, and then of all that make up the most judicious and moving

Discourse

difcourfe that may be : For Example, if an Actour is to make imprecations againft any one, he ought to obferve the order in which they naturally may happen, for it would be abfurd to fee him wifh to his Enemy at laft a curfe which would be but the confequent of his firft imprecation.

To order muft be added Figures, I mean thofe great Figures which exprefs the things themfelves, not thofe little boyifh ones which play in words, fuch as Antithefes, which always fpoil a pathetick difcourfe becaufe they feem affected and Scholar like, fhewing rather a quiet then a troubled mind.

The Figures too ought to be very various, and not ftaid too long upon, becaufe a mind that is in agitation cannot talk long the fame way; the Figures of tendernefs and grief ought to be mingled with thofe of fury and rage: a man is to complain and figh, and not to roar or fcold, and he is feldom to break out into the higheft violence, but when there is enough to make him rave, for that agitation of the mind has no limits and goes much further, then the motions of grief, anger or defpair.

To all this may be objected, that a pathetick difcourfe thus managed and governed by rules cannot fail of appearing affected, and fhew the very art it is made by not reprefenting naturally by confequent the ftate of the humane mind, which acts according to its Idea's and motives without any rule but confufion and diforder. To Anfwer this we muft fay, that this diforder in the words of a man is a fault which weakens even the impreffion which elfe his paffion would make, and therefore ought to be reform'd upon the Stage, which fuffers nothing imperfect; but in doing of it there ought to be a mixture of the greateft

[G]   figures,

figures, that ftill the Image of the Motions of a troubled Mind may remain. Thus by an orderly Method one reforms the defect of Nature in her Tranfports, and by a fenfible variety of figures, one keeps fome refemblance of the diforder of Nature. This is all that I can fay, that is any ways fingular upon fo common a Subject.

Chapter the Seventh.

Of the Figures.

ALL thofe ingenious Varieties of Speech which the Learned have invented, whereby to ex-prefs their thoughts in a nobler way than the vulgar, and which are call'd Figures of Rhetorick, are with-out doubt the moft notable ornaments of Difcourfe ; for by them every thing appears to a greater advan-tage : 'Tis they that give the grace to Narrations, probability to all other reafonings, and ftrength to the paffions, and without them all our Difcourfes are low, mean, and popular, difagreeable, and without effect. Therefore the beft Advice one can give to a Poet, is, that he fhould be perfect in the knowledg of the Figures, by ftudying carefully what the Profef-fors of Rhetorick have writ on that Subject, and which we fhall not here repeat : Yet let him remem-ber, that 'tis not enough to read and know their names and diftinctions, but let him diligently exa-mine their Energy, and what Effect they are like to produce upon the Stage : Neither ought that to fuf-fice without knowing, and that particularly, how to

apply

apply them, and vary them, to produce the Effect we have observ'd in the precedent Chapter ; he must know when to use the impetuous ones, and when to employ the milder, such as Ironies, according to the diversity of his Subject, and the Effect he desires they should produce. For Example ; If it be necessary that an Actor should leave the Stage in a great rage, then he must be mov'd by degrees, beginning by the softer Figures, and at last be raised to the highest Transports a Soul is capable of; but if on the contrary an Actor is to grow calm before he goes off, then 'tis best beginning with violent Figures, and such as most express the impetuosity of a disturb'd Mind, till by little and little he becomes more moderate, and gives room to use gentler Expressions. To make our Poet expert in this, he ought, besides reading of the Antients, to frequent the Stage much ; for there, much better than in Books, he may observe good or ill Figures, and when they are well or ill plac'd, and to help him a little, I will communicate those Observations I my self have made.

First, He will discover that which I have said elsewhere, which is, that nothing is to be expressed without Figures upon the Stage : And if the simplest Shepherds are clothed in Silk, and wear Silver Sheephooks, every thing they say ought likewise to be adorn'd, and have its grace, even so much, that those very things which seem least capable of that Imbellishment, must be order'd with so much imperceptible Art, that no Figures appear, and yet be there secretly and nicely applyed ; for if Poetry is the Kingdom of Figures, the Stage is its Throne, from whence it conveys by appearances well managed by him that speaks, Sentiments into the Soul of the hearers, which are not really in his. [G 2] But

But let him obferve likewife, that as there is great
difference between Tragedy and Comedy, they have
alfo their different Figures. Tragedy, as it is always
ferious and great, employs none but noble Figures,
which draw their force from the Sentiments of the
Stage, and when we mingle Allufions, or Antithefes,
or Equivocal, Proverbial ways of fpeaking, it degene-
rates immediately, and lofes all its Majefty. 'Tis quite
otherwife with Comedy, which having none but
vulgar Sentiments, it rejects not *Proverbs,* nor any
thing that may contribute to make a Jeft, that being
its Character, and the beft part of its Ornaments; nay,
'tis hard *Comedy* fhould rife without a fall, for no
fooner does it aim at folid Difcourfes, or Figures fit
for Tragedy, but we laugh it out of doors, as we
would do a Chambermaid that fhould talk nothing
but Romance; therefore 'tis hard that the Figures for
one of thefe Poems fhould be aptly ufed in the other
without great warinefs, and that *Plautus* has done in
fome of his Plays with fuccefs.

Befides, among thofe Figures which are great and
ferious, the Poet may obferve fome to be fitter for
the Stage than others. For Example, *Apoftrophes,*
which I have always obferv'd to do very well; for
they fuppofe either a true perfon who is abfent to be
prefent, or fome feigned perfon which is but in the
Idæa of Fiction, fuch as *Vertue,* ones *Country*; and
thereupon the Actor talks to them as prefent, which
is extremely Theatral, becaufe it makes two perfons
where there is but one; and though the deceit is vifible enough, yet being an effect of the paffion of
the Actor, it carrys along with it the Imagination of
the Audience, and that particularly when he that
fpeaks is alone; for then there can be no miflake in
the

the Mind of the Spectators ; for 'tis plain, that the
perſon to whom the Actor ſpeaks, is a Fiction of his
own brain, his Diſcourſe not being applicable to any
other. *Monſieur Corneille* uſes this Figure frequently,
and *Stiblinus* eſteems extremely the complaints of
Hecuba in the *Troades* of *Euripides*, by reaſon of
this Figure, which is there frequently and beautifully
made uſe of. But in the practice of this there are
two faults to be avoided ; the firſt is not to have it
too often, for then, beſides the want of variety, which
argues want of Invention to pleaſe ; it grows likewiſe troubleſom, by making too many imaginary
perſons, and in this kind one of our Authors was
faulty, who in the ſame Play, and that a piece of no
great length made an Actor ſpeak at leaſt a dozen
times to Heaven. The other fault to be avoided is,
that an Actor ſpeaking to a King, a Father, a Judge, or
ſome perſon to whom reſpect is due, ought not to
fall into a long *Apoſtrophe* to an Imaginary perſon, becauſe it is againſt the Rules of decency, that a man
ſhould leave addreſſing to a perſon of Authority, to
talk to a thing abſent, or a Chymera of his own brain;
not but that if it were extreme ſhort, and the Diſcourſe preſently continued to the perſon preſent, it
might very well paſs ; as in this Example.

*O Nature ! who knoweſt how true I have always
been to thy Sentiments, ſpeak here in my defence.*

And then continuing and addreſſing to his Father,
ſay,

*'Tis ſhe, O my Father, that muſt juſtifie what I have
done,* &c.

By this ſlight the Figure brings force and variety
to the Diſcourſe, and yet does nothing againſt the
Laws of Reſpect, ſo ſmall a Tranſport being very
                                                    allowable

allowable to a man paſſionate and innocent, and the quick return brings all things in order again.

Proſopopœa's quite contrary are very unlucky upon the Stage ; for though, as well as *Apoſtrophes,* that Figure ſuppoſes perſons that are not, and makes dumb things ſpeak, yet it generally creates confuſion, becauſe the Actor already repreſents a perſon that is not, and this perſon repreſented makes another feign'd perſon ſpeak by his mouth, which makes a double Fiction, and much obſcurity ; for very few of the Audience are either able, or attentive enough to obſerve the Actors paſsing from his own Diſcourſe, to that of the ſuppos'd perſon in this Figure, the leaſt noiſe, or other diverſion at that time being enough to make them loſe the Chain, and ſo confound the Diſcourſes attributed to the feign'd perſon by *Proſopopœa,* with thoſe that the Actor makes in his own perſon.

I dare affirm beſides, that to the people the beauty of this Figure is not ſenſible upon the Stage, but rather troubleſom, becauſe of their want of skill and application to diſtinguiſh things. For Example ; They ſee an Actor who acts the King, and are poſſeſt that all that he ſays is the Diſcourſe of the King he repreſents ; ſo that if he comes to make a *Proſopopœa,* by ſuppoſing that either Vertue, or Love, or ſuch like things ſpeak to him, they are mightily puzzled ; for, though they have ſenſe enough to know that this ſpeech of Love or Vertue does not properly belong to the King, yet they penetrate not the Myſtery of that double Fiction of a King repreſented, and ſpeaking by the mouth of an Actor, and of Vertue likewiſe ſpeaking by the mouth of the ſame King ; therefore this Figure is to be avoided, and cannot well be brought upon the Stage, or if it is ſometimes, it muſt

be

be in Narrations, and then it muſt be very ſhort, or in *Soliloques*, otherwiſe called *Monologues*, where the Poet muſt uſe much Induſtry to ſhew what the thing is he feigns, and makes ſpeak in the *Proſopopœa*, that ſo there may be no obſcurity nor room for miſtake, neither is he to judge of the uſe of this Figure by its being employ'd in Epick Poems and Orations ; for they being generally deſign'd to be read at leiſure, it is eaſie upon any obſcurity to look back and diſcover where the difficulty lyes ; but in the Stage where the beſt part of the Audience is made up of the unlearned, and where the thing paſſes in Diſcourſe of a ſudden without repeal, there is no remedy for thoſe who are once fallen into obſcurity, but to remain in it ; and in Orations, the obſcurity cannot be ſo great, becauſe there the perſon that ſpeaks makes no double Fiction, and ſo is eaſily underſtood.

Irony is a Drammatick Figure, and of its own nature very Theatral ; for by ſaying in jeſt or ſcorn the contrary of that which it really means, it carrys a kind of diſguiſe, and makes an agreeable Effect.

Exclamations are extreme proper for the Stage, as being the marks of a Mind much mov'd with paſſion.

Hyperbole is of the ſame rank, becauſe the words there carrying ones Imagination further than their natural ſenſe, it is fitteſt for the Stage where all things are to be magnified, as if it were continual Inchantment and Illuſion.

Interrogation, which *Scaliger* ſays is only a Figure by uſe, and not of its own nature, is likewiſe the mark of an agitated Mind, and by conſequent Theatral.

And amongſt them all, certainly *Imprecation* will be judg'd Theatral, as being the Effect of a violent
Tranſport,

Transport, and its Discourse ought to be impetuous, with bold expressions, and words full of Extremes.

This I think may suffice for our Poet, without making an unnecessary repetition of what the Rhetoricians may have taught him, and which he may read with great profit in *Scaliger's* Poeticks.

Chapter the Eighth.

Of Monologues, or Discourses made by a single Person.

THough I have not met with the word *Monologue* amongst Antient Authors, who have treated of the Stage ; and that *Scaliger* himself, who has not forgot any curiosity upon this Subject, has nothing of it ; I shall not nevertheless forbear to say something of it according to the meaning of our Modern Poets.

To begin therefore by a necessary Observation we must not confound the *Monodia* of the Antients with that which we call now *Monologue*; for though the first is some piece of Poetry, sung or recited by one man alone, yet custom has fixt its signification to those Funeral Songs which were sung by one of the Quire, in honour of the Dead ; and 'tis thought that the Musician *Olympus* was the first that us'd it, in memory and favour of *Python*, as *Aristoxenes* affirms ; which makes me wonder at one of our Modern Authors, who says, that the *Monodia* was a Poem compos'd under the name of one person, such as the *Cassandra* of *Lycophron*.

Besides, there are among the Learned some who
will

will not receive the Greek word for a Difcourfe made by one man by himfelf, but fay it means a Difcourfe in every thing one and like its felf without variety.

For my part I believe that in our time we have call'd *Monologues* that which the Antients call'd the Difcourfe of a fingle perfon *Monoprofopon*, as many Eclogues both Greek and Latine, and many Difcourfes of the *Chorus*'s in Plays, which *Stillinus* calls *Monodias*, as the Difcourfe of *Electra* alone in *Euripides*, and another of the fame in *Sophocles*, though fhe fpeaks in the prefence of the Quire.

I confefs that it is fometimes very pleafant to fee a man upon the Stage lay open his heart, and fpeak boldly of his moft fecret thoughts, explain his defigns, and give a vent to all that his paffion fuggefts; but without doubt it is very hard to make an Actor do it with probability.

The Antients could not bring in thefe *Monologues*, becaufe of the *Chorus*, which never, or very feldom left the Stage; and except that *Monologue* which *Ajax* in *Sophocles* makes at the corner of a Wood upon the point of killing himfelf while the *Chorus* was gone out to look for him; I do not believe there is any other in the Five and thirty Greek Tragedies which are left. I know very well that in many Scenes there is but one Actor nam'd; but if we obferve narrowly, we fhall always find that he is not alone upon the Stage, and that his Difcourfe is directed to fome that follow him, though they are not fet down at the beginning of the Scenes.

As for *Prologues*, they are indeed made by one fingle Actor, but not in the nature of *Monologues*; 'tis a thing by it felf, which indeed among the Antients was one part of the Dramatick Poem, but not of

[H]   the

the Theatral Action ; 'tis a Difcourfe made to the Spectators, to inftruct them of the Story which begun amongft the Antients as foon as the *Chorus* came on.

The two Latine Comick Poets have many *Monologues* in all their Plays, fome of them are brought in properly and according to reafon, others nor. I fhall not here make any Criticifm upon them, but give my Opinion what Rules are to be obferv'd to make a *Monologue* with probability.

Firft of all, an Actor muft never make a *Monologue*, while he addreffes himfelf to the Audience, with a defign to inform them of fomething they are to know ; but there muft be found out fomething in the Truth of the Action that may be colourable to make him fpeak in that manner. Elfe 'Tis a fault in the Reprefentation, of which both *Plautus* and *Terence* are guilty.

Secondly, When he that thinks he fpeaks alone is over heard by chance, by fome other he muft then be reputed to fpeak foftly, becaufe it is not probable that a man by himfelf fhould fpeak fo loud as Players muft do to be heard by the Audience. I confefs indeed with *Scaliger*, that this is one of the faults of the Stage, which muft be excus'd only by the neceffity of Reprefentation, it being impoffible to reprefent the thoughts of a man otherwife than by his words ; but that which makes this fault the more apparent, is, when another Actor hears all that that man fays, who fpeaks alone ; and though it may happen that a man may fpeak aloud of that which he ought only to think, and which he intends only to fay to himfelf, yet that being a grofs Imprudence, ought not to be reprefented upon the Stage.

Therefore

Therefore in thefe Cafes one muft either find out a probable reafon to make the Actor fpeak aloud, which is very hard to do, or elfe the Poet ought to ufe fuch Art in the Compofition of the *Monologue*, as that the Actor fhould fometimes raife his voice in faying certain words only, and fpeak with a low voice in others, that fo the Actor who is within hearing might be fuppos'd to hear fome fpoke with paffion, and not the others, as being fpoke foftly, and in the mean time the other Actor upon what he does hear might make fome Exclamations, and feem concern'd that he could not hear the reft. Nay, when the Actor, who fhould fpeak the *Monologue*, fhould fpeak foftly, then the other Actor fhould obferve all his Actions, as of a man much taken up with his own thoughts, and in a deep ftudy ; and it may be this way the probability of the Stage might be preferv'd with fome addition of ornament to the Scene in hand; but to execute this well, one muft not meet with proud, impertinent Players, who taking no Advice but from their own Ignorance and prefumption, think they perform all things admirably well ; for a Scene of this nature would hardly fucceed, except as docile Actors as thofe of the new Company of the *Mareft* were wont to be, undertook it.

The third Obfervation about *Monologues*, is to make them fo, as not to chock the probability of the circumftances of time & place: For Example; It would be abfurd to put a *Monologue* in the mouth of a General of an Army, who fhould be in the middle of a Town juft ftorm'd by his Army. There would be likewife little probability if a Lover fhould hear of fome great danger his Miftrefs were in, and inftead of running to her relief, fhould ftand ftill and make

a long

a long complaint againſt the *Stars*, he would be as little forgiven in the Repreſentation, as in the Reality ; ſo that in a word, all that can be done, is ſtill to keep to the Rules of probability and decency as the only Guide of the Stage.

Chapter the Ninth.

Of a Partes, *or Diſcourſes made to ones ſelf in the preſence of others.*

IT often happens upon the Stage, that one Party ſpeaks in the preſence of another who hears and ſees him, and that neverthelefs his words repreſent ſome thought known to no body but himſelf.

There are very few of thoſe to be met with in the Greek Poets, and except a Verſe or two that the *Chorus* ſpeaks after ſome long Diſcourſe of an Actor ; or when a new Actor comes upon the Stage, I do not know of any other Example, and this may ſerve to give us a hint how cautious we are to be in obſerving the probability of the Stage, ſince in a matter of forty Poems they have ſo rarely taken the liberty of re-preſenting a man's ſecret thoughts by words ſpoke aloud.

The *Romans* have taken much more licence in this kind; *Terence* not quite ſo much as *Plautus*, who makes *a partes* very frequently, and often intollerably ab-ſurd. *Seneca* the Tragedian is not more regular in this, than in any other of the Rules of the Stage ; for in his *Agamemnon*, *Clytemneſtra* makes an *a parte* of ſeventeen Verſes. Our Moderns, who have imita-ted

ted the Antients much more in their faults, than in their Excellencies, make likewife fuch abfurd *a partes*, that the moft grofs among the common people can hardly bear them.

I know that thofe *a partes* do fometimes make very good fport upon the Stage, and 'tis often necef-fary to introduce them to make known to the Spe-&ators fome fecret thought of fome A&or, without which they would be in the dark : As for Example ; When an A&or diffembles, but at the fame time it feems a little hard to conceive (though *Scaliger* by a great Indulgence for the Stage allows it) that an A&or fhall fpeak loud enough to be heard by the Audience, and yet not be over-heard by another A&or who ftands by him; and that which is worfe is, that to feign he does not hear him, he is forc'd to make twenty ridiculous *Grimaces*.   Let us fee therefore if by Art we can any ways render thefe *a partes*, if not entirely probable, at leaft fupportable to the Stage.

In order to this I divide them into three forts; the firft, when two A&ors, each of them at one corner of the Stage fpeak as it were to themfelves of their own concerns, making as if they did neither fee nor hear one another.

The fecond fort is, when one A&or fpeaks, fup-pofing the other A&or whom he fees and hears, not to fee nor hear him.

The third fort is, when both A&ors hearing and feeing one another, one of them for fome fudden confideration, fpeaks as if he were not heard by the other.

Now, to order it fo in all thefe occafions, that the Spe&ators Judgment fhall not be chock'd by any im-

pro-

probability, I have bethought my self what might be done.

Firſt then, an *a parte* ought to be very ſhort, and contain very few words ; particularly, when in all the reſt of the Action both Actors ſee and hear one another ; and indeed about half a ſcore, or a dozen words, or one Verſe, are the meaſure of a juſt *a parte*; the beſt of all is an *a parte* of one word, be- cauſe even in the nature of things, one word may ſlip from us, and not be over-heard by him that ſpeaks to us : But long *a partes*, ſuch as *Plautus* makes, are unexcuſable, becauſe they put the other Actor quite out of countenance, and make him, that he knows not at laſt what poſture to be in, to make the Audi- ence believe he does not hear the other, who ſpeaks aloud ſo long, and ſo near him.

Beſides, one muſt take ones time very well to make an *a parte*. An Actor who is ſerious in talk- ing, not being lightly to be interrupted by another, without ſome probable colour for his ſtopping in the middle of a Diſcourſe, which muſt give the other who is to make the *a parte*, an opportunity to make it handſomly ; and if he that is ſpeaking does as it were interrupt himſelf, by ſaying ſomething ſoft- ly, which ought not to be over-heard, he that hearkens muſt wonder at his ceaſing to ſpeak, and either know or think he gheſſes the true reaſon of it, for elſe it would be unnatural that a man ſhould ſpeak and be ſilent by fits, and they that ſtand by, neither be ſurpriz'd at it, nor gheſs at the cauſe. The Poet therefore muſt take either the time of an Ex- clamation, or ſome ſuch other Figure, whereby an Actor may be ſuppos'd to be in a condition not to ſpeak for ſome moments, nor to hearken to what another

another fays, and at that time a few words, or half
a Verfe may be put in another *Actors* mouth, to
make a reafonable *a parte*. If it happens fo that the
time in which one Actor makes his *a parte*, is fenfible to the other, he muft fay fome word that
marks his aftonifhment of the others diftractfulnefs,
either feigning that he did not hear him well, or
miftook him, or fo. We have an Example of this in
Plautus's *Moftellaria*, where *Tranion* having made
an *a parte*, *Theuropides* asks him what it is he
mumbles to himfelf, which fhews the Slave to have
fpoke foftly. The fame Poet does the like in his *Aulularia*, where *Staphila* having faid afide, that fhe
*had rather be hang'd than ferve any longer fuch a co-
vetous, mad Fellow as* Euclio: *Euclio* anfwers, *See how
this Jade murmurs fomething to her felf.* ☞ p. 337.

When two Actors fee not one another, and each
of them make an *a parte*, one of them muft ftill be
fuppos'd to be fometimes filent. For Example; If a
Lover be to make a complaint in fome folitary place,
where another Lady comes to look fomething fhe
has loft, I think the Lover ought to be in fome great
Extacy of grief to give the Lady time to fpeak, and
then the Lady ought to be employ'd in looking what
fhe came for, to give the Lover time to continue his
complaint, and then thefe *a partes* may be longer
than the ordinary ones.

There are fome occafions where they may be
yet longer; as if one of the Actors does not fee the
other, and is doing fomething which requires fome
time, he that fees him, without being feen, may
make a Difcourfe that fhall laft as long as his Action.
For Example; If a covetous man tell his money, the
Thief that fees him may make an *a parte*, that fhall
laft

laſt all that time; nay it is neceſſary there ſhould be one then, there being no greater fault upon the ſtage than to have it ſilent; and whatſoever is doing, ſome body or other muſt ſpeak, and there is to be no ceſſation of that, but in the Intervals of the Acts; nay, if ſomething falls out in the Play, that may ſeem naturally to ſtrike them all dumb, yet one Actor ought to be kept on purpoſe to ſay ſomething of their ſilence, leſt the Action ſhould ceaſe in the middle of an Act or Scene.

From theſe general Obſervations, the Poet may eaſily govern himſelf ſo as to make a judicious *a parte* ; but if he deſires more light upon this Subject, let him read *Monſieur de la Menardiere*, in his ſixth Chapter of his Poeticks, where he makes many judicious Remarks ; only I cannot agree to two Obſervations he makes ; the firſt is, when he ſays that Poets might make more reaſonable *a partes*, if it were written on one ſide of the Stage. For Example ; *This is the Louvre*, and on the other ſide, *This is the Palace Royal*; for the Stage cannot comprehend two places ſo far diſtant from one another. I thought at my firſt reading him, that it was a raillery he made upon our Modern Poets abſurdities, but having afterwards obſerv'd that in the eighth Chapter he makes his Stage contain a whole City, I ſaw he was in earneſt. The other thing in which we diſagree is, that he cites *Scaliger* in the one and twentieth Book of his Poeticks, to ſhew that he condemns all *a partes* upon the Stage ; for *Scaliger* in that place does not ſay one word of it; he deſcribes in that Chapter the *Theatre* of the Antients, and having ſpoke of the *Scene*, which repreſented the Actors Houſes, and of the Proſcenion, or *Foreſcene*, where they appear'd; and

and of the *Orcheſtra* deſign'd for the Muſick and Dancers, he reproaches the *French* Nation with ſo groſs an Ignorance in his time, that they had not ſo much as a Painted Cloth or Hanging to hide thoſe Things and Actors which were not to be ſeen : And theſe are his Words.

In France, ſays he, *they Act Plays ſo, that all things are expos'd to the Eyes of the Spectators ; all the Decorations appear upon the Stage, the Actors never diſappear ; onely thoſe that are ſilent, are reputed abſent : But certainly it muſt be very ridiculous, that the Spectators ſhould know that you hear and ſee, and yet you your ſelf ſhould not hear nor ſee what is ſaid of you in your own preſence, as if you were not where you are : Whereas the true Art of the Poet is to ſuſpend the Attention of the Audience, and make them always expect ſome Novelty ; but there, far from that, Satiety is upon one, before ones Appetite is rais'd.*

Thus it is that *Scaliger* deſcribes the old *French* Stage ; which I have alledg'd elſewhere, to prove the difference between that and our Stage, as it is brought to Perfection at this time, and to what Splendour it might be brought, by following the Example of the Ancients. But *Scaliger*'s Deſign, as it appears, was not here to ſpeak of ill *Apartes,* as may appear to any who ſhall carefully read what he writes there of the **Fabrick** of the Ancient Theatres.

Nunc in Gallià ita agunt fabulas, ut omnia in conſpectu ſint, univerſis apparatus diſpoſitis ſublimibus ſedibus ; Perſonæ ipſæ nunquam diſcedunt, qui ſilent pro abſentibus habentur. At enim verò perridiculum ibi ſpectatorem videre te audire, & te videre, teipſum non audire quæ alius coram te de te loquatur : quaſi ibi non ſis ubi es. Cùm tamen maxima Poetæ vis ſit ſuſpendere animos, atque eos facere ſemper expectantes. At hic tibi novum ſit nihil, ut priùs ſatietas ſubrepat, quàm obripat fames.
Scal. l. 1. c. 21.
Poet.

Chapter the Tenth.

Of the Acts.

WE call *Act* that Fifth part of a Drammatick Poem which is begun and ended with Musick, and consists, in our Plays, of about Three hundred Verses, or thereabouts. The ancient *Greek* Poets knew not the Name, though they had the Thing; for their *Episodes* (which, according to *Aristotle*, were that which was contained between two Singings of the *Chorus*) was the same thing, and our Musick answers their *Chorus*. The *Romans* have had the Word, (as we from them) but not, I believe, always; for at first it signified a whole Play, as the Word *Dramma* did among the *Greeks*: but, I believe, when Comedy came to lose its *Choruses*, and had nothing left but Dancing, Musick, and Buffooning, for Interludes, then the Poets bethought themselves to distinguish their Plays by Acts, for to take off the Confusion that must else have been in reading of them. And this, I think, hapned but late neither; for we see nothing of it in those who were Contemporaries with *Terence*. *Horace* is, I think, the first that has given us any Precepts about it, as well for the Distinction as Number; and 'tis wonderful that *Athenæus*, who cites so many *Greek* Drammatick Poets, does not give us the least hint, from which we might conjecture, that this Distinction was known in his time. But since the *Greeks* have had the Thing, I will treat of it under the name of Acts, without examining in what time, or how it came by that Name.   First

Neve minor,
neve sit quinto
productior actu
Fabula, quæ
posci vult &
spectata reponi.

First then, we must know, that Poets have generally agreed, that all *Drammas* regularly should have neither more nor less than Five Acts: And the Proof of this is in the general Observation of it ; but for the Reason, I do not know whether there be any founded in Nature. Rhetorick has this advantage over Poetry in the Parts of Oration, that the *Exord, Narration, Confirmation*, and *Peroration*, are founded upon a way of Discoursing natural to all Men ; for every one always makes some little Preface, then passes to the thing he has to say, which he confirms by Reason, and, as he makes an end, endeavours to gain the Favour of those that hear him. But for the Five Acts of the Drammatick Poem, they have not been fram'd upon any such ground ; only they owe their being to the many Observations of the Poets, who have studied to find out what would be most agreeable to their Spectators. First then, having perceived that it was not possible for their Spectators to have a continued Attention to the Reciting of Fifteen or Sixteen hundred Verses, without interruption, they used *Choruses* , whose Singing and Dancing eas'd the Impatience of the Spectators , and put them in good humour to hear the Remainder of the *Dramma :* and for the same reason they divided it into Five Parts, which hapned so well, that whether it be that that is a Proportion that just hits the Weakness of the Audience, or that by Custom we are made Friends to it, 'tis certain, that we do not naturally like a Play that has more or less than Five Acts, which divide the Time of so many Hours as we can well spare to a Diversion, without making it a Toil. We see by experience, that the *Italian* Comedians, who fail in this, by making only Three

Acts, according to their ill-received Cuftom, make the Firft Act fo very long, that it is moft importunately tedious. I fhould therefore advife the Poet to make Five Acts, and each of them of about Three hundred Verfes, or little more, having always obferv'd, that the Patience of the Audience feldom reaches beyond Sixteen hundred Verfes ; and every body knows, that two of the moft Ingenious and Magnificent of our Plays have mifcarried for having been too long : For 'tis an ordinary thing to fee the Spectators applaud a Play of a good juft Length, though with fome Faults, rather than admire an exact accomplifh'd one, that is too long. We can find Excufes for the Poet in any thing elfe; but Wearinefs and Satiety have that particular to them, that they make even the beft things infupportable to us.

Let the Poet then feek among the Ancients the Obfervation of this Rule. The *Greeks* have both known and practifed this Divifion of the Drammatick Poem, but not all alike. It is pretty apparent in *Sophocles* : *Æfchylus* had not attain'd in his time the exactnefs of the Rules ; and as for *Euripides*, he always does fo embarafs himfelf with Prologues, that his Plays feem often to have Six Acts, and fometimes Seven. Befides, it feems that in fome Plays the *Chorus* fings in the middle of an Act, and fo interrupts the Sequel ; which is confirm'd by *Horace*, who gives it for a Rule, That the *Chorus* fhou'd fing nothing in the middle of the Acts, that is not proper to the Subject. But this regards a Criticifm not ufeful in our days, by which perhaps we might doubt of the *Chorufes* finging in the middle of an Act : For either the *Chorus* did not

fing,

fing, or the Verfes are ill placed in our Impreffions, as we can make appear by divers Plays of *Ariſto-phanes*, and in the *Bacchants* of *Euripides*.

As for the *Latin* Tragedies, which we have under the Name of *Seneca*, I think our Poet may forbear imitating them in the Structure, as in all the reft, except in the Refinednefs of the Thoughts ? for to me nothing feems fo ridiculous, and withal fo te-dious, as to fee one Man alone make an Act, without any Variety; and that a Ghoft, a God, or fome He-roe, fhall make at the fame time the *Prologue*, and, according to *Euripides*, an *Act* too.

It is not fo eafie to give Advice about *Ariſtopha-nes*'s Comedies ; for they have all of them a Pro-logue, after the way of the *Greek* Tragedy ; but the Plays are not all alike : fome of them are very re-gular, and others fo full of confufion, that it is very hard to name the Acts diftinctly ; as in that called *The Birds*, where it is hard to fay which is the firft Singing of the *Chorus*, nor how many Acts there is, nor where the Second begins : And we fee that the Interpreters have not marked the Acts in our Impref-fions, finding them too much out of order to be ea-fily methodiz'd.   Though, I think, the greateft dif-ficulty has been, either out of the Licence of old or middle Comedy, or by the Corruption of the Co-pies, which Time partly difperfed, and the Ignorance of the Compilers and Printers has ill re-eftablifh'd.

Plautus's Comedies have been liable to the fame Misfortunes in many places, where there are whole Scenes loft, others added, and Acts confounded, as in the *Moſtellaria*, of which the Scene which is rec-koned the Third of the Firft Act, ought to be the Firft of the Fourth : For after the Second Scene of
the

the Third Act, the Stage is empty, and without Action, *Theuropides* and *Tranion* entring into *Simon's* Houfe to vifit him, and no other Actor remains upon the Stage ; fo that the Mufick or the *Mimes* ought to have mark'd the Interval of an Act in this place : but the Scene which is counted for the Second of the Fourth Act, ought to be added to this, which is put for the Firft of the Third Act ; for there is no diftinction neither of Time nor Action between them, the Stage having ftill the fame Perfons prefent, and the fame Difcourfes going on ; and fo thefe two together muft make the Firft of the Fourth Act, fince between that which is put for the laft of the Third Act, and thefe two, there is no feparation ; for *Theuropides* is ftill upon the Stage, being neither gone off, nor come on again : fo that the Interludes have no time wherein they may be inferted to diftinguifh the Acts.

As for *Terence's* Comedies, they may be a Model for a great many things, to thofe who have a mind to gain Reputation, and excel in this Art.

It has been ask'd fometimes, When one may fay properly, that an Act is finifhed ? And it has been answered by *Donatus*, That it is when the Stage is empty, and without any Actor. But if it were fo, we might object, That it would be in the power of the Players to fhorten or lengthen any Act at their pleafure ; for if they did but take away the Mufick, they might appear one after another, without ever leaving the Stage empty : And befides, when the Scenes are broken, as they are frequently enough in our Plays, the Mufick might play, fince the Stage would be empty. Therefore, I think, that the Act ends not when the Stage is without an Actor, but when

when it is without Action. And that which makes me say so, is, that I have obsern'd, that among the Ancients the *Chorus* does both sing and dance, and the Musick play, though there be an Actor upon the Stage , which happens two ways ; the one, when an Actor remains upon the Stage, but incapable of Action, as *Hecuba* in *Euripides,* who falls in a swoon between the First and Second Act ; and the *Amphytrio* of *Plautus,* surpriz'd by a Thunderbolt, between the Fourth and Fifth Act. The other Case is, when the Actor which appears at the end of an Act does mingle with the *Chorus,* as *Electra* in the Intervals of the Acts of the *Orestes* of *Euripides*; and other Actors in the second *Iphigenia,* and in the *Bacchantes* ; this being common enough to Tragedy, Now in the first Case, the Actor which remain'd upon the Stage without Action, stopp'd the Course of the Theatral Action, and so finish'd the Act : And in the second Case, the Actor making part of the *Chorus,* gave easily to understand, that the Theatral Action was ceas'd, and by consequent the Act ended. Therefore I am not of *Donatus*'s Opinion, when he writes, *That the Reason which oblig'd* Menander *to take away the* Chorus *from Comedy, and likewise forc'd Poets to confound their Acts,so as no body could distinguish them, was, that the Spectators were grown so impatient, that they withdrew as soon as the Actors disappear'd from off the Stage, to make room for the Musick, which was to mark the Interval of the Acts.* For, I think, he spoke as a Man not thorowly instructed in the Matters of the Stage. For the Impatience of the Spectators must needs be greater, if their Attention had no ease ; and still more, if the Acts were not broken, nor distinguish'd, as that

must

muft be, if the laft Scene of an Act was immediately rack'd to the firft of the next ; for then the Theatre being never without Actor or Action, you could not naturally part that, which was not feparated by any Interval of Time. Befides, the Muſick among the Ancients was very agreeable, and did not, as now a days, confift of two or three fcurvy Violins, but was one of the greateft Diverfions of their Comedies ; and the Mafters of thofe Muſical Compoſitions had their Names graven in all Publick Infcriptions, with thofe of the Poet, and Chief *Hiſtrio* or Player.

To which, if we add the other Interludes, of *Mimes*, Dances, and Buffooning, we may eafily judge, that there was lefs reafon to be impatient in the Intervals of the Acts, than in the Acts themfelves ; particularly, if fome fcurvy Actor were to come on to fpoil a Part, fuch as formerly was *Pellio*, who acted fo ill in *Plautus's Epidicus*, that the Poet affronted him publickly the next day, when the *Bacchides* was reprefented.

Befides, we do not fee any where but in *Plautus*, that the Acts are not well diftinguifh'd ; (and in him too 'tis the fault of the Printers.) Neither do I think that his Plays were fo little diverting, as to need fuch a fcurvy Contrivance to fix the Spectators Attention; for his Plays have more Action, and are not fo ferious as *Terence's*, and always fucceeded better in the Reprefentation, though *Terence's* pleas'd the Reader better, as having Paffions better govern'd, more elegant Expreffions, and modefter Characters. But to come to *Donatus* ; he fhews himfelf that he was not very fure of what he writ, when he adds, *That the Learned were not all agreed, that it was for this*

reafon

reason that Menander *took away the* Chorus *from* Comedy, *and confounded the Acts.* Besides, that which makes me think that he speaks as a man that did not very well understand the Stage, is what he says of Terences *Eunuchus, That the Acts are there more confounded, than in any other of his Plays, and that none but the Learned can distinguish them well. In which* (says he) *the Poet has made but one Act of all five, that the Spectator might scarce have the time to breathe, and to hinder him in the continuation of the Events from rising before the Scenes were taken away:* For 'tis most certain, that this Comedy is one of those in which the Acts are best distinguish'd, though the Scenes are also best knit together; for at the end of every Act the Actors say precisely where they are going, and what they are going to do; and they that begin the next Act tell whence they come, and why they come on upon the Stage; so that there is not the least suspicion of that imaginary confusion, of which *Donatus* speaks.   Nay, the Latines are generally so careful to make the distinction remarkable, that *Plautus* having made *Pseudolus* go out the last man in the first Act, and come in the first man in the second, because that is against the Rules, and that it might cause some confusion, he makes him say these words as he goes out; *While I retire to my house there to call the great Council of all my Cheats, the Musick will divert you.* And for this reason in the *Heautontimorumenos* of *Terence, Menedemus,* who makes an end of the fourth Act, and begins the fifth, says precisely, *That he had been some time absent, that he had been in the remotest part of his house, where he had seen* Clitipho *shut himself up with* Bacchide; so that there is no room to believe that confusion of Acts, as *Donatus*

Would have it, and indeed may fay, that in moſt of the Latine Comicks, it is only by the ignorance of thoſe who have marked the Acts, that there is any confuſion, as in the *Amphytrio* of *Plautus,* where the fourth Act ought to begin by that Scene which is put for the laſt of the third Act; and in the *Heautonti-morumenos* of *Terence,* where the fourth Act ſhould begin at the Scene cited for the ſecond, that which is mark'd for the firſt belonging properly to the third Act, it is then much more reaſonable to believe what we have ſaid, which is, that the Actor in theſe occaſions where he ſeems to continue an Act, did mingle with the *Mimes,* and other Interlude Actors, as in *Tragedy* with the *Chorus,* or that the Copys are corrupted, and Scenes loſt; or at leaſt ſome Verſes which might have juſtified the Poets Art; as it has happened to *Plautus* in many places, of which I ſpeak more at length in my Obſervations. But let us come now to the Inſtruction of the Poet about the diviſion and ſtructure of his Acts.

Having then choſen his Subject, he muſt remember to take the Action he has a mind to repreſent in its laſt point, and he muſt believe, if he be not very ſterile indeed, that the leſs matter he ſhall borrow, the more liberty he ſhall have for agreeable Invention; therefore let him ſo ſtrengthen himſelf, as in appearance not to have wherewithal to make above one Act; things paſs'd will furniſh him with matter to fill up the others, either by bringing the Events of the Story ſomewhat nearer, or by *Recitals,* or other ingenious Inventions. Thus *Euripides* in his *Oreſtes* opens his Stage with the very moment in which thoſe that were guilty of *Clitemneſtra's* death, were to be judg'd. One would think that there were

not

not matter for one Act, and that the *Cataſtrophe* muſt preſently follow; but he prepares allſo dextrouſly by the coming of *Menelaus,* and *Hermiones* abſenting her ſelf from the Pallace, that this Tragedy is one of the moſt Noble and Excellent ones of all Antiquity. *Corneille* does ſo in his *Horatius* ; he begins his Story juſt after the Truce agreed upon by both Armies, and the Combat of the three againſt three reſolv'd upon for the deciſion of the Cauſe; then he furniſhes his Stage with thoſe paſſions which he draws from *Sabina's* Marriage.

After this, he muſt conſider that which *Ariſtotle* ſays of *Epiſodes* ; for the Drammatick Poem has three things differing from each other, which are the *Conſtitution of the Fable or Story, the Compoſition of the Tragedy,* which is properly, the diſpoſing of the Acts and Scenes, and the *verſification* or Poetry.

The conſtitution of the Fable is the Invention and Order of the Subject, whether from Story, or receiv'd Fables, or the Imagination of the Poet. *Ariſtotle,* by the Conſtitution of the Fable, means only that part of the Story or Subject which comprehends the Theatral Action, that is, which happens after the opening of the Stage, and is of Opinion, that all that is done before, is out of the Conſtitution of the Fable ; and for this reaſon, ſpeaking of probability, he ſays, *That it is lawful for the Poet to ſuppoſe ſomething againſt probability, provided it be without the Fable,* that is, in thoſe things which are done before the opening of the Stage, and are to be made known afterwards by ſome Actor; and he brings for Example *Sophocles* in his *Oedypus,* in which he ſuppoſes in the part which happens before the overture of the Stage, that *Oedypus* did not know how

King *Laius* died, which was not at all probable.

But for my part, I am of Opinion that the Conſtitution of the Fable ought to comprehend the whole Story of the Stage ; for that which happens before the opening, is as much of the Subject, as that which happens when the Stage is open ; and I cannot conſent that the Poet ſhould ſuppoſe any Incidents againſt probability in thoſe Adventures which precede the Action repreſented, becauſe that they being a foundation for things which happen afterwards upon the Stage, it breaks all the Chain of Events, it being againſt all order that a thing probable ſhould be built upon an improbable one; and the Poet is leſs to be excus'd in this, than in any thing ; for the Incidents which are before the opening of the Stage, are in his power, whereas often in the ſequel of the Play the Events conſtrain each other, and take away ſome of the Author's liberty.

The Compoſition of the Tragedy is the diſpoſition of the Acts and Scenes, that is, of the *Epiſodes,* which are to be added to the Conſtitution of the Fable, to give it its juſt proportion, in which often conſiſts the greateſt beauty of the Poem, as it is the greateſt Art of the Poet ; for the ſame Subject, that is, the ſame Conſtitution of Fable, without altering the Fund or the Events, may have a Diſpoſition of Acts and Scenes ſo differing, that is, the *Epiſodes* ſo diverſly order'd, that there may be a very good, and a very bad Tragedy made of it. For Example, that *Cinna* had reſolv'd to kill *Auguſtus,* and engaged divers of his Friends in the Deſign, is of the Conſtitution of the Fable, but that he comes and tells the Deſign to *Emilia,* repeating to her the very words he had us'd to excite the Conſpirators, that is of the
Com-

Compofition of the Tragedy, or Difpofition of the Acts ; for without changing either the Fund of the Events of the Fable,another befides *Cinna* might have related the Confpiracy, and to another perfon than *Emilia* ; but fuch a Narration would not have had the fame Effect ; and 'tis in that that Mr. *Corneille* does particularly excel ; for he has an Art of placing in his diftribution of the Acts and Scenes, fuch Incidents as afford him moft lively,moving paffions, and another man, without changing any thing in the Subject, would place the fame Incidents fo as to draw little of beauty from them.   This has made me often wonder at fome Learned men, and well read in *Ariftotle*, who have confounded the Conftitution of the Fable with the Difpofition of the Tragedy.   For the *Philofopher* fays in exprefs words, *That after having conftituted the Fable, you muft infert the Epifodes*, that is, all the Pathetick Difcourfes, Narrations, Defcriptions, *&c.* and take care that they naturally flow from the Fable or Subject.   As to the verfification, which is the laft part, that depends upon the Talent the Poet has receiv'd, and his ftudy in the Art,which will help him to cultivate and polifh Nature.   To come then again to our Subject, the Poet muft examine if the Conftitution of his Fable can fuffer *Epifodes* ; and if fo, of what kind, which will be the moft taking, and in what place they will appear, and have their beft Effect ; and after this he muft divide his Acts fo, as if poffible, they may not be very unequal, and that the laft Acts have ftill fomething of ftrength and ornament more than the firft; either by the greatnefs of the Paffions, the fingularity of the Events, or the rarity of the Show and Decoration.

To

To do this well, we muſt have a full Idæa or Pro-
ſpect of his whole Subject, and have it entire before
him ; for he that comprehends the whole, can eaſily examine the parts, and range them ; but he that
knows his Subject only as he divides it, runs the hazard of dividing it very unequally.

Some have maintain'd, that every Act is to be
opened by a new Actor that has not appear'd before. I ſhould not diſlike this if it could be done
ſo as that the new Actor brought no confuſion upon
the Stage, and that his coming on be ſo prepar'd, as
that this variety may ſeem natural to the Subject,
and not appear to be the bare Invention of the Poet,
*for Art that diſcovers it ſelf, is againſt the Rules of
Art upon the Stage.* Yet I do not think it neceſſary
to be always thus practiſed, the Poet having other
ways of diverſifying his Acts by Incidents, Paſſions,
or ſome ſuch thing; not that I would confine the
Poet neither to one *Epiſode* in an Act, but if he produce more, he muſt be careful that they do naturally,
and without affectation, create one another; and one of
our beſt Plays was condemn'd for being too richly
various in this kind, ſo as the Audience had not time
to breathe after the impreſſion of a moving Paſſion ;
the Graces of the Stage muſt have time to be relliſh'd,
and like other humane pleaſures, we loſe the Enjoy-
ment of them, if we are either cloy'd with them, or
have not the leiſure to taſt them thoroughly.

Sometimes it happens that there are in a Story
ſuch circumſtances, that they are not agreeable, nor
decent in the Repreſentation, and yet they might
give riſe to noble Narrations, and produce Sentiments, of which the Expreſſions would be admirable.
In theſe occaſions there is nothing to be done, but to
ufe

ufe the Antients Artifice, which is to fuppofe the
things done. For Example; It would have been
hard and ridiculous to reprefent *Ajax* upon the
Stage killing of Sheep, which he miftook for the
Greeks in his rage, and whipping a great Ram whom
he thought to be *Ulyffes*, and yet it was fitting to
give fome Image of this to the Spectators; therefore *Sophocles* does not only make the recital of it,
but fuppofing this Maffacre, arriv'd in the night, he
opens *Ajax*'s Tent, where appear thefe creatures
flaughter'd, and that poor Prince overwhelm'd with
grief and madnefs. Where we may take notice, that
the Poet avoided to open the Stage by the beginning
of *Ajax*'s fury; for he could not fo well have govern'd his Subject, neither would he let it quite pafs
over, becaufe then he fhould not have rais'd compaffion in the minds of his Spectators. *Euripides* likewife is very ingenious, when he avoids making
Phædras Nurfe corrupt *Hyppolitus* upon the Stage
(as *Seneca* and our French Poet *Garnier* have done)
becaufe he muft either have made her fay things
weak, and of no effect to her defign, or have made
her ufe expreffions againft the Decency and Majefty
of Tragedy; therefore by making that young Prince
appear angry at the old Womans Difcourfe to him,
he preferves to the Stage all its Sentiments of Vertue,
and yet informs the Audience of the thing that was
neceffary for them to know.

In a word, the moft general Precept is fo to caft
your Subject, as to throw between the Acts all that
can be troublefom to the Poet, or difagreeable to the
Spectators. That which I have faid before, that the
fame Actor ought not to finifh one Act, and begin
the next, in ftrict regularity is true, becaufe that
the

the Actor that goes off, is suppos'd to do it upon
some important business, which requires some reasonable time, for the Execution of it ; and if he come
in immediately upon the playing of a Tune or two,
the Spectators are surpriz'd to see him come back so
soon ; but yet there are some Exceptions; for if the
Actor have but little to do, or go but a little way,
he may begin the next Act ; and 'tis ordinary for
Plautus so to do; and *Terence* does it sometimes :
But Comedy suffers this better than Tragedy, because
that the Actors in the first being but of mean condition, they may do any thing hastily, without indecency ; but in *Tragedy*, the persons being all Ladys,
and great Men, their Actions must be more grave
and serious. If the Antient Tragick Poets begun an
Act by the Actor, that had just ended the preceding
Act, it was when he stay'd upon the Scene, being
mingled with the *Chorus*;a thing pretty ordinary with
the Women, and of which the Examples are frequent.

Above all things, methinks the first opening of
the Stage ought to be magnificent, either by the
number, the Majesty of the Actors, or by the Pomp
of the Decoration.

The Greek Tragedys begun generally by a Machine, which brought on a God or Goddess ; that is
very noble,but must be but seldom practis'd amongst
us, they had a veneration for their Gods, and Plays
were a part of their Religion ; but we are ignorant
of those Mysteries, and despise them; and I for my
part should rather approve of any other Invention or
Contrivance, which should raise some great Expectation, or a strong desire of knowing something that
were past.

Principium debet esse illu-stre. Voss. lib. 1. cap. 7. Poet. Sumendum principium ex illustri re, ta-que tùm cog-nata, tùm proxnma. Scal. lib. 3. cap. 95. Poet.

The

The *Orestes* of *Euripides* begins very finely, by exposing that unhappy Prince lying upon a Couch, wrapp'd up in his Cloke, sleeping with disquiet and starts; his Sister at his Feet weeping, the *Chorus* scarce daring to tread for fear of waking him, and so raise his Fury: all that is pleasing, and raises an expectation of something extraordinary. The waking of *Herode* in the *Mariamne*, is a fine opening of the Stage. These are things not to be neglected; for they are to the Poet what an *Exordium* is to the Orator, to gain the Attention of the Audience, and the Good-will of his Judges.

Chapter the Eleventh.

Of the Intervals of the Acts.

PAinting and Drammatick Poesie, besides many other Points that they meet in, do also agree in this, that they cannot possibly give the entire Image of that which they design to represent, and can comprehend but the least part of their Design. A Picture cannot shew any Person entire, nor any Story but by halves, and by the visible Parts onely. So the Stage cannot represent an Action in all its Circumstances: Battels of Armies must be suppos'd, which cannot be seen; and many other things, either undecent, or frightful. But likewise as the Excellence of the Painter consists in finishing so rarely well all that he does shew, that by that the Spectator may judge of what he hides; so the Poet must work with so much Industry, that those things which

he

he shews upon the Stage, may lead the Spectator to an easie comprehending of those which he either cannot or ought not to shew. 'Tis for this reason that the Drammatick Poets have made use of the *Intervals* of the *Acts*, to perform those things which could not so well be done upon the Stage : And the Ancients fill'd up that space of time with *Choruses*, and other Interludes, as we do now with Musick. Some may say, perhaps, That these Intervals are not so very necessary, because one might so continue the Scenes of a Play without Interludes or Musick, that the Actors who should disappear, should be reputed to do off of the Stage, all that either could not, or ought not to be done there, while other Actors should appear and act their Parts. This in it self may be true ; but Experience teaches, that Mankind has not Attention enough to support the reading of one entire Play, without interruption : for even one Act too long is a most insupportable trouble ; and, as *Cicero* says, That *no Man would make an Oration of one Period, though he had Breath enough to recite it* ; so no Auditor would be content with a *Dramma* without any pause or stop, though he had an Attention strong enough to mind it. Variety is our greatest Charm ; and by that means Beauties will pass upon us more agreeably, than a great and excellent one, always the same. But besides, it happens sometimes, that all the Actors are to be busied for some time off of the Stage, which then remains empty ; and so that time must be fill'd up, that the Audience may not expect with disgust and tediousness. Moreover, if there were always some Actor present upon the Stage, the Spectators could not naturally imagine that an Actor had employ'd

ploy'd any more time in what he had been about,
than while the other Actor was speaking ; and yet,
it may be, that first Actor must be suppos'd to need
two or three Hours to do his business in, which cannot be thought to have pass'd away in half a quarter
of an Hours Talking by another, whom the Audience has seen all the while.   But the *Intervals* make
this probable enough ; for the absence of all the
Actors, with the Musicks playing, and the cessation
of the Audiences attention, do all contribute to deceive the Imagination ; so as we may take a few
Moments for whole Hours : and then when the
Actors return, and say what they have been doing,
we do not wonder that they have perform'd so
much in so little a time.   Besides, the impatience
we are in to see the Continuation of the Story, makes
us think we have staid a great while, and so give the
more allowance for the things we hear have been
done in that time.

The Poet then must consider well in his Subject
what things cannot well be expos'd to view, and
throw them in the Intervals ; but if they are to afford Matter to any great Passion or Narration, there
the Poet's whole Art will be necessary, and the
Reading of the Ancients to boot, who will afford
him great light in managing those Contrivances.

Sometimes the Beauty of an Action lies in its beginning onely, and then you must shew the first
Strokes and Preparations of it, and finish it in the
Intervals, and behind the Stage : So we see that
Eteocles and *Polinices* dispute their Pretensions before their Mother ; but they do not fight and kill
one another before her. Otherwhile it happens, that
an action has nothing but the latter part of it fit for

[L 2]   Repre-

Reprefentation, and then the beginning muft be fup-pos'd to be done in the Intervals, and the laft Touch-es onely made fenfible, and prefent to the Spectators. *Sophocles*, as we have obferv'd in the preceding Chapter, has done this in his *Ajax* ; not that the Poet is bound to do this always at the end of an Act ; for fometimes the thing may come to pafs fomewhere further than the Place reprefented by the Stage, and then the Bufinefs may be related in the next Scene.

The greateft Advantage the Poet has from the Intervals of the Acts, is, that by that means he can throw off all the troublefom Superfluities of his Sub-ject. But he muft have a care not to fall into one Errour, common enough among our Poets, which is to fuppofe a thing done in the Interval of an Act, which in all probability could not have been done without having been feen by the Audience . And this muft happen when it is fuppos'd to have come to pafs upon the Place reprefented by the Stage ; for that being open, and expos'd to the Spectators Eyes, nothing can probably be perform'd there, that fhall not be feen. I remember, upon this Subject, that I was once at a Play, which otherwife was no ill Dramm-atick Poem, in which there was a Baftion of a be-fieg'd Town, upon which were armed Men for its de-fence ; and then in the Interval of an Act this Town was fuppos'd to be taken by Affault, and yet this Ba-ftion was neither attack'd nor defended upon the Stage ; and fo the Spectators remain'd with an ima-gination that the Town was not taken. Whereas the Poet might at leaft have faid fomthing of the pro-bability, if he had found a way to let the Audience know that the Town had been carried by an Affault

in

in another 1 lace, and so there had been no need of defending it there.

I shall not here enter into a particular deduction of the Kinds of Interludes with which the *Romans* mark'd the Intervals of the Acts in new Comedy, after having taken away the *Chorus's.* I shall not neither say at what time it was that the *Mimes* and the *Embolarii* took possession of the Stage, nor what their Dancing, Musick, and Buffooning was; why they made use of *Flutes*, and of what sort they were that are nam'd in ancient Inscriptions of Comedy *equal* and *unequal*, right or left : all that concerns onely the understanding the Stage of the Ancients, and not the Art of making a Drammatick Poem. I had undertaken to treat of all this in a Book which I should have called *The Restoring of the Theatre in France,* to shew what Ornaments might be added to ours from Antiquity ; but I should here go too far from my Subject, if I should lanch into this Matter. I will onely say, That much of it may be learn'd out of *Scaliger, Vitruvius, Julius Pollux, Vossius,* and others, though they speak of these Matters with ill Methods, and not much Application.

Chapter the Twelfth.

Of the Scenes.

I Was in some doubt whether I should explain here all the different Significations of the Word Scene, because the Learned will meet with nothing but what they know a'ready ; however, having con-
                                                    sider'd,

fider'd, that others may have by it fome Inftruction about the Matters of the Stage, I thought it not amifs to do it,

Firft then, the Word *Scene*, in its original and proper Signification, is taken for a Covering of Boughs made by Art, from whence the Feaft of the Tabernacles of the *Jews* was call'd *Scenopegia*; and from thence too fome People of *Arabia* were call'd *Scenites*. Sometimes too it fignifies a natural Shade of fome Grotto, or folitary place; fo *Virgil* has it,

Tum Sylvis Scena corufcis--------
Defuper horrentique atrum nemus imminet umbra.

But becaufe the firft Comedies, or rather the firft Buffooning, was under fome green Shade, the name of *Scene* was given to all Places where Comedy was reprefented; and Tragedy too, though transferr'd into great Cities, yet preferv'd the name of *Scene*, with that of *Theatre*, which fignifies a place for Spectacles. But then the Word *Scene*, even in Drammatick Poetry, was taken in different Significations; for fometimes it fignific'd the Place of Acting, as we fay, to be upon the *Scene*; and *Pliny* has it, That *Lucia, an old buffooning Woman, recited upon the Scene at the Age of a hundred years.*

Sometimes it fignifies that which we call the Decoration of the Stage; that is, all the Ornaments of painted Cloth which reprefent the Place where the thing is acted; and according to the three kinds of Drammatick Poetry, *Vitruvius* teaches how to make three forts of Scenes or Decorations of the Stage, fit for *Tragedy*, *Comedy*, and *Paftoral*; and from this Signification is come the Word *Profcenion*, or Fore-fcene, scene, attributed by the *Greeks* to that part of the Stage where the *Histrions* or Actors did both act and speak. At last its Signification became so extended, as to express at once the Place where the Actors acted, and that where the Spectators were. And it is in this sense that the Jurisconsult *Labeo* defines the Scene, according to *Ulpian.* Sometimes likewise it signified all that pompous Structure of Buildings, Galleries, Walks, Seats, and other places, where the *Romans* us'd to represent their Games.

From these different Significations have proceeded many Mistakes amongst the Modern Writers, because they did not rightly understand the Ancients, and so have confounded the *Proscenion* with the Decoration, and that again with the whole Building.

The last sense in which the Word *Scene* has been taken, and which we particularly need here, is, when it signifies that part of an Act which brings any Change upon the Stage, by the change of Actors.

The *Greeks* never us'd it in this Signification, tho they had the same distinction of Acts which we have. The *Latins* first brought it in use, with the Word *Act,* in *New Comedy,* having taken away the *Choruses.* I do not find any thing about this, in any Author ancienter than *Donatus*; but since we have receiv'd it, it will not be amiss to put here some Instructions to correct the Irregularities of Scenes.

The Ancients, who had no Division of their *Acts* into Parts, have always very exactly observ'd the Union or Dependance of *Scenes* upon one another; for knowing that the whole *Act* could not contain above one sensible Action upon the Stage, they judg'd very reasonably, that there was no need of
separating

Fabula quidem in Actus divisio vetus est & à Poetis ipsis: Actus autem in Scenas distributio est à Grammaticis & à vet. Terentii & Plauti cod. abest. Vossius, l. 2. c. 5. Poet.

separating the Parts that should compose it. But when our Poets begun to write for the Stage, they hardly knew what an *Act* or a *Scene* was; they plac'd a Man upon the Stage, to recite there what they had compos'd for him, and they took him away again when the *Capricio* of their Muse pleas'd, and then brought on one or more, which went off too with as little reason; so that one might have transpos'd any of their *Scenes*, without any injury to the *Play*, every one of them making as it were an *Act* by it self. We have seen upon our Stage a Captain, a Poet, and a Visionary Lover, all without having any thing to do with one another; and what they said, was more like so many Scholars Declamations, without any dependency upon each other.

Now I have observ'd, that there are four ways of uniting the Scenes together; to wit, an Union of *Presence*, another of *Seeking*, a third of *Noise*, and a fourth of *Time*.

The Union of *Presence* is, when in the following Scene there remains upon the Stage an Actor of the preceding Scene; which may be done three ways: Either by bringing on at once all those that are to be employ'd in that Act, and make them retire one after another, according to the diversity of their Interests; for still those who remain make a new Scene, which is united to the precedent Scenes by the Presence of those who rest. And this is a noble manner for a First Act. The second is, when the Actors come upon the Stage one after another, and none of the first go off; for then all the new Actors make new Scenes, which are united to the preceding ones by the Presence of those who were already upon the Stage. And this manner is very

good

good for a laſt Act.   The Third Way is, when the
Actors go and come according to their Intereſts and
Buſineſs : As when two Actors meet upon the Stage,
if there goes off but one, the ſecond who remains
makes a new Scene, and knits it with the firſt, by
other Actors who are to appear ; and this way is
capable of as much variety as the Poet pleaſes.

The Second Way of uniting the Scenes is, by ſeeking when an Actor who comes upon the Stage, looks
for him who went off ; and the Examples are very
frequent among the Latine Comick Poets ; but one
muſt be very careful that the reaſon for which one
Actor looks after the other, be a reaſon taken from
the Subject in hand, and ſenſible to the Spectators,
or elſe it would be a falſe Colour affected, and of no
effect ; and we muſt remember beſides, that if the
Actor who was upon the Stage goes off, for fear of
being ſeen by him that comes on, that does not make
an union of Scenes, except he that comes on, comes
with an Intention to look for him that goes off. Some
of our *Moderns* have fail'd in this, in withdrawing
their Actors for fear of being ſeen by the comers on,
when the New Actor had no Intention to look for
him that went off; for in this, far from being an union
of *Seeking*, it is rather one of *avoiding*, and ſo the
Scenes would be united by the very Actor who
broke them.

The Union of *Noiſe* is, when upon ſome Noiſe
which is made upon the Stage, an Actor, who probably might hear it, comes to know the cauſe, and
finds no body upon the Stage, that Scene made by
him is very well united to that which was made by
thoſe who went off, ſince the Stage does not remain
without Action, and that a *Chorus* or Muſick could

[M]   not

not be brought in without interrupting the Sequel of the Story. *Plautus* has many Examples of that.

As for the laſt which is made by *Time*, 'tis whe n an Actor, who has nothing to do with thoſe who go off the Stage, comes on, but in ſuch a nick of time, that he could not reaſonably be ſuppos'd to do it ſooner or later. We have a preciſe Example of this in the *Eunuchus* of *Terence*, in the third Act where *Antipho*, who has nothing to do with *Chremes*, nor thoſe who go off the Stage, ſays, *That he is in much trouble not to find* Chærea, *who was that day to take care of the Dinner for a Club of young men, that the hour of the Aſſignation was paſs'd, and that he is going to look him,* and ſo popt upon him. Now 'tis moſt certain *Antipho* comes on naturally at the due time, and that *Chærea* had fail'd by being taken up in the Intrigue, in which *Parmeno* had ingag'd him by making him paſs for an Eunuch, with a young Woman that he was in love with. Yet I muſt ſay this, that this Union of Scenes, except it be done with very natural Colours, and great Exactneſs, is not to be much practis'd.

Some have put the Queſtion, What ought to be the number of Scenes in each Act? The Poet muſt uſe in that his own Judgment; if there be very few, the Act will want variety; if there be many, and ſhort, the Act will be perplex'd; there will be little ſaid, and much confuſion. But we muſt obſerve that Comedy endures many more Scenes than Tragedy, as being more active, and leſs engaged in great paſſions which take up time. The Antients have ſometimes made up an Act of one ſingle Scene, but I do think that tædious, and much more when as in *Seneca* there is but one Actor for that Scene. I think in Tragedy
there

there ought to be at leaft three Scenes in an Act, and that if there be above eight, it cannot pleafe; I believe experience will juftifie this ghefs of mine.

I fhall now add here a thing, which it would be difficult for me to place any where elfe with more order, which is a difficulty which has often puzzled our beft Poets; and I fhall at the fame time fhew them how to avoid it. It happens then very ordinarily in Drammatick Poems, that to give a foundation to fome things which are to be fpoke, or to clear fome others which have been faid already, there is a neceffity of doing it in a *Theatral* way, and by confequent by an Actor, but as often fome other of the Actors are not to know or hear of it; it is then neceffary to make a new Scene, to drive off thofe who are to be ignorant of the thing, and to bring on others who may fpeak of it; and this I call a Scene of *Neceffity,* when it precedes what is to be done; and a Scene of *Efclairciffement,* or clearing, when it follows, and takes away any miftake or confufion that might have been: But it is good to obferve, that fuch Scenes, being as it were independent and loofe, they break the Union of the others, and often make the Stage dull; both which to avoid, I think we may take this Method.

Firft, To chufe the perfon that is to fpeak upon this occafion, and the place where the Speech fhall be; all that depends on the Poets Judgment, who to gain Obfervations, may read *Plautus* and *Terence;* both which have many of thefe *Scenes;* and for thofe of Neceffity, fometimes they are in the beginning of the Play, as *Sofia* in *Andria,* and *Geta* in *Hecyra,* where both thefe Slaves are of thofe Actors whom we call *Protatick,* who appear only at the

opening

opening of the Stage, to give intelligence about the Subject of the Play; and this way is not to be us'd without great dexterity.

As for that dulnefs which fuch Scenes bring along with them when they are not in the beginning, but in the body of the Poem, it muft be corrected, by making the Difcourfe of him that fpeaks eager and quick, which cannot be done but by great Figures, fuch as *Admiration*, *Exclamation*, &c. or by fome motions of fear or joy ftrongly expreffed; for elfe, though the thing which is expreffed be neceffary, yet it will be cold and dull, without any grace, becaufe there will be a plain affectation, which is the greateft fault a Poet can fall into.   As for the coming off of fuch Scenes, which is often very troublefom, he may avoid it by introducing in the beginning of an Act the perfon whom he intends to employ in any fuch Scene, provided that may appear probable, and confift with the following Scenes; or elfe he may retain at the end of an Act one or two perfons to this end. But the moft refin'd way of performing this is, to do it in the middle of an Act by fome body retain'd on purpofe to unite the following Scene; and who in that interval of time makes alone a Scene of Necef-fity, or of *Efclairciffement*, by taking occafion to fpeak of the different concerns of the Actors, who are gone off, or of thofe who are to come on; for this way neither the perfon, nor the thing, are af-fected, and the Scenes are not broken, and the Stage being warm'd by the pafsions of thofe who are gone off, is kept fo eafily by thofe who are to come on next.   In all this neverthelefs I leave the Judicious Poet his liberty, only I have thought fit to warn him of thefe Inconveniencies.

Chapter

Chapter the Thirteenth.

Of Spectacles, Machines, and Decorations of the Stage.

Having treated at length in my *Terence* justified about the construction of the Theatres of the Antients ; together with the *Decorations, Ornaments* and *Machines,* which were employed in the Representation of their Drammatick Poems, I can say little here that's new upon that Subject; therefore I shall not repeat any of it here, my design being only to instruct the Poet, and not the *Decorator*; but some Advertisements may not be amiss to the first, to teach him some ways how to add some external Ornaments to the Inventions of his Brain, to make them appear with more grace and perfection.

'Tis certain that the Ornaments of the Stage with the Scenes, Machines, and Decorations, make the most sensible delight of that ingenious Magick which seems to make *Hero's* live again in the world after so many Ages ; it sets before us a new Heaven, and a new Earth, and many other wonderful appearances of things which we imagine present, though we know at the same time that they are not so, and that we are agreeably deceiv'd : These Ornaments make the Poems themselves more illustrious ; the people takes them for Enchantments, and the men of understanding are pleas'd to see the dexterity of the Artists (who deservedly attract admiration) with the concurrence of so many Arts and Professions employed in the Execution of these contrivances, to

which

which all run with joy and delight. It was for this that the People of *Greece* and *Rome*, though as Martial as Learned and Ingenious, did bestow the richest Decorations upon their *Theatres*; there one might see the Heavens open, where appear'd their Imaginary Gods descending to converse with Men; the Air was often full of the noise of Thunder and Lightning; the Sea shew'd Tempests, Shipwracks, Men of War, Gallys, and Battles: The Earth did not only produce Gardens, Deserts, and Forrests, with magnificent Temples and Pallaces, but it often opened, and shew'd flaming *Abyssus*'s, Mountains came out of its bosom, Furies, Dæmons, and all the Prodigies of their fabulous Hell: In a word, the Objects of the diversion of these People were taken from all the supernatural Effects of the Divinity, the Miracles of Nature, the Master-pieces of Art, and all the beautiful contrivances that Imagination could form for the adorning their Theatre. Their Magistrates always strove to surpass one another in these magnificencies, and the People gave the highest dignities of their Government at this price: therefore the Poets, who saw that in the fortune of great Men there always was, and would be a fund for these Illustrious Expences, did not spare to fill their Poems with Incidents, where the richest Artifices were employed; and the Workmen were pleas'd in adding their labour and contrivance to acquire those riches and fame which certainly attended the success of their undertakings.

But for our times, though the Court does not dislike these Ornaments, and that the People crowd to see them, yet I would not advise our Poet to busy himself much in these *machine* Plays; our Players are neither Rich, nor Generous enough to make the Expence

pence of them, and their Decorators want ability in the performance ; I muſt add that our Authors them-ſelv's have been ſo negligent in acquiring the know-ledge of the Ancients ways in this matter, and in their means of Execution, that we need not wonder if we ſee ſo many ill Invented Embelliſhments of this kind.   Yet one would think that our Age, as ſoon as any might recover the priſtine glory of the *Theatre*, conſidering the Liberality of our Princes, the Application of our Poets,the Ingenuity of our Work-men, and the Care of our Comedians,and that which we have ſeen already perform'd in this Kingdom, is, it may be, but a pattern of what we may expect in the plenty of Peace.   Therefore that we may not be wanting to any thing that may contribute to the accompliſhment of ſo great a work, I ſhall here com-municate ſome Obſervations upon publick *Spectacles* and *Machines*, which I hope will be of ſome uſe.   I conſider all publick Spectacles and Decorations of the Scene three ways.

Some are of *things;* when the Spectacles are per-manent and immovable; as a Heaven open, a ſtormy Sea, a Pallace, or the like Ornaments.

Others are of *Actions;* when the Spectacle depends principally upon ſome extraordinary Fact ; as that one ſhould throw himſelf headlong from a Tower,or from a Rock in the Sea.

The Third ſort is of thoſe that are mingled with *Things* and *Actions*, as a Sea-fight, where at the ſame time is the Sea and Ships, and Men acting upon it.

Theſe may be all further diſtinguiſhed into natural, artificial, and marvellous.

The Natural ones are thoſe which repreſent the moſt agreeable things in Nature, as a Deſert, a Moun-tain on fire, *&c.*   The

The Artificial are thofe which fhew us the moft magnificent works of Art, as a Temple, a Pallace.

The Marvellous are thofe which fuppofe fome Divine Power or Magick Production, as the defcent of fome God from Heaven, or the rifing of fome Fury from Hell.

And of all thefe, the leaft confiderable are the laft, becaufe there goes little contrivance to the inventing of them, there being hardly any wit fo mean, who by this may not bring in, or carry off a great Intrigue. I faw once a Play, in which the Author having brought on a Rival, and concern'd him fo deeply in his Subject, that he did not well know how to bring him off, bethought himfelf to kill him with a Thunderbolt ; the contrivance was pretty fure; but if this fort of Invention be admitted in *Dramma*'s, we need not much trouble our felves to wind up the Plot any other way ; therefore all thefe Machines of Gods and Devils are to be us'd with great difcretion, and great care to be taken that in the Execution they play eafily, for elfe the people are apt to laugh, and make Railleries of a God hanging in the Air, or coming down too faft.

I fhould not likewife advife our Poet to ufe frequently thofe, where Actions are to make the greateft Effect, becaufe that all the fuccefs depends upon the Exactnefs of the *Comedians*, who are often fo negligent in the performance, that they will neither ftudy the manner, nor time neceffary; or elfe they are fo poffeffed with an Opinion of their Abilities, that they think it beneath them to be inform'd ; fo that either their Idlenefs, or their Vanity, moft commonly fpoils that which was well invented, and ought to have made the beauty of the Play. That which
remains

remains then is the permanent Decorations, of what nature foever they are ; and to thefe I would confine the Poet, but ftill with many Precautions: For,

First, They are to be neceffary, infomuch as the Play cannot be acted without thefe Ornaments ; or elfe they will not take, though never fo ingenious. And in this, I think, our *Andromeda* has not all its Regularity ; for in the Firft and Fourth Act there are two noble Buildings, of different Architecture, and no mention made of them in the Play ; fince thefe two Acts might be reprefented with any of the Decorations of the other three, without offending the Poet, or fpoiling any Incident of his *Dramma*.

Secondly, Thefe Ornaments muft be agreeable to the Sight ; for 'tis for that, that the People flock to them.   Not that I would abfolutely forbid the Poet to put in things monftrous or horrible; but at leaft then the Painting muft be exquifite, that the Art may be admir'd.

They muft likewife be modeft, and not againft that Pudour which the moft diffolute love the appearances of.   I believe that the fhewing of *Mars* and *Venus* furpris'd in a Net by *Vulcan*, would not be allowed for a fine Decoration.

They muft, befides, be eafie to put in execution ; that is, that the *Machinifts* do difpofe their *Machins* to play fo well, that there may be no need of great numbers of Hands, but they do of themfelves perform to a Minute ; for the People cannot endure to expect long the Effect of a *Machin*, and when they do not hit the Minute, they do not agree with the Motion and Pretence of the Actor upon the Stage, and fo fpoil his Part.

It will likewife be reafonable to confider, whether

[N]   the

the Place reprefented by the Scene, will bear in truth that which is to be fhewed in Image ; for elfe it would be a grofs Fault againft Probability : For example, If the place of the Scene were a Palace, and that clofe to it were a Prifon, or fome noifom place ; for Princes and Great People do not live near fuch places.

There muft not likewife be any Decorations made which are not agreeable to the Unity of Place ; as to fuppofe the Scene the Palace or Chamber of a Prince, out of which there fhould be an immediate Paffage to a great Foreft : For all thefe Fictions, though pleafing to the Eye, yet are otherwife, to our Reafon, which knows them to be falfe, impoffible, and ridiculous.

But particularly, the Poet muft fo order it, as that out of this Shew and Decoration fome notable Event may refult in the Body of the Play ; that is, fomething that may contribute either to the perplexing of the Plot, or the eafier unweaving of it ; for if all this Shew is onely for fhew, and not of the Effence of the Piece, the Men of Underftanding will value the *Decorator* for executing, but not the *Poet* for inventing fo ufelefs an Ornament. In the *Rudens* of *Plautus*, the Shipwrack that is there reprefented, makes both the Knot and the Unweaving of the Intrigue. The *Frogs* of *Ariftophanes* have a vaft Decoration, which ferves to all the Acts, and almoft to all the Scenes. And we fhall find few among the Ancients, but what agree with our Rules.

I cannot omit here to advertife the Poet of two important Confiderations : The firft that regards himfelf, which is, That when the Spectacles are of *Things*, that is, of Permanent Objects, they muft,

if

if poffible, appear at the firft opening of the Stage, to the end that the Surprife and Applaufe of the People, which generally attends fuch Sights, may be over, before the Actors begin to fpeak: or, that if there be any neceffity of changing the Decorations, let it be done in the Interval of an Act, that the Workmen may have the time neceffary for their Machins moving, and the Actor that is to appear, that of dreffing himfelf at leifure. But if, by the neceffity of his Subject, fome great Change is to be in the middle of an Act, let him contrive his Actors Part fo, as he have but little to fay at that time, and thofe too Words of Admiration, Grief, or Aftonifh-ment, to give fome time to the Murmur of the Spe-ctators, which is always rais'd upon fome fuch new Appearance.

The other Confideration regards the *Comedians*; which is, when the Spectacles confift of Actions: that is, when the Actors are to be in fome pofture extraordinary: The Actor, I fay, muft ftudy this Pofture with care, before he comes to act it upon the Stage; or elfe 'tis odds but he performs it very ill and not without danger fometimes to himfelf: all which does not a little trouble the Beauty of the whole Piece.

THE
ART
OF THE
STAGE.

Book the Fourth.

Chapter the First.

Of the Quantitative Parts of the Drammatick Poem, and particularly of the Prologue.

THE Drammatick Poem is so chang'd since the time of *Aristotle*, that though we should make an Allowance for his Translators and Intepreters Errours, yet we think we have great reason not to be altogether of his mind, particularly in the Matter of which we are going to treat.
He

He writes, That Tragedy has Four parts of Quantity, to wit, the *Prologue*, the *Chorus*, the *Episode*, and the *Exode* ; and to make them the more intelligible, he defines three of them thus. *The* Prologue (says he) *is that part of the* Tragedy *which is before the Entrance of the* Chorus. *The* Episode *is all that is between the two* Cantos *of the* Chorus. *And the* Exode *is that part after which the* Chorus *sings no more.* This I cannot conceive to be true, according to the present state of the *Greek* Tragedies ; neither can I allow, that *Aristotle* has well distinguish'd the parts of Tragedy as it was in his time, at least according to the Works of those three excellent Tragick Poets which have been transmitted to us.

To understand this aright, let us begin with the *Prologue*, and consider how many sorts of *Prologues* there were among the Ancients.

The first sort was of those which were made for the Interest of the Poet, either in answering the Invectives of his Adversaries, or in expounding his Proceeding in the Play. Many of this kind are to be found in *Plautus* and *Terence*, particularly in the last ; which made some say, as he himself relates, *That without the Reproaches and Cavils of the old Poet, the new one would not have known what Subject to have taken for his Prologues.*

Vetus si Poeta non lacessisset prior, nullum invenire Prologum potuisset novus. Prolog. in Phorm.

There were other *Prologues* that regarded the Interest of the *Comedians*, either to obtain the Judges or the Peoples Favour, or to bespeak their Attention. Such is that of the *Pseudolus* of *Plautus*, and some others.

There are some likewise which make a Mixture of the Subject of the Play, with the Poets or Comedians Interest ; and this was indeed the most ordinary

dinary one with *Plautus,* as appears in his *Captives,* his *Pœnulus,* and his *Menechmes.*

Now thefe three forts of *Prologues* were particular to *Comedy* ; for we meet with none fuch among the Tragick Poets ; neither do I think, that if they had us'd them, that *Ariftotle* would have reckon'd thefe fort of *Prologues* amongft the Parts of Quantity of a Tragedy ; for they are things by themfelves which may be omitted, without injuring the Poem, or otherwife leffening its true Proportion. 'Tis for this reafon that the Learned *Voffius* fays, *That the Prologues of Comedy and Tragedy are very different, becaufe in Comedy the Prologue is as it were alien to the Subject ; but in Tragedy it is incorporated with it, and makes a part of it.* And yet I muft fay, That I think he is miftaken in both; for fometimes in Comedy the *Prologue* is fix'd to the Body of the Poem, as in the *Ciftellaria* of *Plautus,* where it contains three Scenes : and, on the other fide, the Tragedian *Prologues* are not always fo twifted with the Subject, as to make a part of it.

The firft and moft ordinary *Prologues* of the *Greek* Tragedies were made by one of the Chief Actors, who came and explain'd to the Spectators all that had paffed in the Story before the opening of the Stage. We have of this fort divers in *Euripides,* where the Actor having done this, ends with fome Verfes which give a beginning to the Action of the Poem.

But it cannot be faid, that thefe *Prologues* make a part of the *Tragedy* ; firft, becaufe they are Difcourfes made to the Spectators, and by confequent, faulty, by mingling the Reprefentation with the Theatral Action : Neither are they neceffary, becaufe thofe things which precede the beginning of the
Play,

Play, ought to be dexterouſly told in the Play, in different parts of it; and this *Æſchylus* and *Sopho-cles* always obſerve. So that it is moſt certain, that theſe *Prologues*, which contain the Argument of the Play, are uſeleſs, defective, and may be eaſily ſepa-rated from it. And therefore we do not ſee that Monſieur *Corneille*, whom I always cite as a great Maſter for the Stage, has ever us'd ſo ill an Artifice; and I cannot but condemn thoſe *French* and *Italians* who have had recourſe to it.

Euripides makes another ſort of *Prologue*, more faulty and defective ſtill; to wit, when he employs ſome of the Gods to explain, by his Omniſcience, not onely all that was paſs'd, but things to come in the Play, even to the *Cataſtrophe*; by which means all the Events were foreſtall'd, than which there could not be a greater Fault, ſince it deſtroys all that Expectation and Suſpenſion which makes the Sur-priſe and Novelty of the Play. Now I do not think that *Ariſtotle* means this ſort of *Prologue* neither, when he ſays 'tis a Quantitative part of the *Dramma*.

The two ſorts of *Prologue* which remain for us to conſider, ſeem to agree better with *Ariſtotle's* Definition: *The* Prologue, ſays he, *is that part of the* Tragedy *which precedes the arrival of the* Cho-rus *upon the Stage:* By which he ſeems rather to teach us the Place of the *Prologue*, than its Nature: And according to this Definition, thoſe *Tragedies* that begin with the *Chorus*, have no *Prologue*: Such are the *Rhæſas*, the *Perſians*, and the *Suppliants* of *Euripides*; and by conſequent, according to this Doctrine, they have not their due Proportion, being depriv'd of their firſt Quantitative part: (And by the by, we may by this diſcover the Miſtakes of thoſe who

who have given us Arguments and Preambles upon these Greek Tragedies) for they say at the beginning of these three Plays which I now mention'd, *That the Chorus makes the Prologue*; for since the Prologue, according to *Ariftotle*, ought to contain all that is said before the *Chorus* comes on; 'tis impoffible for the *Chorus* to make the Prologue; or if the *Chorus* could make the Prologue, then *Ariftotles* definition is good for nothing: But now let us come to these two laft forts of Prologues.

One of them did ufe to contain in three or four Scenes made before the coming on of the *Chorus*, fome things which concern'd the Theatral Action, but which in truth were not neceffary parts of the Poem. We have two Examples of this in the *Phœnicians*, and in the *Medæa* of *Euripides*. In the firft *Antigone* appears upon the Walls of *Thebes*, with her Governour, who fhews her the Army of the befieging Princes, with fome Difcourfes about the Commanders of it, and this in fome fort does regard the *Dramma*, but does not in rigour make a part of it; and the Author of the Argument fays expresfly, that all that *Antigonus* does upon the Walls of the Town, is abfolutely out of the Theatral Action.

In the other Tragedy *Medæa*'s Children appear with their Governour, to whom *Medæa*'s Nurfe recommends them, expreffing fome fear for them in the fury and rage of *Medæa* againft *Jafon* their Father; and this at firft feems to belong to the Subject, but yet it makes no part of the *Dramma*; for if you begin the Play juft after the firft *Chorus*, you will not mifs any thing in it; and therefore in both thefe Plays the Prologues are not infeparable from the body of the *Dramma*; and that which may ftill

[O]   contri-

contribute to convince us of this is, that in these Prologues the Poets often put things which were inconsistent with the Rules of the Stage; as in the *Agamemnon* of *Æschylus*, where one of the Guard that speaks the Prologue seems to see things which could not come to pass in the time prescrib'd by the Drammatick Poem ; and if this Prologue were to be suppos'd part of the Play, it would make it defective, and against all the Rules.

The other sort of *Prologue* plac'd before the *Chorus*, contain'd not only such things as regarded the Poem, but such also as were proper, and incorporated with its Subject, making a true part of it; as in the *Sphigenia* in *Aulide*, where the disquiet of *Agamemnon*, and the Narration he makes to an old Man, whom he sends his Letters by, to his Wife, do certainly begin the Play, and make an inseparable part of the Subject ; and if the definition that *Aristotle* gives of Prologues can be reduc'd to any rational meaning, it must be to this sort of Prologue ; but yet I cannot understand neither why this must be call'd a Prologue sooner than any other part of the Play; 'tis properly an *Episode*, and its being before or after the *Chorus* changes nothing in its nature, but only alters its place ; and this, in my Judgment, is not enough to make a just and true distinction of the parts of a *Dramma*, who ought to have more Essential differences between each other. My Conclusion then is, that that which is properly Prologue, cannot be reckon'd a part of the Play ; and that which is a part of the Play can no more be nam'd a Prologue, than the other *Episodes* that compose the Play.

If in opposition to this any one shall say, that in the beginning of all the Tragedys of *Sophocles* and *Æschylus,*

Æschylus, we meet with the same word that is in *Euripides* (and which fignifies to fpeak a Prologue) though neither of thefe Poets defign'd a Prologue, except *Sophocles* in his *Electra*, and *Æschylus* in his *Agamemnon*) I fay, that is not fo much to be minded, becaufe the words fignifie likewife to *fpeak firft*, and are fo tranflated in the Latine Verfion; and this may ferve to avoid a miftake upon this Subject.

As for the *Chorus*, of which *Ariftotle* makes the fecond part of Tragedy, it muft be confider'd in two different ftates; the firft is, when the *Chorus* fpeaks with the other Actors in an *Epifode*, or the continuation of an Act, for then the *Chorus* is perfectly an Actor concern'd, and working in the Intrigues of the Stage, according to the Doctrine of *Ariftotle* and *Horace*; and in this fenfe the *Chorus* can in no wife be counted a diftinct part of the Play.

The other ftate in which we are to confider the *Chorus* is, when it fings to mark the Intervals of the Acts, and therefore is defin'd by *Voffius* a part of the Fable after an Act, or between two Acts. Now I will not deny but *Chorus*'s may have been true parts of Tragedy, as long as they fung things concerning the true Subject of the Poem upon the *Theatre*; but they were not neceffary parts, fince they have been fo eafily omitted, no more than our Mufick that plays between the Acts can be faid to be an Effential part of our Plays. *[margin: Chorus pars fabulæ poft actum vel inter actum & actum. Voff. l. 2. c. 5. Inft. Poet.]*

Ariftotles Exodus, or laft part of Tragedy, is not, in my Opinion, any whit better diftinguifh'd; for if the *Exodus* contains all that is faid after the *Chorus* gives over, it is no more than our fifth Act; and therefore *Voffius* would have the *Cataftrophe* and the *[margin: L. 2. cap. 5. Inft. Poet.]*

[O 2]   *Exodus*

Exodus to be the fame thing ; but in that he does not agree with *Ariſtotle*, for according to him the *Cataſtrophe* often begins towards the end of the fourth Act, and fometimes it does not begin till towards the middle of the fifth Act,ſo that then you would be ob-lig'd to cut off from the *Exodus* all that ſhould be ſaid after the *Chorus* gives over, or elſe according to *Voſſius* it would be cut in two by a *Chorus*;both which are againſt *Ariſtotle*'s Doctrine. But beſides, what will become of this *Exodus* in thoſe Tragedys that end with a *Chorus*, as all *Euripides*'s, and the beſt of *Sophocles* and *Æſchylus*'s do ; for the laſt Verſes of their Tragedys were according to the moſt receiv'd Opinion ſung by the *Chorus*,and ſo there could be no *Exodus* in thoſe Plays, who by conſequence, accord-ing to *Ariſtotle*, muſt want that part of quantity. It will not be amiſs to obſerve here by the by, that *Exodus*, and *Exodion* are not the ſame things ; for the *Exodus* is the laſt part of the Play, and the *Exo-dion* was a piece of *Buffoonery*, as the *Mimes* and *Embolimes* were, and were acted when the Play was done, by thoſe they called *Exodiarii*, which may prevent a miſtake, apt elſe to be made in reading the Antients.

From all this that we have ſaid, it appears that either *Ariſtotle* did not explain himſelf well in his Definitions, or that thoſe Plays which we have of the Greek Poets, did not ſerve him for the Rules of his Poeticks; ſo that of thoſe four parts of quantity of Tragedy, of which *Ariſtotle* makes mention, we have but one left, which alone makes up our whole Tragedy, and that is the *Epiſode* ; for ſince the *Epi-ſode* contain'd all that was between the Antient *Cho-rus*'s, and that our muſick with which we begin and end

end our plays is to us in the place of the Ancient *Chorus*'s,it is manifeſt,that five*Epiſodes* make our five *Acts* ; but becauſe we divide our *Acts* into *Scenes*, and that we ſeparate our Acts by a conſiderable diſtance of time, neceſſary to the Theatral Action, I therefore think that a Drammatick Poem can be properly ſaid to have but two parts of quantity, to wit, *Five Acts ſubdivided into Scenes, without any limited number* ; and the *four Intervals* of thoſe Acts. If any one elſe has more light to ſhew us other parts, I ſhall eaſily ſubſcribe to his Opinion.

Chapter the Second.

Of Epiſodes *according to the Doctrine of* Ariſtotle.

TO underſtand this matter well, we muſt look back to ſome things that have been ſaid already,and know thatTragedy &Comedy begun thus.

Bacchus having found out the Art of cultivating the Vine, and making Wine, taught it *Icarius*, who then was Maſter of a little Territory in *Attica*, to which he gave his name. *Icarius* having preſently put his Skill to tryal, met with a Goat in the Vintage time, that was eating his Grapes, therefore looking upon him as an Enemy to *Bacchus*, ſacrificed him to him ; and having call'd his neighbours to this Sacrifice, they all together fell a dancing and ſinging ſomething in the honour of *Bacchus*, whom they had thus reveng'd of his Foe. This appear'd to them both ſo religious, and ſo pleaſant, that they continu'd it every year at the ſame time,and call'd it *Tragœdia*, that is, a Vintage-ſong.   The

Hygin. l. 2.
Aſtronom. in
Actoph. Ex
Eratoſtene.
Virg.Georg.2.

Caſſiod. li. 4.
Var. Varr.l. 1.
de vit. pop.
Rom. Plutar.
Sympoſion.19.
qu. 1.

The *Athenians* having in proceſs of time tranſ-
ferr'd this Ceremony to their Town; their beſt Poets
began to be concern'd in the Hymn to *Bacchus*, and
to ſtrive with one another for the honour of excel-
ling in it. They brought in beſides great *Chorus*'s of
Muſick and Dances, with many turnings and wind-
ings, and ſo transferr'd it from the Temples to the
Theatres, without any irreverence; nevertheleſs, becauſe thoſe very Theaters were dedicated to *Bacchus*,
and the Victim that was ſacrificed to him, was a
Goat, as deſtructor of the Vine; from whence this
Hymn was called *Tragedy*, as who ſhould ſay, the
Goat-Song, and ſo much of it as remain d among the
Country people in Villages, was called *Comedy*, as
who ſhould ſay a *Country-Song*: All this appears
clearly from many famous Authors of Antiquity.

Athen. l. 2.
Caſſiodor. l. 1.
Plut. Sympoſ.
l.1.q.1. Snidas.
Initium Tra-
gædiæ & Co-
medi e à rebus
Divinis Incenſis Altaribus, & admoto hirco id genus carminis quod ſacer Chorus libero patri red-
debat Tragedia dicebatur. Donat. in Terentium.

Thus were diſtinguiſh'd theſe two Poems, though
they had the ſame beginning in the ſame Country
of *Icaria*, and by the ſame adventure, according to
Athenæus, of whoſe Opinion are *Donatus Maximus*
of *Tyr*, and *Euſtathius*.

Now it happening that by little and little the Subjects that the Poets took to praiſe *Bacchus*, being ex-
hauſted, they were forc'd to add little Stories or
Fables, which they handled merrily at firſt, in honour of *Bacchus*. To confirm this, *Ariſtotle* writes,
that *from little Fables made with mirth and fooling,*
Tragedy roſe by degrees to that perfection it acquir'd in
Sophocles *time*. Some are of Opinion that *Epigenes*
the *Sycionian* was the Author of Tragedy, whether
it were that he firſt brought the Song from the Vintage

tage to the Town, or that he first instituted the Dispute between the Poets, in which the Conquerour receiv'd for reward the *Goat* that was sacrific'd to *Bacchus*, after a formal Procession; the Ceremony of which describ'd by *Plutarch*, was simple enough at first, though much alter'd in his time : However, Tragedy remain'd a great while in the same state ; for between this *Epigenes* and *Thespis*, who first added an Act to this Hymn, there are reckon'd fourteen famous Tragick Poets, almost all Successors to one another; and 'tis of the Tragedies of that time that *Diogenes Laertius* is to be understood, when he writes in the Life of *Plato*, that the *Chorus formerly acted the whole Tragedy.* These words at first did extremely puzzle me, because the neglect of *Chorus's* in our days, hinder'd me from penetrating the true sense of the Author. I consider'd Tragedy as I found it in *Sophocles*, and there I could not see any conformity with *Laertius's* mind ; and all I could then imagine in order to make something of it was, that they that made the *Chorus* were likewise the Histrions and Actors of the Tragedy : But besides that thereby I made no distinction between the Histrions who were Actors, and the *Thymelicks*, who were Musicians, against all truth of Antiquity. I found the difficulty still grow upon me, when I read in *Athenæus, That antiently all fort of Tragedy was compos'd only of the Chorus, and had no Histrions or Actors at all:* For these last words did entirely destroy all my first thought, neither could I any ways relieve my self by any of the Interpreters of these two Authors, though so many Learned men have commented them, without saying one word of this ; therefore I began to go back to the first Original of
things,

things, and confidering that Tragedy at firft was nothing but an Hymn of the Pagan Religion, danc'd and fung by *Chorus's* of Muſick, I eaſily found the folution of all my difficulties; for 'tis moſt certain, that in that time, and for almoſt fix hundred years after Tragedy was reprefented only by the *Chorus*, as *Laertius* has it, and had no Actors, as *Athenæus* truly affirms.

At laſt *Thefpis* bethought himfelf of putting in an Actor, who ſhould recite without finging, that the *Chorus* might take breath, and reſt themfelves ; not that I think that Actor fpoke alone, but he made a Dialogue with the *Coryphæus*, or fome other perfon of the *Chorus*, who anfwer'd him fomething to the purpofe, to give him Subject to continue his Difcourfe, as we may yet fee in fome fragments of *Epicharmus*, who liv'd in that time. We muſt not think neverthelefs, that *Thefpis* was the Inventor of Tragedy, as *Horace* feems to believe, but only that he introduc'd the firſt Actor without finging. And *Plato* tells us, that Tragedy was in great credit in *Athens* long before *Thefpis*'s time. And as for what is faid alfo of him, *That he carryed his Actors about in a Cart, from whence they fpoke many Railleries and witty Jeſts againſt paſſengers*, that muſt not be underſtood of ferious Tragedy, for which there were already publick Theaters, but of *Satyrical Tragedy*, in which they reprefented the Dances, and groſſeſt poſtures of *Satyrs* and *Silenes*, who were fuppos'd to have accompany'd *Bacchus* in his Voyages, (for this Satyrical Tragedy was at firſt without Actors, as well as the ferious one, according to *Athenæus*) and came at laſt to that perfection, that it was one of the four Poems which made the *Tetralogy* of *Dramma*'s, in which

which the Poets of *Athens* difputed the Prize at their four great Holidays.

Thefpis likewife added to his Jefts and Railleries the dawbing of his Actors with Lees of Wine, as *Horace* has it; or with Cerufe and Vermillion, as *Suidas* reports: And this was done to imitate fo much the better the Satyrs, who were always repreſented with red Faces, as *Virgil* paints *Silenus's,* dawb'd with the Juyce of Elder berries and Mulberries.

Que canerint agirentque per- uncti f cibus ora. Horat. de art. Poët. Virgil in Silen. Sanguineis frontem moris & tempora pingit.

At laft Tragedy having receiv'd a total alteration, by Recitals in the Intervals of the Mufick, it acquir'd fhortly after its utmoft Perfection; for *Æfchylus,* who liv'd fifty years, or thereabouts, after *Thefpis,* added one Actor more, and fo made up two Actors: and indeed we never fee more than two, in any Scene of his, talking together, except it be for a word or two put in by a third, and that tco very feldom, whatever *Scaliger* fays to the contrary; he invented likewife a convenient Drefs for his Actors with Co-thurnes, or High Shoes to make them appear tall like *Heroes. Sophocles* who was born Ten or Twelve years after the Death of *Æfchylus*, encreas'd the number of the Chief Actors to Three, and caus'd the Scenes to be painted with Decorations fitting for his Subiect. So that in lefs than Fourfcore years Tragedy attain'd to its higheft perfection, with all the Glory of which it was capable.

Diogen.in Plat. & Philoft. in Sophift. Et de vit. Apollon. l. 6. c.6.

As for Comedy, *Donatus* feems to think it was invented by Shepherds and Country People, who us'd to dance about the Altars of *Apollo* firnamed *Nomian,* and fing at the fame time fome Hymns in honour of him; but I had rather believe *Athenæus,* who makes it take its rife with Tragedy, and they

[P]   were

were both confecrated to *Bacchus*, and not to *Apollo*:
Except *Donatus* would judge of all Theatral Actions
by the *Apollinary* Games, which indeed were *Scenick*, and celebrated in the Honour of *Apollo*.

I fay then, That Comedy and Tragedy were born
together ; and accordingly we find in *Clemens Alexandrinus*, that the Invention of Comedy was attributed to one *Sifarion* of *Icaria* ; it may be, becaufe
he was the firft that compos'd the Hymns of *Bacchus*, after the Sacrifice of the Goat by *Icarius*. And
this may fuffice to appeafe the Quarrels of the
Learned upon the Origine of Comedy , fince they
are not agreed neither in Times, Places, nor Perfons.

But Comedy had not the fame progrefs with Tragedy, it being long detain'd in Confufion and Diforder : Nay, even in *Ariftophanes's* time, which was
after *Sophocles* and *Euripides*, it was full of fatyrical
Reflections and fcandalous Slanders. It will be hard
for us to mark the degrees of its progrefs, from the
time that it was a Rural Hymn, to that of its perfection upon the Stage ; becaufe, as *Ariftotle* fays,
*it being not fo noble as Tragedy, there has been lefs
care to make Obfervations upon it ; and the Magiftrates were a great while before they concern'd themfelves in giving the* Chorufes, *but us'd to leave them
to the Difcretion of thofe who made the Comedy.* Neverthelefs, if I may venture to bring to light things
buried in fo long an Obfcurity, I think that it begun
to have Actors about the fame time as Tragedy did,
that is, under *Epicharmus* the *Sicilian*, the Contemporary of *Thefpis* ; and before that time I have
not obferv'd any Speakers. And 'tis from this, that
the *Sicilians* do maintain, That Comedy was invented at *Syracufa*, becaufe *Epicharmus* was that Countryman ;

tryman : not that they can pretend that there was
no Comedy before him, (for we have yet the Fragments of *Alcæa*, a Comedy two hundred years before his time) but becaufe he firft introduc'd an
Actor with the *Chorus*. We may fay as much of
Sannyrion, who was the firft that added Masks and
Buffoons, according to *Athenæus* ; and the fame of
Cratinus, who fetled three Actors, and made the
whole Compofition regular ; the fame of *Ariftophanes*, who gave Comedy a further perfection ; and fo
of all thofe whom *Diomedes* calls the firft Comick
Poets, though they came a great while after Comedy was invented.

Now we are to take notice, that the Recital of
that Actor or Player introduc'd by *Thefpis* in Tragedy, and the number of which was fince encreas'd
by other Poets, receiv'd the name of *Epifode*, as who
fhould fay, an additional Difcourfe, thrown as it
were acrofs another ; therefore *Suidas* fays exprefly,
that *Epifode* fignifies a thing which is befides the
Subject of another, and to which neverthelefs it is
joyn'd.   So when *Æfchylus* and others did infert into their Tragedies Actors that recited a Story which
was nothing to the Praifes of *Bacchus*, the Priefts
of *Bacchus* began to complain of that neglect, and
faid, that in thofe *Epifodes* there was nothing that
was proper either to the Actions or Myfteries of
their God ; which gave occafion to that *Greek* Proverb, 'Ουδὲν πρὸς τον Διονυσον, *Nothing to Bacchus.*
And this Explication of the Proverb, which is according to all the Ancients, feems moft reafonable :
For to think, as fome do, that in Drammatick Poetry they call'd *Epifodes* all the Defcriptions, Narrations, and pathetick Difcourfes, as things not belong-

[P 2]   ing

ing to the Subject, seems very abfurd, since without those things the *Episodes* themselves could not be.

These Complaints of *Bacchus's* Priests did not at all stop the Progress of Tragedy, which by little and little went its Course, and at last grew to such a distance from its Originals, as that the *Episodes* became the Tragedy it self. Therefore now all the Doctrine and Precepts of *Aristotle* about the *Episodes,* how to make them succefsfully, is no more than the Art how to make a *Drammatick Poem* ; for we have neither *Prologue, Chorus,* nor *Exode* to make the Parts of our Tragedy : so that having none but the *Episode* left, that alone must be called the *Dramma* ; and when we read in *Athenæus, That* Alexander, *at the last Feast he made before his death, recited an* Episode *of the* Andromeda *of* Euripides, we must not understand it as *Natalis Comes* does in his Marginal Note, calling it *a Piece added to make Mirth* ; but rather in the sense of *Aristotle,* that it was some part of that Tragedy, either a fine Description, or some pathetick Expression in some Act of the Play.

It being then agreed, that the *Episodes* contain all that is between the *Choruses,* that is to say, Five Acts, distinguish'd by five Concerts of Musick, *Aristotle* gives three principal Instructions in composing of these *Episodes.*

The first is, *That having chosen your Story, and resolv'd how much of it you will bring upon the Stage, you must then cast your* Episodes, that is, the Descriptions, Discourses, Passions, and other things that are to entertain the Stage. And this is one of the greatest Dexterities of the Poet.

The second is, *That the* Episodes *be proper and na-*
tural

tural to the Story or Fable ; that is to fay, drawn from the very Essence of the Subject, and so fit, as to seem to jump naturally, and of themselves, with the whole Concourse of other Events. And 'tis out of the secret Knowledge Men have of this Precept, that we have often seen them blame upon the Stage Narrations that were not necessary, superfluous and vain Descriptions, Complaints, and other Passions, introduc'd out of order, and without which the *Dramma* might not onely have been, but have been better.

The third Rule is, *That the* Episodes *ought not to be too long.* And that is it which even the Common people every day condemn upon our Stages ; for the finest Discourses, and the most necessary ones, have a Measure, after which they become tedious.

To these three Precepts of *Aristotle*, I add two Observations of my own; That the Drammatick Poet must have a care in these *Episodes* not to enter too much and too strongly into the particular of things; but he must onely touch the beautiful places of his Subject, by some strong Thoughts ; because elfe there will appear an Affectation, and be too unlike a Natural Discourse, which in all things he is to imitate.

The other Observation is, That often the Business of the Stage does not suffer that the Actors should make long Discourses, not even of a thing necessary ; as if they were to go in haste to succour some afflicted Person, or to avoid their Enemies. I should therefore advise the Poet, in such occasions, to use some other Means to instruct the Spectators of that which they are not to be ignorant of, or to do it at least in very few Words, so as to keep the Rules of Probability.

Probability.   One great flight in thefe fudden Occafions, is to explain fome Circumftance of the Story, which may ferve for the underftanding of the
neareft Events, and fo referve to ones felf the Liberty of explaining the reft at leifure.

As for the other general Inftructions that *Ariftotle*
gives about the *Epifodes*, they are to be found in his
Interpreters ; but the Poet muft ftill remember, that
they are to be applied to the Acts and Difpofition
of Tragedy, as it is now treated amongft us ; it
being moft certain, that Drammatick Poems which
comprehend the Events of two Stories in the unity
of one Theatral Action, were never called by the
Ancients *Epifodick Fables* ; becaufe thofe *Drammas*
which contain but one Story, are as much Epifodick
as the others ; that is, they have as many Acts or
Recitals between the *Chorufes*, as we have already
fufficiently explain'd.

Chapter the Third.

Of the Chorufes *of the Ancients.*

WE have faid already, That *Tragedy* in its firft
Original was nothing but a Sacred Hymn
fung and danced to the Honour of *Bacchus* ; and that
by little and little the *Epifodes*, which we call *Acts*,
were added between each *Chorus*. And we know likewife, that now adays *Tragedy* has quite loft its *Chorufes*,
as *Comedy* had loft his, even before the Age of *Plautus*.   So that it may feem to fome, that a Difcourfe
of *Chorufes* may be now an unneceffary thing for the
Practice

Practice of our Stage. But besides that they may one day be re-establish'd upon our Theatres, when we are well inform'd what they were amongst the Ancients, I think it very necessary for me to explain here my Thoughts about them, and which will scarce be found any where else.

To take the *Chorus* not as it was at first, when alone it made the whole Tragedy; but as it was in the time of *Sophocles* and *Euripides*, that is to say, in its perfection among the *Grecians*, I think we may define the *Chorus* thus.

The Chorus *is a Troop of Actors, representing the Assembly or Body of those Persons who either were present, or probably might be so, upon that Place or Scene where the Action is suppos'd to be transacted.*

These Words are of importance, and we are not to proceed without well weighing of them. Thus we see, that in the *Hecuba* of *Euripides*, the *Chorus* is of *Trojan* Women who were Slaves in the Camp, it being most probable that they were at the Tents of *Hecuba*, who was under the same Captivity with them. And in the *Cyclops* the *Chorus* is of *Satyrs*, and that very ingeniously contriv'd; for no other sort of Men cou'd venture to stay before the Den of cruel *Polyphemus*. In the *Antigone* of *Sophocles* the *Chorus* is of the Old Men of *Thebes*, because being sent for by *Creon* to Council, none could more reasonably be thought to be before his Palace. In the *Ajax* the *Chorus* is of Seamen of *Salamis*, who come very naturally before the Tent of their Prince, to endeavour to do him some Service, upon the noise of his being furious and mad. In the *Prometheus* of *Æschylus* the Nymphs of the Ocean make the *Chorus*, because in probability hardly any other

Persons

Perfons could be fuppos'd near that unfortunate Man, who was faftned to a Rock far from the commerce of the reft of Mankind ; and alfo in the Seven before *Thebes* , the Young Women of the Town make the *Chorus*, becaufe it was more reafonable to affemble them before the Palace, and make them ftay there full of fears and apprehenfions, lamenting the Calamity of the War, than to have plac'd Men there, who are fuppos'd neceffary to the defence of their Countrey. And from this we may judge likewife with what Induftry and Ingenuity *Ariftophanes*, in his Play againft *Socrates* , makes a *Chorus* of Clouds, becaufe he fuppofes *Socrates* to invoke them to appear at his *Sophifms*; as in another place he has made a *Chorus* of Birds, which two *Athenians* come and entertain in a place full of Trees, and out of the way, talking to them about building a Town in the Air. I make no Citations here out of thofe Tragedies which go under the name of *Seneca* , becaufe they are very ill Models to imitate ; and particularly, the *Chorufes* are very faulty : for fometimes they fee all that's done upon the Scene,hear all that's faid, and fpeak very properly to all ; and at other times one would think they were blind, deaf, and dumb. In many of thofe *Drammas* one can hardly tell who they reprefent, how they were drefs'd, nor what Reafon brings them upon the Stage, nor why they are of one Sex, more than of another. Indeed the Verfes are fine, full of Thoughts, and overloaded with Conceit ; but may in moft places be very well fpar'd, without fpoiling any thing, either in the Sence, or in the Reprefentation of the Poem. Befides, the *Thebaida* has none at all, whether it be loft by the fault of the Copyifts and our Printers, which

which I can hardly believe, becaufe there would at leaſt have remain d ſome fragments, conſidering that they were pieces inſerted into the very body of the Poem in many places ; ſo that I am apt to believe that the Author made none at all for that Play ; and this with ſome other conjectures, has given me occaſion to doubt of the truth of what *Scaliger* affirms ſo poſitively ; to wit, that Tragedy never was without *Chorus*'s ; for I incline to think that in the time of the debauch'd and looſe Emperours, where *Mimes, Embolimes,* and *Buffoons* came in for Interludes in Tragedy, as well as in Comedy, the *Chorus* ceas'd by little and little to be a part of the *Drammatick Poem,* and became only a Troup of Muſicians and Dancers, to mark the Intervals of the Acts; but thoſe four Greek Poets,whoſe works we have, have been much more exact in their *Chorus*'s than the Author of *Seneca*'s Tragedys, as underſtanding a great deal better than he, the Art of compoſing ſuch *Poems ;* and out of them likewiſe it is that we learn that the *Chorus* might be compos'd of all ſorts of perſons, without diſtinction either of Age or Sex,nay of living creatures. or inſenſible things, as *Ariſtophanes* has done, from which we may likewiſe obſerve, that they who thought the *Chorus* repreſented the people were ſomething out; for we ſee that in his *Knights* the people of *Athens* is acting, ſpeaking and judging the conteſt between *Cleo* and *Agoracritus,* and that the *Chorus* is of *Athenian* Knights,perfectly diſtinguiſh'd from thoſe who repreſent the people.

And when *Ariſtotle* and *Scaliger* after him name the *Chorus* a *kind of idle Client, which gives but ſmall aſſiſtance to thoſe he pretends to help.* It muſt be underſtood only in compariſon of the other Actors,

who

who are generally more bufie ; as alfo becaufe the *Chorus* never forfakes the place of the Scene ; whereas the other Actors often perform great things off of the Stage ; but yet the Greek Poets have never chofen for their *Chorus* either idle people (though they might be eafily fuppos'd prefent) or thofe who had no concern in the bufinefs in hand, becaufe all that they could have faid or done would have been weak and languifhing, of fmall, or no effect upon the Spectators, who do not willingly hear unconcern'd perfons in a Tragedy. Befides, according to the Art of Poetry, both of *Ariftotle* and *Horace*, the *Chorus*, befides its finging, ought to act a part of fome concern, and advance and forward the Affairs of the Stage, as other Actors do ; and therefore it is obfervable, that when the Subject did naturally furnifh the Poet with a *Chorus*, he never borrowed it any where elfe ; as in the *Rhæfus* of *Euripides*, where the Scene is before the Tents of the Generals of the *Trojan* Army, and all things coming to pafs in the night. The Guard makes the *Chorus*, becaufe it would have been againft probabilty that any other perfons fhould have been affembled there at that time. Nay, if the Principal Actors themfelves were enough in number, they made the *Chorus* of them, as in the *Suppliants* of *Euripides*, where the feven Princes of *Argos*, that imp'ore *Thefeus*'s help to bury the dead bodies of their Husbands before *Thebes*, make the *Chorus* themfelves.

But if they were put to invent a *Chorus*, they always did it conformably to the nature of their Subject, and to the Rules of probability. This *Ariftophanes* has ingenioufly enough obferv'd in Comedy, as where he makes a *Chorus* of Frogs to fing while *Bac-*

chus

chus paffing the *Stix in Carors* Bark ; and another of
Wafps in the houfe of *Philuclea*, whofe Son would
hinder him from going abroad ; for though thofe
are very ridiculous Imaginations, yet they are
Comical; well enough invented in mirth, and are not
againft the Rules of his Art.

From hence we may likewife judg why the *Chorus*
was at laft left out in new Comedy, and of this I
think no body hitherto has given a true reafon. *Horace* thinks that the malignity and fatyrical humour
of the Poets was the caufe of it ; for they made the
Chorus's abufe people fo feverely, that the Magiftrates
forbid them at laft to ufe any at all ; but I think,
that if the Rules of probability had not likewife feconded this prohibition, the Poets would have preferv'd their *Chorus* ftill, with conformity to their Subject, and that without too much Satyr ; therefore I
imagine the thing came to pafs thus.

Comedy took its model and conftitution from
Tragedy ; and when the downright abufing of living perfons was prohibited, they generally invented
feigned Subjects, which they govern'd according to
the Rules of Tragedy ; but as they were neceffitated
to draw Pictures of the life of the Vulgar, and were
confin'd by confequent to mean Events, they generally chofe the place of their Scene in fome Streets
before the houfes of thofe whom they fuppos'd concern'd in the Story ; and it was not very probable
that there fhould be a Troup of people in fuch a place
managing an Intrigue of inconfiderable perfons from
morning to night. Comedy loft of its felf infenfibly
the *Chorus*, which it could not preferve with any
probability.

[Q 2]   Comedy

Comedy therefore having loft its *Chorus* long before Tragedy, that which was called new Comedy
receiv'd Dances, Mufick, and Buffoons, in the room
of the *Chorus*, as more proper for the genius of Comical Poetry.

Since therefore we are now fully inform'd what
the *Chorus* was, let us fee how it acted upon the
Stage.

At firft it was plac'd a little lower than the
Theatre, and was feated by it felf, from whence it
rofe to fing and dance; afterwards it was plac'd up
on the Stage it felf, and at laft it came upon the very
Scene, that is, behind the Hangings or Decoration,
as may be feen in *Scaliger, Caftelvetro,* and other Authors, with many other things which I forbear to
repeat here.

But we may obferve befides, thar the *Chorus* did
not ordinarily appear upon the Stage, till after the
Prologue, that is, as we have explain'd it, till after one
or many Scenes, which open'd the Play, and were
preparatives to the better underftanding of the
piece, not being reckon'd among the Acts or Epi-
lods. This too is to be underftood only in ftrictnefs;
for fometimes there was no *Prologue,* and all that
pafs'd before the coming on of the *Chorus* was the firft
Act, and to be reckon'd of the body of the Tragedy, as in the *Ajax* of *Sophocles;* at other times the
Chorus its felf opened the Stage, as in the *Rhæfus* of
Euripides, becaufe being compos'd of the Guards,
which had watch'd all night, 'twas not probable any
fhould be there before them.

We muft obferve befides, that when the *Chorus*
once came on in regularity, they were not fuppos'd
to go off till the end of the Play ; and this appears
by

by all the Greek Tragedys, where the *Chorus* often
shews the Pallace or Houfe to ftrangers, complains,
or feems aftonifhed at fudden noifes made within; by
all which it may be concluded, it ftayed all along upon the Stage. 'Tis true, that fometimes we may
obferve it to come in and out, but that is extraordinarily, and by fome remarkable Artifice of the Poet,
who has a mind that fome Action or other fhould be
perform'd upon the Stage without witnefs : As when
Sophocles has a mind that *Ajax* fhould kill himfelf
upon the Stage, he fends out the *Chorus* under pretext of affifting *Tecmeffa*, who is endeavouring to find
out *Ajax*, to prevent the Effects of his fury (he having juft left her with a Sword in his hand.)

Another reafon the Poets have of fending out the
Chorus is, when 'tis probable that they who reprefent the *Chorus* have done an action which could not
naturally have been perform'd upon the Stage : So in
the *Oratrices*, or pleading Women of *Ariftophanes*,
the Women which compofe the *Chorus*, go out at
the end of the firft Act in Mens difguife, to go to the
Council to have it there decreed, that the Government of *Athens* fhall be put into their hands ; and at
the end of the fecond Act, they come back upon the
Scene to bring their Husbands cloths which they had
ftolen in the night : Where by the by we may take
notice of the Ignorance of fome of our Pedants in
their Latine Tragedys, when at the end of each Act
they bring on a fingle Actor to reprefent the *Chorus*,
and declaim fome fcurvy Verfes of Morality, bringing him on, and driving him off as they pleafe, thinking thereby to fulfil *Ariftotles* Rules, and perfectly
imitate the Antients ; whereas their *Chorus* was compos'd of many perfons, who fung and danced with
great

great Art, and were always brought upon the Stage for some good reason; nor are we to imagine, as some have done, that the *Chorus* sung and danc'd always; for that was only when there was need to mark the Intervals of the Acts. In other places the *Chorus* was considered as any other Actor, and the *Corypheus*, or chief of them us'd to hold Discourse for all the rest; or else being divided in two (as sometimes it was half on one side of the Stage, and half on the other) the Chiefs of each side discours'd together of the Affairs of the Stage, as is to be seen in the *Agamemnon* of *Æschylus* upon the death of that King.

We see likewise sometimes that the *Chorus* after some Discourses falls a singing, or is commanded to do it, by which it appears, it did not sing before; The Example is precise in the seven before *Thebes*, where Prince *Eteocles*, after having discoursed with the *Chorus* a good while, bids him at last leave off talking, and sing, to know now whether they all danc'd, and whether the same persons danc'd that sung, and if they danc'd and played on Instruments together, and of what sort is that great diversity of Song we find among the Antients, all this I say cannot contribute any thing to the composition of a Drammatick Poem; and therefore need not be examin'd, but in order to instruct our Musick, in case we should have a mind to bring the *Chorus*'s upon our Theatres.

But we must not forget here, that the chief Actors did frequently mingle with the *Chorus*, as *Electra* in *Euripides* and *Sophocles*. Queen *Æthra*, with King *Adrastus* in the *Supplicants* of *Euripides*; and in these cases I am of Opinion, that those Actors were the *Coryphæi*'s.

Some

Sometimes there was divers *Chorus*'s, when it was not probable that the same persons could be twice upon the Stage, as in *Chriſtophanes*, when *Bacchus* paſſes the River *Stix*, to go to the Pallace of *Pluto*, the *Chorus* is made by Frogs ; but when he is at the Gate of the Pallace, the *Chorus* is made by the Prieſts, and the fraternity of his Myſteries.

Sometimes likewiſe the *Chorus* did not come back time enough at the end of an Act, being ingag'd ſome-where elſe, and then that Act was mark'd by ſome *Mime*, Muſick Dance or buffooning, taken from the Subject, as in the *Oratrices* of *Ariſtophanes*, the Women being all elſewhere at the end of the fourth Act, the Poet makes a farce of two old Women, and a young Girl, who ſing and dance to Inſtruments, in expectation of ſome Man to come by, and are already diſputing who ſhall have him to make him obey the Womens Laws.

From all theſe Obſervations it is moſt apparent, that the *Chorus* is nothing but what we have deſcrib'd it to be; and that we have much reaſon to wonder that the Learned, who have afforded us ſo many curioſities upon the Drammatick Poem, have not nevertheleſs diſcover'd any thing like this to us, though very important, to underſtand antient Tragedy, and juſtifie the probability of all the Rules of the Theatre.

For firſt, if the Antient Greek Poets have made but few *Monologues* upon the Stage, it is becauſe it was not always eaſie to find a pretext to ſend out the *Chorus*, and to have it come in again; and on the other ſide, a man could not in probability be ſuppos'd to ſpeak aloud of ſecret things, without being heard by perſons who were ſo near him.

Secondly,

Secondly, The Ancient Poets feldom make any of their Actors die upon the Stage, becaufe it was not probable, that fo many Perfons as compos'd the *Chorus*, fhould fee fuch a thing done, and not endeavour to hinder it. Thus *Æfchylus* makes *Agamemnon* be kill'd in his Palace, and his Crys and dying Groans to be heard without by the *Chorus*, which deliberates whether they fhall call the People, or break in to his Relief; when *Clytemneftra* her felf comes out, and owns the Murder, and its manner, fhewing them likewife her Husbands dead Body; which has made fome imagine, that *Agamemnon* was kill'd upon the Stage. On the other fide, *Sophocles* makes the *Chorus* leave the Stage, and brings on *Ajax* in a fedate, calm Refolution of dying; where after having fpoke a moft paffionate *Monologue*, he kills himfelf with his own Sword, from which none could hinder him, he being alone upon the Stage. And by the by, that may ferve to oppofe to thofe who fo peremptorily maintain, that the Ancients never fhed any Blood upon the Stage; for they have both done it, and avoided it, and ftill with decency and probability.

Thirdly, The *Chorus* oblig'd a Poet to a Continuity of Action; for if the Action ceas'd, it was not probable the *Chorus* fhould ftay there any longer, its Bufinefs being onely depending upon the Action. Thus we fee, that as foon as *Ajax* s Fury feem'd to be a little over, the *chorus*, which was made up of his Subjects, who came to enquire of his Condition, has a defign to be gone; but is ftopp'd by a Meffenger, who tells them the Arrival of *Teucer*, *Ajax*'s Brother, and the danger that *Minerva* had put *Ajax* in all that day.

Moreover,

Moreover, we may here conclude, That the *Chorus* oblig'd the Poet infenfibly to a neceffity of keeping the Unity of the Scene ; for fince it was regularly to ftay from the beginning of the *Dramma* to the end, without going out, tis moft undoubted, that the Place could not change : for it would have been moft ridiculous, that Perfons who never ftirr'd, fhould have been tranfported from *Europe* to *Afia*, or from *Athens* to *Thebes*, without ever having difappear'd from the Spectators Eyes ; and therefore thofe Poets, whenever they did make the *Chorus* go off from the Stage, were very careful to make them tell where they went, that it might not be imagin'd that in carrying off the *Chorus*, they meant to tranfport the Scene too.

And not onely the Unity of Place, but likewife the Meafure of Time convenient to the Drammatick Poem, may be learn'd from the *Chorufes* : for if the Poet had comprehended in his Play a Year, a Month, or a Week, how could he make the Spectators believe, that People who had always been in their Eye, fhould have pafs'd fo long a time without either eating, drinking, or fleeping   I know it will be anfwered, That there is an Illufion to be allow'd upon the Stage ; and I own it . But the Spectators muft ftill be deceiv'd, fo as not to perceive that they are fo ; and though they know before-hand that they are to be deceiv'd, yet it muft not be done fo grofsly as to be perceiv'd without reflection, and at firft fight.   Therefore that which in our days has help'd thefe irregular Plays to pafs upon us, was the Intervals of the Acts, where none remaining upon the Stage, and our Mufick not being look'd upon as a Continuation of the Action, the Spectator's Imagination

[R]   gination

gination was at liberty to help the Poet, and to
shorten Years and Months into Moments, the Eyes
having nothing before them to contradict this Imagination.

From hence then it results naturally, That the
time of the *Dramma* ought to be very short, as we
have shew'd in a Chapter on purpose.

To make an end of this Matter, we must observe,
That the *Chorufes* made all the Grandeur and Magnificence of the ancient Tragedies ; not onely because
the Stage was always full, but because there was
need of making a vast Expence : for there was a
great number of Actors, Musicians, Dancers, Clothes,
and often very costly Machins, as in the *Clouds* of
Ariftophanes ; and it was among the *Grecians* an honourable Profession to instruct and direct the *Chorufes*, as appears by *Plato* the Philosopher, who follow'd that Employment the best part of his Youth ;
and *Ariftophanes*, we find, had the direction of his
Chorufes, particularly of that of the Clouds. The
Richest of the Nobility often bore the Charge ; as
Dio, in favour of *Plato*, who at first was one of the
Tragick Poets. The Magistrates likewise, to make
the time of their Administration more Solemn,
did the same thing. Sometimes the State it self,
when they would do an extraordinary Honour to
some of their Tragick Poets, order'd, that the
Charges of the *Chorus* should be allow'd by the Publick Treasury: And this the *Athenians* have often
done. And I believe, that when the Great Men
forsook the Care of the Stage, it soon fell into Contempt, the *Chorufes* being retrench'd, by the impos-
sibility that the Players and Poets were in to answer
such an Expence ; and afterwards, the Ignorance of

following

following Ages thought fit to look upon them as uſeleſs, and unfit to be put in practice. New Comedy it ſelf loſt its *Choruſes,* even in the moſt flouriſhing Drammatick Age ; but that was rather becauſe it was much harder to give *Choruſes* their due Probability in Comedy, than in Tragedy, though its *Mimes,* Muſicians, Embolaires, and ſuch like, were not of a leſs Magnificence than the *Choruſes* of Tragedy it ſelf ; and thoſe who were the Maſters and Directors in them, had as much Fame when they ſucceeded, as either *Æſopus,* or *Roſcius,* or any of the Chief Actors of the Age. This may be ſeen by ſome ancient Inſcriptions of *Terence*'s Comedies, and other very conſiderable Proofs in Antiquity.

If then our Age could ſuffer the re-eſtabliſhment of the *Chorus,* as being the moſt glorious and magnificent Ornament of Tragedy, our Poets ought in the firſt place to ſtudy the Art of the Ancients in that point, how ingeniouſly they invented them, how neceſſarily they brought them on, and how agreeably they made them ſpeak and act ; and then the King. or our Great Lords, ſhould be at the Expence : Which I think not the hardeſt to compaſs, conſidering the Profuſion we have ſeen in Ballets, Balls, and Tragedies in this Kingdom.

And laſtly, It would be neceſſary to have Muſicians and Dancers capable of executing the Inventions of the Poets, after the way of thoſe lively ſpeaking Dances of the Ancients, which, to ſay truth, I think impoſſible for us *Frenchmen* to attain to, and I believe it very hard for the *Italians.* Therefore I ſhall not expatiate here upon the Method of adding *Choruſes* to our Tragedies, nor ſay what might be left out, and what taken from the Ancients, in conformity to

our

our Cuftoms ; for that would deferve a particular
Treatife,   I pafs now to things more neceffary to the
true Underftanding of the Drammatick Poem, and
the Practice of the Stage.

Chapter the Fourth.

*Of the ancient Actors or firft Reciters of Epifodes,
againft the Opinion of fome Modern Writers.*

THough in all this Work I have had no other
Defign than to inftruct the Poet in many Particulars which I thought very important for the making of a *Dramma* ; yet being carried, by my own
Study and Enquiries, into the Difcovery of an Errour
of fome of our Moderns, about the ancient Reciters
of Tragedy, I could do no lefs than endeavour to re-
ctifie that Miftake, though it do not perfectly regard
my firft Defign, which was onely to deliver Precepts
about Drammatick Poetry.   But if my Readers are
curious enough to be willing to know fome Circumftances about the progrefs of Tragedy, I fuppofe
this Difcourfe may not be difagreeable to them.
   We have laid down, as a moft conftant Truth, That
for many Years Tragedy was nothing but a Pagan
Religious Hymn, fung and danced in the Honour of
Bacchus ;   That *Thefpis* introduc'd an Actor to recite
fomething Forreign to that Subject, which was call'd
an *Epifode* ;   That *Æfchylus* brought on two Actors,
and *Sophocles* three, with other Ornaments, which
brought Tragedy to its perfection.   And this we
have juftified by the Teftimonies of *Ariftotle*, *Dia-*
                                              genes

genes Laertius, *Athenæus*, *Plutarch*, *Donatus*, and many other ancient Writers ; to whom I may add all those who since have writ of Drammatick Poesie. But *Castelvetro*, *Ricoboni*, and some others, are of opinion, that the *Chorus* signifies sometimes the Band of Comedians or Tragedians, and that 'tis in that sense that we must understand that Passage of *Diogenes Laertius*, in the Life of *Plato*, which says, *That formerly the* Chorus *alone acted the whole Tragedy* : By which, says *Castelvetro*, *it appears, that the* Histrions *acted formerly without Musick or Dancing.* And as one Absurdity generally engages us in another, to maintain this Errour, he commits a greater, when he adds, *That the Actor introduc'd by* Thespis *was a Buffoon who used to Sing, and Dance, and play upon some Instrument, and that Æschilus after him brought on two such, separating Dancing from the Singing, and playing upon Instruments, and that* Sophocles *at last brought on three Actors for these three things.* So that he pretends, that before *Thespis* the *Chorus* was a Troop of Players or Actors, and that those brought on by *Thespis*, *Æschilus*, and *Sophocles* were not so, but Singers and Dancers which certainly is both false and ridiculous. First, there is no passage in any of the Ancients that can be cited to prove, that they who associated themselves to Act Plays were ever called by the Word *Chorus*, but by that of *Company* : We have many Examples of this in *Plautus*, who very often makes them appear under this Name at the end of his Plays to thank the Spectators, and in Terence. *Ambivius Turpio* complains, *That the Poets carry'd to other Companies those Plays that were easy to represent*; besides, it is so far from being true, that antiently the

Plays

Plays were acted by *Histrions* without Dancing or Musick ; that on the contrary 'tis most certain, that they were originally danced and sung by a *Chorus* of Musicians without *Actors* or *Histrions*.

To Illustrate fully the truth, I think that it is a strange mistake to say that the *Chorus* of which *Diogenes, Athenæus,* and *Donatus* do speak, when they say, *That Tragedy was at first acted by the* Chorus was a Company of *Comedians,* or reciting Representatours without either Dance or Musick, for one need only read those Authors to be convinced of the contrary ; and when *Athenæus* saies, *That Tragedy had none of those* Histrions *which the* Greeks *call* Hypocrites, or, Representers of other Men ; he cannot be understood of Buffooning, Dancing or Singing Actors, because the *Greeks* had a great many of them , in Tragedy ; particularly in that which was called *Satyrical Tragedy.* Besides, in the time, and before the time of *Thespis,* they used a little sort of Stage called *Eileos,* where was placed a Musician to answer the rest of the *Chorus,* and as Tragedy was then nothing but a Sacred Hymn in the honour of *Bacchus ,* the *Chorus* was composed of those who were Ministers to his Ceremonies, and who were hir'd for Money often to Sing and Dance in great Feasts, so that if the Actor brought on by *Thespis,* had done nothing but Sing and Dance without reciting, he had done nothing new, and the Priests'of *Bacchus* would not have had reason to complain of it, but there is more in it still, for even in the time of *Thespis* the *Choruses* were composed of Dancers and Singers, and *Athenæus* saies, that he and *Pratinas,* and *Phrinicus* with other Poets of that time, were Nicknam'd *Dancers,* because they fitted their Poetry to the Dance of

the

the *Choruses* whom they used to teach with care themselves, to represent well in Dancing, that which
they had expressed in Verse.

This *Pratinas* was a *Tragick Poet* who lived a little
after *Thespis*, and was contemporary with *Æschylus*, and as *Athenæus* tells us, he writ as an observation of his time, *That when the People saw the Players of Instruments come upon the Stage without Dancing
with the rest of the* Chorus, *and the* Chorus *sing and
dance without playing upon Instruments, they were
angry at it, as a piece of Novelty against a received
custom.* By which it appears, that the Division of
Musick from Dancing, which was then made by the
Poets, was a change in the *Chorus*, and not an Introducing of new *Interludes*; these *Choruses* were
composed of such great numbers, that *Æschylus* was
forc'd to lessen them, as we have it from *Aristotle*,
and this he did after the representation of his *Eume-
nides*, and that *Chorus* is well distinguished from the
Persons who recited. If then it were or could be
true, that in the time of *Thespis* the *Chorus* was the
company of *Comedians*, or *Histrions*, we must be
told how that Name was transferr'd from the Reciters to the Musicians, and who first brought into
Tragedy that great number of Dancers and Singers
of which we could not be ignorant, the *Greeks* having
been pretty well informed of their own History ever
since the settling of the *Olympiads*, which was
near three hundred years before that time.

To this we may add as very considerable, that
which *Aristotle*, and *Diogenes Laertius* say, *That by
the means of the three Actors introduc'd by those three
lights of the Stage,* Thespis, Æschylus, and Sophocles, *Tragedy received all its splendour, and its last perfection;*

fection; for if before them there were companies of Players that reprefented reciting, as they have done fince, and that thefe three Actors added, were only to fing, dance, or play upon the Inftruments; fure thefe Authors would not have judg'd that fo great a thing as to make the perfection of Tragedy confift in it; and when in thefe latter times, Tragedy having recovered its glory without all this *Mufick*, *Mimiking*, and *Dancing*; did ever any one yet object the want of that for a fault, and that its true fplendour confifted in thofe ridiculous Interludes? Befides *Thefpis* brought fo great a change upon Ancient Tragedy, that he was called the Inventor of it, and if there had been before his time, whole companies of reciting Comedians, I doubt whether he would have deferv'd that name for only adding a Buffooning Actor to the reft.

There is yet another thing to confirm this, which in my opinion is important enough, which is, That if before *Thefpis*'s time there had been Stage Players, or *Hiftrions*, they muft have acted without a Stage, and without Clothes conformable to their parts, and without any decoration, for all thefe things were moft certainly brought in by thofe three Poets, and in different times.

And it is moreover true, that *Æfchylus* having Introduc'd the Second Actor, divided the recitals of his Actours upon the Stage, and *Ariftotle* for this reafon calls the Firft Actors part, *The Principal Difcourfe*, or the *Principal Canto*; and *Philoftrates* fpeaking of this Second Actor of *Æfchylus* writes, *That by this means he took off from the Stage thofe long and tedious* Monodias *of a fingle Actor, putting in their room a Dialogue of Difcourfe of different Actors.*

Actors. So *Scaliger* writes, that at the beginning Tragedy was *Monoprosope*, that is, of One Actor, and that *Æschilus* brought in the Discourse of two, by which it appears that these Actors were Reciters and not Singers or Dancers, but to finish the proof of this matter we must know that by the general Interpretation of all the Greek and Latine Authors that writ since these three Poets; the *Histrion*, or Player introduc'd by *Thespis* is named *Protagonist*, that introduced by *Æschylus Deuteragonist*, and the Third added by *Sophocles Tritagonist*; that is, First, Second, and Third Actor, and not Dancer or Musician. By the First they understood that Actor who in Tragedy represented the chief Person of the *Dramma*, and had the chiefest part, as appearing most upon the Scene, and by the two others they understood those who acted the second and third parts of the Stage. Upon this *Cicero* writes, *That amongst the* Greeks *he that has the second or third part, though he happen to have a stronger voice than the first Actor, yet he moderates it that he may not drown the first.* And *Porphyrius* says, *That the* Tritagonists *always acted with a low voice* ; and 'tis in that sense that these names have in other cases been applied to those Persons who had the first, second, and third parts, which made *Demosthenes* to affront *Æschynes* call him *Tritagonist*, insinuating thereby, that he had been a Player, and that only of the third rank, and no body will say, that in all these comparisons there was any thought of these Actors being Musicians or Dancers.

Indeed something like the imagination of *Castelvetro* has happened in *Comedy* : for where it was first received in *Rome*, it had no *Chorus* but *Interludes* of

S   Singers

Singers, Dancers, and Players upon Inftruments, who altogether marked the intervals of the Acts, and according to my opinion, were tranflated to the Stage from the *Ludi Scenici*, or Scenical Games.

That they fung danc'd, and play'd upon Inftruments all at once, appears by *Livius Andronicus*, who being grown old took an occafion from the weaknefs of his voice to have a youth fing for him, which made his dancing fo much the more agreeable, as being freed from the conftraint of managing his motions to his voice: Some while after he laid afide his Inftruments likewife, and then having his Arms at liberty to give the full grace to his dancing, he brought that Art to great perfection. This he did in Imitation of the *Greeks*, for we fee in *Lucian*, that in Tragedy thefe three Actions were formerly united and performed by the fame Perfon of which the furprifal of the people mentioned by *Pratinas*, and which we have already alledged, is a fufficient proof.

Not but that there are fome paffages in Ancient Authors which feem to fay, that formerly *Tragedies* and *Comedies* were fung and danc'd, and that fo Artificially that the Mufick and the poftures gave fenfible Images of the things expreffed by the Verfes; but this was either becaufe the Mufical Games (even in *Plato*) comprehended under them all the Exercifes of Poetry even to the Drammatick; or elfe, becaufe the Hymns of *Bacchus* which were originally at firft both Tragedy and Comedy, were always accompanied with Mufick and Dances, or becaufe in the intervals of the Acts they had people who reprefented by their dancing; thefe things which had been fpoken in the Act, as is to be feen in *Plutarch*

and

and *Lucian,* or rather, moſt probably, becauſe not only they had at the ſame time, and in the ſame places, Actors who recited Tragedy, but likewiſe *Choruſes* for Tragedy ; and *Mimes* for *Comedy,* who ſung and danc'd to the ſound of Inſtruments with poſtures which repreſented the Perſons both of Men and Gods.

Let us then conclude, that before the Age of *Theſpis* the *Chorus* was nothing but a company of Muſicians ſinging and dancing Tragedy as a Hymn in the honour of *Bacchus,* and that *Theſpis* brought on the Firſt Actor, who by reciting, divided the ſinging of the *Chorus,* and gave a beginning to the *Epiſodes,* and of this truth beſides Ancient Authors we have for *Guarantees* many modern ones, as *Robortel, Piccolomini, Bernardo Segni, Scaliger, Benius , Eugubinus, Voſſius, Heinſius, Victorius,* and other Interpreters of *Ariſtotle* who have all proved this Aſſertion, though by reaſons differing from thoſe which we have here declared.

Chapter the Fifth.

Of Tragicomedy.

THis New Word which ſeems to have been introduc'd to ſignifie ſome new ſort of *Drammatick* Poem, obliges me to explain it more clearly, and at length, then any of our Modern Authors have done, and to that end I muſt ſhew all that in our Plays is different from, or conformable to the Works of the Ancients.

[S 2]   The

The Stage by little and little being come to its last perfection, became a sensible and moving Image of all humane life: Now there being three sorts of conditions or ways of living, that of Great persons in the Courts of Kings, that of Citizens, and Gentry in Towns, and that of the Country people in the Country, the Stage has likewise receiv'd three kinds of Drammatick Poems, to wit, *Tragedy*, *Comedy*, and *Pastoral.*

Tragedy represented the Life of Princes and great People full of disquiets, suspicions, troubles, rebellions, wars, murders, and all sorts of violent passions, and mighty adventures; whence it was well call'd by *Theophrastus*, The State of an Heroick Fortune.

Now to distinguish Tragedys by their *Catastrophe*, they were of two sorts; the one were calamitous and bloody in their Events, ending generally by the death, or some great misfortune of the *Hero*; the others were more happy, and concluded by the felicity of the chief persons upon the Stage, and yet because the Poets out of complaisance to the *Athenians*, who loved spectacles of horrour, ended often their Tragedys by unfortunate *Catastrophes*; many people have thought that the word *Tragical* never signifi'd any thing but some sad, bloody Event; and that a Drammatick Poem could not be call'd a *Tragedy*, if the *Catastrophe* did not contain the death of the chief persons in the Play; but they are mistaken, that word, in its true signification, meaning nothing else but a *Magnificent, serious, grave Poem, conformable to the Agitations and sudden turns of the fortune of great people.* And accordingly in the nineteen Tragedys of *Euripides*, many of them have a happy conclusion; and which is very remarkable is, that the *Orestes*, which

which begins with fury and rage, and runs upon such
strong Passions and Incidents, that they seem to promise nothing but a fatal, bloody Event; it nevertheless terminated by the entire content and satisfaction
of all the Actors, *Helena* being plac'd among the
Gods, and *Apollo* obliging *Orestes* and *Pylades* to marry *Hermione* and *Electra, which made one of the Antients say, that that Play had a Comical Catastrophe;*
but in that he is much mistaken, as well as *Victorius*
and *Stiblinus,* who say the same thing of the *Electra*
and *Alceste.*

Comedy was the picture of the Actions of the
people, in which were general'y represented the Debaucheries of young people, with the tricks and acts
of Slaves and Courtezans, full of Railleries and Jests,
and ending in Marriages, or some other pleasant Adventure of common life; and this Poem was so much
confin'd to represent a popular life, that the style of
it was to be low and mean, the expressions taken out
of the mouths of ordinary people; the passions were
to be short, and without violence. In a word, all the
Intrigues were to be upheld by slight and cunning,
and not by the sublime and marvellous part of humane life; therefore *Scaliger* is in the right to find
fault with *Plautus* for making *Aleesimark* appear
with a Dagger, and a design to kill himself, because
that is an undertaking too generous for the Comick
Theatre. Donatus likewise blames *Terence* for making
his passions too strong and lasting, with expressions
something too noble for his Art, and *Comedy* its self
does not always in *Plautus* end happily as may be
seen in divers of his Plays.

Pastoral or *Satyr* had a mixture of serious and
pleasant; *Hero's* and *Satyrs* were its Actors; and
this

this fort of Poem ought to be confider'd two ways ; at firft it was nothing but a little Poem call'd *Idyllium*, or *Eclogue*, fung or recited by one man alone, and feldom by two or more ; and they were generally Shepherds, Gardners, Husbandmen, Satyrs, Nymphs, and all forts of Country people ; there was nothing but complaints of Lovers, cruelties of Shepherdeffes, difputes for Singing. Embufcadoes of Satyrs, and ravifhing of Nymphs, with fuch like diverting, eafy Adventures ; but the Poems were all loofe pieces, without any ftory, or neceffity of Action. We have many Examples in *Theocritus* and *Virgil*, and many Modern Poets have imitated them in Latine. In the Reign of *Henry* the Second in *France*, divers *French* Poets made *Eclogues* in their own Language, of which we have fome Examples in *Ronfard*.

The other fort was a Drammatick Poem, carryed on according to the Rules of the Stage, where *Hero*'s and Satyrs were mingled together, reprefenting both grave and pleafant, ridiculous things ; and for that reafon this Poem had the name of *Satyrical Tragedy*.

This fort of Poem had not any courfe among the *Romans*, at leaft that ever I could obferve either in their Hiftorians or Poets ; that which they call'd *Satyr*, being only a Copy of Verfes made to flander or reprove, and never us'd for the Stage, but with the *Mimes*, and by way of *Interlude*.

But among the Græcians, Satyrical Tragedy was highly valued ; for at the Feafts of *Bacchus*, call'd *Chytres*, the Poets us'd to vye with each other, and difpute for the Prize by this fort of Poem. *Athenæus*, *Plato*, *Plutarch*, and *Suidas*, alledg many Examples of this kind, and we have fome fragments, but

but no entire Poem of this kind, except the *Polyphe-mus* of *Euripides*: And I incline to think that his *Alcefte* is one of that kind too, by reason that *Her-cules* is very pleafant there with a Slave, and does very Comical Actions ; but I fhall wait the Opinion of the Learned, before I fhall determine any thing in that Point.

Thefe three forts of Poems are not now upon the Stage, in the fame manner as they were antiently; for to begin with *Paftorals*, they are now a Drammatick Poem, according to the Rules of all other *Dramma's*, compos'd of five Acts, and many agreeable Events and Intrigues, but all regarding a Country life ; fo that we have borrowed the matter of the *Eclogues* from the Antients, and applyed it to the Rules of *Sa-tyrical Tragedy*.

Comedy among us has remain'd long, not only in meannefs and obfcurity, but look'd upon as infamous, being chang'd into that fort of *Farce*, which we ftill retain at the end of fome of our Tragedys; though they are certainly things without Art, or Grace, and only recommendable to the Rafcally fort of Mankind, who delight in obfcene, infamous words and actions. I know indeed that fometimes our Poets have endea-vour'd to reftore the Comedy of the Antients, either by tranflating their Works, or by otherwife imita-ting them, but that has feldom happened, and then without fuccefs too, for many reafons ; but particu-larly, for not having chofen Subjects that had any conformity with our manners and cuftoms ; or for not having chang'd in the Works of the Antients, that which was not fo conformable to our Sentiments : Neither can we fay that the Comedy of the *Italians* has fucceeded to thofe of *Plautus* and *Terence*, for they

they have obferv'd neither the matter nor form of them ; their Subjects are always mingled with ferious Adventures, and *burlesk* ones, *Hero*'s and *Harlequins* ; and generally they confift but of three Acts, without any order of Scenes, nor any thing of the Conduct of the Antients. And indeed I cannot but admire how it comes to pafs, that the Defcendents of the *Romans* fhould be fo unlearned in the Art of their Fathers.

As for Tragedy, it has been preferv'd a little better among us, becaufe the manners of our Nobility being ferious and heroick, they have with more pleafure feen upon the Stage the Adventures of fuch perfons, and have fhew'd no difpofition at all to that mixture of ferious and burlesk which we blame in the *Italians.* But befides the Niceties of the Art, which as well as the *Italians,* we have long been ignorant of; we have done two things, one of which is very reafonable, and the other without any good grounds. The firft is, that we have rejected all thofe Storys full of *horrour* and *cruelty,* which made the pleafure of the *Roman* and *Athenian* Stages ; and for this very reafon one of the nobleft Tragedys that we have, and the moft worthy of a Græcian *Theatre,* could never fucceed well upon ours, but gave always fome difguft both at Court, and to the people. I have already given a reafon for it in another place. But the fecond thing which we do without any ground at all is, that we have taken away the name of Tragedy from all thofe Plays where the *Cataftrophe* is happy, and without blood, though both the Subject and Perfons are heroick, and have given them the name of *Tragicomedys.* I do not well know whether our Poet *Garnier* was the firft that brought it up,

Alboin.

up, but he gave that name to his *Bradamante*, which many since that have imitated.

I shall not absolutely fall out with this name, but I shall shew that it is at least superfluous, since the word Tragedy signifies as well those Plays that end in joy, as those that end in blood ; provided still the Adventures be of Illustrious persons.   And besides, the signification of the word *Tragicomedy* is not true in the sense we use it ; for in those Plays that we apply it to, there is nothing at all Comical, all is grave and heroick, nothing popular and burlesk.

But moreover, this title alone may destroy all the beauty of a Play, which consisting particularly in the **Peripetia,** or return of Affairs, it may discover that too soon ; since the most agreeable thing in a *Dramma* is, that out of many sad and Tragick appearances, the Event should at last be happy, against the Expectation of the whole Audience ; but when once the word *Tragicomedy* is prefix'd, the Catastrophe is presently known, and the Audience the less concern'd with all the Incidents that trouble the designs of the chief Actors ; so that all their *Pathetick* complaints do but weakly move the Spectator, who is prepossessed with an Opinion that all will end well; whereas if we were ignorant of the Event, we should tremble for them, and be likewise more delighted with the return of good Fortune that should deliver them.

One thing which surprises me the most in this occasion is, that there are men of Learning and Parts, who out of complaisance to popular Errours, do maintain that this was a word us'd by the *Romans* ; for, for my part I cannot imagine where they can find that a *Dramma*, containing the Adventures of heroick persons, and ending in a happy *Catastrophe*, had the

[T]   name

name of *Tragicomedy*. We fee nothing of this in what remains of the Works of the Antients, nor in thofe who have compil'd fragments, or written their own fenfe about the Art and Maxims of the Stage. 'Tis true that *Plautus* in the Prologue to his *Amphytrio*, ufes the word *Tragicomedy*; but as he is the only *Roman* that has us'd it, fo has he done it in a fenfe very remote from the ufe we make of it. That he is the only Poet of the Antients that has us'd this word, is out of difpute; and our Moderns cannot alledge any other *Roman* Author, while the *Roman* Tongue was a living Language; fo that *Plautus* was the Coiner of this word, which alfo fell with him, and died in its Cradle long before the *Roman* Language; but if others after him had made ufe of it in the fenfe he employs it, that could not autho-rize the word *Tragicomedy*, as it is now employ'd; and quite contrary,'tis by *Plautus*, that we will fhew the miftake of its fignification, and the ill ufe that is made of it.

To underftand this well, we muft repeat here, that *Tragedy* and *Comedy* were two Poems fo diftinct,that not only the Adventures, Perfons, and Stile of the one, had nothing common with the other; but even the *Tragedians* never acted Comedys, nor the *Comedians Tragedy:* They were as it were two different Trades or Profeffions; and accordingly Story gives us the names of divers Actors, who excell'd in the one or the other, but never, or at leaft very rarely of any that excell'd in both.

We are to take notice befides, that the *Mimes*, *Pantomimes*, *Embolarii*, the *Buffoons*, the *Dancers*, *Muficians*, *Players of Inftruments*, nay even the *Actors* of the *Atellane Fables* (which were the modefteft of all)

all) were not admitted among those who acted *Tragedys*, nor likewise among the Comedians, or those who acted *Comedy* ; both these being reputed much more honourable than the Actors of those *Farces* and *Interludes* ; but the chief distinctive mark of these two Poems was the matter of their *Incidents*, and the condition of the persons in each Poem ; for where Gods and Kings acted according to their gravity and dignity, that was call'd *Tragedy* ; but when the *Intrigues* of the Stage were founded upon the tricks and behaviour of young *Debauchees*, Women and Slaves, that was Comedy. And if we seek a further reason for this, it will appear that the Hymn or Song of *Bacchus*, which was sung and danc'd before his Altars, having been transferr'd from the Country, to Towns and Citys, the Subject of it was always taken by the Poets out of illustrious and serious Storys and Fables, and treated in a grave and sublime style ; but the very same Hymn remaining in the Country Villages, took its Subject from the common people, and their actions ; and being treated in a low, familiar style, was call'd Comedy, though that name too at first was common to both sorts of Poems, till their Characters being so very different, made them be distinguish'd by different names. Now let us see in what sense it is that *Plautus* employs the word Tragicomedy in the Prologue of his *Amphytrion*, where *Mercury* speaks ; and having desir'd from the people a favourable Audience, continues in these words. *After this I will explain to you the Subject of this Tragedy, What, you frown, because I have call'd this Play a Tragedy ? but I am a God, and therefore can change it presently if you will, and without altering a Verse of it make it a Comedy.* Then having jest-

ed

ed a little, he goes on; *I will by a mixture make it a Tragicomedy; for I do not think it reasonable that a Play should be call'd all Comedy, where Gods and Kings come and act; how shall we do then since a Slave too is one of the chief Actors? why, as I told you, we will make it a Tragicomedy.*

After such plain and intelligible words, I cannot imagine how any body can say, that *Plautus* had us'd the word *Tragicomedy*, as we use it; for he never dreamt of that signification; all that he says is a jest, wherein he joyns the names of those two Poems, as he had done the persons by which the great distinction that was between them does more evidently appear; and that therefore we have very ill apply'd that name to a Poem, where all the Persons and Adventures are heroick. 'Tis for this that *Plautus* never call'd his *Amphytrio* a *Tragicomedy*, but because his Gods and Kings do not act according to their dignity, but rather very far from it, playing the fool almost continually, insomuch that *Jupiter* and *Amphytrio* go to Fifty-cuffs; he therefore often boldly calls it Comedy, in many places of his Prologue. *Jupiter*, says he, *will act himself in this* Comedy, and by and by, *Hearken now to the Argument of this Comedy*; so that his Interpreters and Commentators have not also call'd it by any other name, no more than such Antients as speak of *Plautus* and his Works; as *Cicero, Quintilian, Varro, Aulus Gellius, Volcatius* in his Treatise of the Comick Poets, *Servius, Sextus, Pompeius, Macrobius, Rufinus, Donatus, Petrus Crinitus, Lilius Geraldus*, in his History of Poets, *Scaliger* in his *Poetica*; none of these, I say, have called his *Amphytrio*, no more than all his other Plays any thing else but a *Comedy*. And when *Vossius* explains
                                                              this

this word of Tragicomedy, he fays, *Plautus* gives it
to his *Amphytrio*, becaufe he in that Play mingles
the dignity of perfons with the lowneſs of Comical
Diſcourſes; and *Feſtus* making a diviſion of the
Fables among the *Romaus*, fays, that the *Tabernariæ*,
were ſuch as admitted of perfons of Quality, mingled
with people of mean Extraction, upon which *Voſſius*
adds, that the *Amphytrio* of *Plautus* is of that fort,
and that ſuch a Play may be call'd *Tragicomedy*, or
Hilaro-Comedy, which is a new word invented by that
Author.   And *Scaliger* before him, fpeaking of the
name of Tragicomedy given to this Play, fays, It is
done in *Raillery*, becaufe the Poet had made a mixture of the meanneſs of Comedy, with the dignity
of great perfons; let us not therefore affirm any longer, that this word Tragicomedy was us'd by the
Antients in our fenfe; for *Plautus* is the only one
that has it, and that in a quite different fenfe from
ours, who by that word do mean *a Drammatick
Poem, of which the Subject is Heroick, and the End
or Cataſtrophe happy*; and that indeed is a noble and
agreeable fort of Tragedy much us'd by the Antients.

The fame fault, in my Opinion, is committed by
thofe who would have the *Hilaro-Tragedia* to be a
Dramma, or Theatral piece in ufe among the Greeks,
and of the nature of that which we call *Tragicomedy*,
which feems not to be very probable. *Suidas* indeed
does fay, that *Rintho*, a Comick Poet, invented a fort
of Poetry call'd by him *Hilaro-Tragedia*; but to conclude from thence, that it was a regular Drammatick
Poem, of which the Subject was Heroick, and the
End happy, feems againſt all appearance, firſt, becauſe that it was a Comick *Poet* that invented it, and
they

they feldom or never undertook to treat any grave Subjects; or when they did, it was always to turn them into *Ridicule*, as this *Amphytrio* of *Plautus*, and the Comedys of *Ariflophanes*. *Suidas* calls this Play of his a *Farce*. *Hefichius* calls the Author Jefter and Laugher; and *Varro* puts the name of *Riortho* for a Jefter. Befides, this Invention of his had no progrefs, and we have not heard ever fince, of any regular *Dramma* that has carryed this title, nor of any Poet that fucceeded him in this kind.

What I fhould think then of this *Hilaro-Tragedia* is, that it was a little piece of Poetry, of the number of thofe call'd *Mimes*, wherein were mingled ferious and pleafant things, fung with Voices and Inftruments, and danc'd upon the Stage with geftures, expreffing the fenfe of each word, according to that wonderful way of the Antients, fo little known in our days; and this feems to be fo much the more probable, becaufe *Voffius* fays, that the *Hilaroedia* is the fame with the *Hilaro-Tragedia*; and 'tis certain, that that, and the *Magedia*, were two Poems of that fort, fung and danc'd upon the Stage by thofe who were thence call'd *Hilaroedians*, and *Magedians*; and they were not Drammatick Poems reprefented by *Tragedians* or *Comedians*, as fome by miftake have imagin'd, for the *Hilaroedians* (who were likewife call'd *Simoedians* from one *Simon Mages*, who excelled in that Art) did dance and fing a piece of Poetry agreeable, but ferious; and though not fo ferious as *Tragedy*, yet much of the fame nature; and as for the *Magedians*, they at firft recited only Difcourfes of Magick or natural Caufes, fuch as is the *Pharmaceutra* of *Theocritus* and *Virgil*; but in procefs of time they came to act all fort of lafcivious
Farces

Farces in the Comick Character, but much below it. The *Magedians* represented Men in Womens cloths ; but there were another sort who represented only Women in Mens cloths, and those were call'd the *Lisoedians* *Athenæus* remarks many more particulars about them not proper to our Subject.

But that none may have cause to wonder at what I say about *Hilaro-Tragedy*, we must observe that most of the Poems of the Antients were sung and danc'd with ingenious Gestures, either in their Temples, or upon the Theatres, or at their Feasts In a word, in all publick Pomps and Shows, either sacred or profane. Sometimes they took *Odes* and *Idylliums*, and other small pieces of Poetry, as *Mnafion* did by the *Jambicks* of *Simonides*, and some others. by the Verses of *Phocilides*, and other Poets. The *Lacedemonians* did the same thing by the Songs of *Thaletas* and *Aleman*, and the *Pæans* of *Dionisiodorus*, at the celebration of the Feast for the *Tyrean* Victory. Sometimes they took a *Cento* out of some great work, as out of *Hesiod* or *Homer* ; and these reciters were call'd *Homeristes*, being first brought upon the Stage by *Demetrius Phalereus*; and one *Hermodorus* was famous among them.

We find also by a certain *Jason*, cited by *Athenæus*, that in the great Theatre of *Alexandria*, *Hegesias* the Comedian was a famous Actor of those Poems, written by *Herodotus Lozominus*, a noted Poet of those times, different from the Historian of that name.

Nay, there were people who us'd to sing and dance some parts of Tragedys and Comedys at Feasts, and great Entertainments ; and sometimes the entire Plays were thus sung and danc'd, not only in the time when Tragedys and Comedys consisted of the Hymn

of

of *Bacchus*, (of which we have spoke in its proper place) but even since they were reduc'd into Rules, and made up of many *Episodes* inserted between the *Chorus*'s, as we have them now.

From whence we see *Aristotle* calls *Æschylus*'s *Dancer Divine*, for having so rarely danc'd a Play of his call'd the *Seven* before *Thebes*; and we see *Seneca* makes use of *Pylades*, a rare Tragedian Dancer: and *Batyllus* as rare a one for Comedy, to insinuate, that no one ought to undertake any thing but what they are excellent in, if they mean to succeed. 'Twas this *Pylades* who rais'd a Dispute before the people of *Rome* against *Hylus* his own Scholar, which of them two represented *Agamemnon* best, either *Hylus*, who to make him great, rais'd himself upon his Toes, or *Pylades*, who made him pensive and thoughtful, as being the best *Idea* of a Prince that was to take care of his Subjects good. *Plutarch* likewise in his *Table Conversations* makes two great Discourses about this ingenious way of representing by motions and postures, persons and actions, insinuating that Poetry is nothing but a speaking Dance, and Dancing a dumb kind of Poetry, and condemning at the same time the Dances of *Pylades* in publick Feasts, as being too serious and passionate.

But, though these Discourses about the Antients may be agreeable and useful, they carry me too far from my Subject, upon which I have already been too tædious to explain only the word *Tragicomedy*, our Poets may reflect whether they think fit to use it still in its vulgar acceptation, or whether according to the true notion of Tragedy, they will use this word indifferently in all those *Dramma*'s, of which the persons are Heroick, whether the *Catastrophes* be

happy

happy or fatal, that fo they may hinder the Spectator from difcovering the Event of their Plays be-
forehand.

An Analyfis, or Examen of the firft Tragedy of So-
phocles, entituled Ajax, *upon the Rules deli-*
ver'd for the practice of the Stage.

IF the Curious that have read thefe Remarks, are
willing to receive fome fatisfaction for their
pains, and to judg equitably of the labour I have
undergone, it will be neceffary for them to read in
the Original this *Dramma*, which I am going to examine, and till then, if they condemn or praife me
any where, I muft except againft them as unfit either to cenfure or applaud my Endeavours. All *Cri-*
ticifms have this property, that they oblige the Readers to view the piece they *criticize*; for if they have
not prefent in their minds all thofe particulars, upon
which the Rules are to be applyed, they are fubject
to doubt of the beauties and faults that are fhew'd,
and of the truth of all the Criticks Obfervations. I am
not ignorant that fuch a Difcourfe is none of the
moft agreeable of its felf, and therefore ought not to
impofe the reading of another Book; but there is no
way to make this Lecture eafie, but by taking in
both. It may be a bolder man than my felf would
tell you, that thefe Remarks, though by the crab-
bednefs of their *Criticifm* they may fail of pleafing
one way, yet they will in fome meafure atone for that,
by fhewing the hidden graces, and the great dexterity of thofe great Mafters which have hitherto been

[V] litt!e

little taken notice of, or at least regarded as casual beauties.

Supposing therefore that my Reader has just read *Sophocles*'s *Ajax*, I begin to examine it by the *Subject*; for 'tis there that the Poet himself ought always to begin.

The subject of this Poem is nothing but the just Indignation of *Ajax* against his Country men the *Græcians*, for preferring *Vlyffes* before himself in their dispute about the armour of *Achilles*. This affront in the person of a King and the bravest man of the whole army unjustly and basely us'd by those whom he had so valiantly defended, and that by those Generals who could not be ignorant of his great Actions done in their presence, could not but be most highly resented and therefore afforded a noble Theme for great passions. The fund, I confess, seems to be sterile, and to promise little; but there lies the greatest art of chusing such improvable subjects, to give the Poets Imagination the greater Play; who it may be upon this Anger alone Invented both his rage and manner of dying, for I do not find History to have positively determined either of them: *Ovid* speaks onely of his Anger, and some have said that he was killed by *Paris*; others that he was stifled in mud by the *Trojans*, because he was Invulnerable, otherwise; for my part, I believe that those who tell his death *Sophocles*'s way, have had it from him, which is no new thing in Theatral stories, the very Fables, from thence having by the Poets Inventions passed at last for Authentick Histories.

These two Incidents then I think to be the Poets Invention, who in that has with great Art, followed the Rules of probability, for a Soul as fierce and
passionate

paffionate for Glory   as that of *Ajax*, might well entertain the refolution of being reveng'd upon his
Judges and his Competitour, and thereupon run mad ;
After which coming to himfelf again, and feeing the
extravagant and fruitlefs Effects of his tranfport, he
might well kill himfelf out of fhame and fome remainder of rage.   That which makes this ftill feem to
be the Poets Invention, is the prohibition that *Menelaus* and *Agamemnon* lay upon *Teucer Ajax*'s Brother,
that he fhould not bury *Ajax*'s dead body, for 'tis
very probable that thofe two Princes were not fo in-
humane; but *Sophocles* added that to create the greater
compaffion for *Ajax*'s calamity, feeing his brother
hardly permitted to pay him thofe funeral rites which
were due to fo great a man and a King ; in this indeed he makes fomething bold with the generofity of
Menelaus and *Agamemnon*, but *Ajax* is his *Hero* to
whom he Sacrifices all things; and this refufal of theirs
to let him be folemnly Interred againft the law of all
Civiliz'd Nations, contributes not a little to perfwade that they had ufed him Unjuftly in the point
of *Achilles*'s Armour, all which, makes him ftill be
the more pityed; not but that thofe *princes* might have
fome fhadow of reafon for their feverity, confidering
Ajax as one who had meditated the ruine of the chief
Captains of the *Græcian* Army, and made himfelf as it
were a publick Rebel whofe punifhment among them
was to be prohibited the folemnity of fepulture. I am
not Ignorant, That *Cointus Calaber*, an Epick Poet,
makes them much more generous and with him they
perform honourable obfequies to his body. And in that
he aims at preferving the dignity of his Poem and
Hero's, as *Sophocles* does of his, befides this Ingenious
Fiction in his Subject he brings in *Tecmeffa Ajax*'s
[V 2]   Wife

Wife whence he draws three or four very paſſionate Scenes; now let us ſee what other changes he makes to adjuſt the time and place neceſſary for the compoſition of his Poem.

As for the time, he ſhews that indeed there needs no longer a one for the repreſentation than for the real action. Since in the third Act 'tis ſaid, *That Minerva's Anger againſt* Ajax *is to laſt but a day, and that if they could but watch him for one day, he might avoid deſtroying himſelf.* Now *Ajax* after this is all alone, and kills himſelf, by which we may naturally conjecture, that the Play ends the ſame day that his madneſs began; for all that's done after his death, is nothing but a conteſtation about his being buried, which is ſoon over, as happening near the dead body; and to ſhew that he does not employ the whole day upon his Stage, he opens his Theater in the morning, after *Ajax* had already run through the whole *Grœcian* Camp, exercis'd his fury upon the Flocks of Sheep, and carry'd ſome of thoſe Animals bound into his Tent, which takes up naturally more time than is ſpent from the hour that *Ulyſſes* comes to ſpy what *Ajax* did, to the time that *Teucer* carrys away his dead body to have it bury'd; ſo that a ſmall part of the day is taken up by his Actors.

The only Incidents in this piece is the return of *Teucer*, who was in *Myſia* with an Army; and that this coming of his might not appear affected, he makes *Ajax* complain of the long ſtay of his Brother, who ſhould have been back long before, and who was expected by him with great impatience; ſo that when *Teucer* comes at laſt, that does not appear ſo much a contrivance of the Poets to make him be there to diſpute about his Brothers Obſequies, as a

natural

natural effect; the Spectatours being so prepared
that they are wishing for his return of themselves
before he comes, that he might save *Ajax*'s life, in
which we may observe another change that *Sophocles*
makes in the Story by this absence of *Teucer*, the
reason of which change is, that if *Teucer* had been
present in the Camp during his brothers Madness,
the Scene being before *Ajax*'s Tent, 'tis very
probable that *Teucer* would have taken care to se-
cure him, whereas all other Authors who speak of
this adventure, as *Cointus Calaber* particularly, leave
Teucer in the Army, but not able to save his brother,
because he was gone out of his Tent to kill and Maf-
sacre the Flocks of Sheep, and no body knew what
was become of him.

Observe moreover with what art he chooses the
place of his Theater.   In following the Fable as it is
generally receiv'd, none of the Actors have any Stable,
or particular place.   *Ajax* is abroad in the Fields;
Teucer, *Ulysses*, *Menelaus*, and *Agamemnon* are in the
Camp; his Wife *Tecmessa* laments with her litt'e
Son in his Tents, and his Subjects the *Salaminians*
are either upon their Ships, or abroad to seek out
their Prince.   There was nevertheless a necessity of
bringing all these people together, and to make them
appear in one and the same place with probability,
and thus he brings it to pass.

He places his Stage before *Ajax*'s Tent as being
the most probable place where all things should come
to pass; particularly considering that there was a
necessity of making an afflicted Lady appear before
the Audience, it would not have been decent to
place her any where else, nor to make her run about
the Fields after a Mad-man; but because likewise he
was

was refolv'd to bring the body of *Ajax* upon the
Stage, that he might the better fhew the Paffions
of *Tecmeffa* and *Teucer*, and the conteftation about his
burial ; he fuppofes that there was a Wood Clofe
by the Tent, and to make that fuppofition the more
likely, he places *Ajax*'s Tent the laft of all the
Camp, which is very artificially intimated in the
firft Verfes that *Minerva* fpeaks, and to fhew that the
Wood is hard by his Tent, he makes the *Salaminians* hear from the Camp, the voice of *Tecmeffa*, when
fhe falls into loud complaints in the Wood upon finding the Dead Body : Then to bring *Ajax*, who was
the chief Actor, to his Tent, he fuppofes againft the
receiv'd Fable, that he did not immediately kill himfelf after the flaughter of the Sheep; but that he
brought into his Tent, a great Ram which he took
for *Ulyffes*, and other Creatures which he took for
the Chief Captains among the *Græcians* with an in-
tent to make them linger under the torment of his
Stripes.

But let us fee in particular how each Actor is
brought upon the Stage, and goes off according to
reafon.   *Ulyffes* comes to fpy what *Ajax* was doing,
and *Minerva* to affift him againft the fury of *Ajax*,
Ajax appears by the command of *Minerva* to give *U-
lyffes* the content of feeing his Enemy in the condition that fhe had put him; *Ajax* returns to his
Tent to whip the Ram that he took for *Ulyffes*, then
Minerva and *Ulyffes* go off of the Stage where they
have nothing more to do, and that's the Firft Act.
In the Second Act *Tecmeffa* comes out of her Tent to
defire fuccour from the *Salaminians*, who are the
Chorus in this Tragedy, and then opens her Tent to
go in again, where appears *Ajax* in the midft of the
flaughter'd

slaughter'd Beasts, but somewhat come to himself, which gives subject to very fine Discourses between him, his Wife, and his Friends.   In the Third Act he comes out of his Tent feigning to go wash himself in the Sea to purify himself; but indeed to hide the Sword that *Hector* gave him; his Wife comes out to follow him, but by his command retires into her Tent again, and he goes on. Then appears a Messenger, who bringing the news of the return of *Teucer*, orders from him that *Ajax* be carefully kept; upon this news *Tecmessa* goes out again, and desires the *Salaminians* to help her to look *Ajax*, which they do very willingly, and so ends the third Act.   In the Fourth Act *Ajax* appears in the Wood near his Tent, making complaints of his misfortunes, and so falling upon his Sword, the Hilt whereof he had put into the ground, which circumstance shews that his Death was at the same time an effect of shame for what he had done, and some remainder of the rage he was possessed with; at the very moment that he expires the *Salaminians* come upon the Stage from different parts weary, and vex'd that they had sought him in vain, and *Tecmessa* who alone had gone towards the Wood, finds *Ajax* just expiring, and cries out, which being heard by the *Salaminians* they go to her: In the mean time the seeking of him with so much noise had easily made every body think that he was gone out of the way on purpose to kill himself, and fame which ordinarily fore-runs great events, having carried the news of his death to *Teucer* obliges him to leave the *Greeks* with whom he was wrangling about his Brother, and come to his Tent to hear some news of him; and at the same time almost *Menelaus* who had likewise heard the news of his death comes thither to
forbid

forbid his being buried ; then goes back to tell *Agamemnon* of *Teucers* difobedience to his Commands ;
who at the fame time goes out to find a burying place
for his Brother, having firft fhut up *Tecmeffa* with
her Maids. In the Ffith Act *Agamemnon* comes himfelf
to put his Orders in execution ; and *Teucer* who fees
him afar off, comes back to be near his Brothers
dead Body,to defend it; *Ulyffes* arrives to appeafe*Agamemnon,* who at laft yields and goes out ; *Teucer* defires *Ulyffes* to withdraw, left his prefence trouble
the deceafed Ghoft or *Manes* of *Ajax* who had been
his Enemy ; he does fo, and *Teucer* carries off his Brothers Body : Now all thefe pretexts and colours for
the going off, and coming on of all the Actors, are
without doubt very natural and probable ; but the
Art with which the Poet brings all to pafs, is fo fine,
and fo ingenious, that one cannot fay that he affects fo
much as a word in it all, every thing being fo well
contriv'd, that all appears neceffary, and therein lies
the fecret of the Art.

You do not neither fee any Actor upon the Stage
whofe name you do not prefently know, or at leaft
their quality or concern as much as is neceffary to
prepare the Attention of the Spectators. At the
opening of the Stage *Minerva* (eafily known to the
Ancients by the marks of her Divinity) difcovers
Ulyffes's name who comes to her, and the defign he
has to fpy what *Ajax* does ; and when *Ajax* appears, one fees in what condition he is, for *Minerva* declares it, and calls him by his name. The
Chorus in its firft Verfes fhews, that it is made up
of *Ajax*'s Friends, the chief of them faying, *That he
had been always partner of the good and ill Fortune of
that Prince,* hardly has *Tecmeffa* fpoke three lines,
but

but the *Chorus* asking her about *Ajax*, she tells them
that she can best inform them, being from his Mistress
and Slave become his lawful Wife. The Messenger is presently known by his Dress, and by the first
words he speaks. When *Teucer* comes in the Fourth
Act, the *Chorus* says they hear his voice, and his
name alone is enough to raise the expectation of some
generous Sentiment from him, and the *Chorus* bids
him consider what to say to *Menelaus* who draws
near, and by that prepares an incident of some new
trouble. When *Agamemnon* arrives , *Teucer* says,
That he came back quickly, because he had seen Agamemnon *at a distance with the marks of Anger in
his Countenance.* Thus by the Poets most agreeable
Artifice, the spectators are not uncertain in the knowledge of the Actors, and their designs, which always
ought to be; except where the ignorance of their
Names and Interests is to produce some rare effect
in the incidents of the *Dramma.*

Could these Acts have been more judiciously divided? The first contains *Ajax*'s fury, the second his repentance, the third the preparations for his death, the
fourth his death, and the fifth the Dispute about his
burial, not that these Actions are meerly single, for they
are accompanied with many circumstances which
much embellish, and altogether compose the Acts; and
as for the Scenes they are extreamly well knit together, as because there always remains some body of
the precedent Scene in that which follows except in
the Third Act, where the Messenger who brings the
Order to watch *Ajax*, and not to abandon him, arrives upon the Stage just as *Ajax* goes off, which is one
way of uniting a Scene, when he that comes on
seeks him that gois off. And in the Fourth Act,

[X]   though

though *Ajax* talks no longer with the *Chorus* which comes back juſt upon the point he kills himſelf, yet thoſe two Scenes are united by the time, and the ſpectacle of his dead body, which remains as an Actor to whom the others arrive. As for the Intervals of the Acts, they are ſo neceſſary and ſo well fill'd by what is done off of the Stage, that the continuity of the Action is moſt manifeſt ; for in the firſt Interval, *Ulyſſes* tells the *Greeks* what he has learn'd concerning *Ajax*, and *Ajax* continues his Madneſs in his Tent : In the Second *Ajax* ſeeks for *Hectors* Sword ; and in the ſame Interval *Teucer* comes to the Camp and ſends a Meſſenger according to *Calchas*'s advice. Between the Third and Fourth Act there is no Interval, becauſe the *Chorus* is gone off of the Stage which remaining empty, makes very well the diſtinction of thoſe two Acts ; not that *Ajax* had been doing of nothing all that while, for he ſays himſelf that he had been fitting his Sword to kill himſelf : The Fourth Interval contains the return of *Menelaus* to *Agamemnon*, with their Diſcourſe about *Teucers*'s diſobedience, and the care that *Teucer* takes to find a fit place to bury his Brother in ; ſo that from the firſt opening of the Stage there is not one moment that the Actors are not buſie each according to their Deſigns.

Conſider beſides how well he has choſen the *Chorus* in this piece, and how induſtriouſly he makes him Act. He makes his *Chorus* of *Salaminians*, who more probably then any others might be ſuppoſed to come to *Ajax* , their Princes Tent upon the news of his madneſs, as alſo to pity his diſtraction with their own ill fortune ; nevertheleſs he does not bring them upon the Stage at the beginning, as he does

does his *Chorus* in other Plays, becaufe they were not to hear the Difcourfe between *Minerva* and *Ulyf-fes*, and befides too they could not without fear have been in *Ajax*'s prefence fince *Ulyffes* himfelf thinks himfelf not fafe near him, though under the protecti-on of *Minerva* ; but he brings them on at the end of the Firft Act, and makes them go off again at the end of the Third Act under pretext of looking after *Ajax* ; but indeed becaufe that having a defign to make *Ajax* kill himfelf upon the Stage, it would not have been probable that his Subjects fhould have feen him undertake fuch a thing and not hinder him.

To take this Tragedy according to the truth of the Action It feems not that the Poet has done any thing in favour of the Spectatours, fo naturally do all things fall out, and are depending of each other, and yet his making the *Chorus* go out that *Ajax* may kill himfelf upon the Stage, is contriv'd on purpofe to fhew the *Audience* a generous Action worthy their compaffion, and to move them yet to more tendernefs, the very body of fo great a *Hero* is deny'd burial.

We cannot but admire befides, the Art of his Nar-rations, for he makes *Minerva* tell the Defign which *Ajax* had fecretly refolv'd upon the Night before againft all the Græcian Princes, and how fhe had made him run mad to hinder the execution of it, which are things that *Minerva* alone could know ; and then he makes *Tecmeffa* tell the remainder of what he had done when he was in his Tent. This divifion pro-duces two different effects upon the Stage ; the firft a Sentiment of Admiration for the care that *Minerva* takes of *Ulyffes*, but with furprize for fo great a

[X 2]   misfortune

misfortune in the Perfon of *Ajax*. The other is a Sentiment of Pitty, when the Spectatours fee a Lady beautiful and well beloved fitting near a Mad-man her Husband. We muft not neither let flip the Narration which *Tecmeffa* makes fummarily of the ruine of her Family, and the death of her Parents, her Captivity, and then happy Marriage with *Ajax*; nor that of *Teucer* about the exchange that *Ajax* made of a Belt with *Hector* for a Sword which he received from him; the firft having ferv'd to faften the Body of *Hector* to the Chariot of *Achilles*, and the other having been the Inftrument of *Ajax*'s Death, for though both thefe Narrations are inferted in the moft lively paffions of the perfons that make them yet are they touched with fo much Art, that they do not at all weaken the Paffions, but quite contrary heighten them by giving an Image of fome new misfortunes; befides that all the ftory of *Ajax*'s Country, his Family, and his Warlike Exploits are induftrioufly told in different places without any affectation, and only for a more perfect underftanding of the Subject.

I do not knew whether the Conteftation of *Ajax*'s Sepulture would be agreeable and pathetick in our age, but I make no queftion but that in *Sophocles*'s time it muft have taken extreamly; for then it was a mark of the higheft Infamy, and the extreameft misfortune that could befal any body to be forbid burial, and without doubt the Spectatours were moved with great compaffion feeing the body of fo great a Prince ready to receive fuch unworthy ufage by the effect of *Minervas*'s anger and as the Difcourfes of the two Princes, *Agamemnon* and *Menelaus* feem well grounded upon reafons of State to deprive

prive him of the honour of Sepulture; and on the other side, the reasons of *Teucer* have Piety and Generosity on their side, I believe that this debate which was conformable to the manners and customs of the Ancients must needs have been very agreeable to them, particularly considering that *Euripides* has founded the Tragedy of the *Suppliants* in honour of the *Athenians* upon that sole consideration; and that it is not probable that so great a Poet would have taken a weak Subject to establish the glory of his Country.

As for the shew or spectacle he might have made *Ajax* appear in all his Madness ; but besides that it is a Passion below a *Hero*, except some great cause excite it, and that the effects of it are Illustrious; I believe he avoided doing of it, because it would have been hard to represent him making a great slaughter among the Sheep and Goats without making him ridiculous and so deprive the *Hero* of that compassion due to so great a Calamity; therefore to shew the deplorable condition of so great a Prince, and yet not to rob the Stage of any thing of ornament, he makes him appear in his frenzy indeed, but something abated by the presence of *Minerva* (which is a Figure of the rage of Great Men, which ought not to be quite abandoned by prudence, as the madness of the vulgar is) and so shews him sitting in his Tent in the first abatement of his fury, having those slaughter'd Animals all about him with his Wife, his little Son, and his Friends in a mournful posture near him ; all which does in my opinion afford a well invented spectacle, apt to raise compassion; when *Ajax* comes alittle to himself, and that all his looks, words, and actions have the character of
shame

shame, courage, and fury painted in them, the better
to manifest the excess of his misery; add to this the
tears and complaints of his Wife, the presence of a
little Infant who cannot speak it self, but whose presence gives occasion to many tender expressions;
and lastly, the heavy consolations of his Friends,
I say, that it is hard, but all this must produce a
very pathetick and moving shew. After this the
Poet brings him to his Senses entirely, but then the
prophetick words of *Calchas* which threaten him
that day particularly with death, bring new ter-
rour upon the Stage, and that so much the stronger,
because the Spectatours thought him safe by being
returned to his Senses. After this he dies by his
own hand and his very Sepulture becomes a Subject of contestation; all these are new Objects of
Compassion which shew us the mastery of the
Poet in supplying his Stage with variety by changing continually the Face of things.

A Project for Re-establishing the French Theater.

THe Causes which hinder the French Theater,
    from continuing the Progress it had made
some years ago in Cardinal *Richelieu*'s time may be
reduced to six.

1. The common belief that to frequent Plays
is a sin against the Rules of Christianity.

2. The Infamy with which the Laws have noted
those who make an open profession of being Players.

3. The failings and errours committed in the representation of Plays.   4. The

4. The Ill Plays which are indifferently acted with the good.

5. Ill Decorations.

6. Diforders committed by the Spectatours.

To begin by that *Generally received Opinion.* 'Tis true that the Ancient Fathers of the Church always forbid Christians to frequent the Theaters for two reafons.

The firft, (which few have taken notice of) was becaufe that the reprefentation of Plays was Anciently an Act of Religion, making a part of the Cult and Worfhip performed to the Gods of the Heathens; this is out of difpute, and may be eafily proved, if need were, by a thoufand Teftimonies of the Ancient Writers of Antiquity; the Firft Fathers of the Church condemned therefore the Chriftians that affifted at thofe Spectacles as being participant of Idolatry, which they had renounc'd by their Baptifm, as we may fee in the writings of *Minutius Felix, Tertullian,* St. *Cyprian,* St. *Auftin, Lactantius,* and others.

The fecond Reafon was founded upon the Indecencies and obfcenities faid and committed there by the *Mimes, Pantomimes,* Dancers, and others who acted their *Dythirambes, Phales, Itiphales, Priapeas* and other impure reprefentations which were proper to the Cult of *Bacchus,* to whom the Theater was Confecrated as to its Author, and to *Venus* as the companion of *Bacchus.* As to the firft Reafon then of the Pagan Religion, that ceafes now, fince Plays are no longer a piece of Worfhip, but rather an Innocent Recreation without any Impious Ceremonies in honour of the Idols, but the Publick muft be well informed of this.

As

As for the second Reason, though in Cardinal *Richelieu's* time all *Obscenity* was banished from the Stage in his presence, yet the Publick Theaters do retain something of those Indecencies in *Farces* and other Poems where the Authors endeavouring to please the rabble represent Impudent Stories, and set them out with filthy jests; which is a thing that Christian Religion justly condemns, and which all good Men abhor; and till that be taken away, and the Publick Theater as pure as it was in *Cardinal Richelieu's* presence, Plays will be look'd upon to be against good Manners and the strictness of the Gospel

As to the Infamy of those who take up the profession of Players, it was justly inflicted upon them formerly, but now is no longer so.

To understand this point, we must know that there was two sorts of Actors among the Ancients, the *Mimes*, and *Dancers*, and the *Comedians* or *Players*, who are those that now act among us, and as these two sorts of people were very different in the things that they represented as well as in the manner, places, and habits of representing, so were they very differently esteemed.

The first in the later end of the *Roman* Empire were declared Infamous though at first they were not so, neither among them nor amongst the *Græcians*.

But the *Comedians* and *Tragedians* never were so disgrac'd, but on the contrary, always us'd with civility and kindness by all persons of worth and quality, which may be made out by many proofs, but particularly by this, that the *Drammatick* Poets themselves acted often the chief parts in their own Plays, though some of them have been Generals of Armys,

and

and had other noble employments in the State; and if it has happen'd that the Actors have in some Reigns at *Rome* been us'd somewhat severely, it was by Maxim of State, for having sided openly with Princes reputed Tyrants, but not at all for being Enemies to good Morals.

In *France* our first Acting begun in Churches, representing then only holy Storys, but it soon degenerated into buffooning and satyr, both of them as opposite to good Government, as to the purity of the Christian Religion. Amongst these Actors who were nam'd *Basochiens* and *Baslelours, Comedy* remain'd with as much shame as ignorance for many Ages ; the Libertinism of that sort of life drawing away many young men of good Families, our Princes very justly noted them with infamy, to hinder by that means young Debauchees from continuing in a Society which was made incapable of keeping company with any other honourable sort of men; and from this likewise followed, that persons of quality scorn'd to contribute any thing to so mean a diversion, and were far from imitating the Antients in their generous liberality to *Comedians.*

From these two Considerations arises a third, which still stops the progress of *Drammatick* 'Poesie, which is *the fault of Representation.*

The Esteem that the Antients had Plays in, made many of the most excellent Wits apply themselves that way, and the Glory of the Magistrates, as well as the Fortune of the *Choragues* or Undertakers being depending upon the success of the Play, they did take great care in chusing their Actors, and instructing of them in the perfect performance of their parts, so that they attain'd to have many rare Actors in all

[Y]   kinds,

kinds; whereas with us very few ingenuoufly bred, have mounted the Stage, being hindered from fo doing, either by the fear of committing a fin, or by the apprehenfion of incurring the Infamy affix'd to the profeffion by the Laws, from whence it has follow'd, that thofe who did undertake it, being ignorant of their duty, perform'd it very ill in all its parts; nay, fo little knowing they were in their own Tongue, that they often expreffed very imperfectly, what they were to fay; and if there did fometimes rife up an Actor worthy of the Antient Theatre, he was fo ill feconded, that upon his failing any way, the Stage was ready to fink, and that even in our days has brought Plays towards their decay.

The fourth Caufe is founded upon ill *Dramma*'s or Plays, and this does not fo much regard our Modern Poets, who, to fay truth, have gain'd a very juft applaufe by many excellent pieces of theirs; but yet fomething may be faid, which is this;

The Antients could not leave us any ftore of ill *Dramma*'s, becaufe all their Plays were feen and examin'd by the Magiftrates; and befides, their Poets were not mercenary, but wrought for glory as much as for gain, there being a folemn Prize appointed for their reward, which was deliver'd with great Ceremony at their greateft Feftivals, to thofe who had beft fatisfied the Judges, and the Spectators; but we are far enough from that Method.

In the beginning of our Plays, as our Poetry was bad, fo was the reft of the Play, as to the Rules of the Stage; I have feen fome of eight and forty Acts or Scenes, without any other diftinction. In the time of *Ronfard*, Comedy was a little more regular, being cultivated by *Jodelle*, *Garnier*, *Belleau*, and fome others,

others, who contented rhemfelves with making fine
Difcourfes, but without Art, nor any contrivance
in the Reprefentation. *Hardy* did quite contrary,
endeavouring to pleafe the people by the variety of
things reprefented, but without any knowledge of
the Rules, which his Poverty did not give him leave
to fpend any time to ftudy. At laft *Cardinal Richelieu* encouraging by his noble generofity the Induftry and Labour of our Poets, brought Plays to the
State, where we now fee them far enough from their
true perfection, nay, and fomething decay'd fince
his time.

For, as every day there appears new Poets animated either by the defire of glory or reward, and
that they cannot all be excellent, we fee often fuch
Plays as ought not to be acted, which proceeds from
the little experience and prefumption of thofe new
Poets, as alfo from the ignorance of the *Actors*, who
being capable of judging only of fome things, are
neverthelefs the only Judges of all *Dramma's*, whether they fhall be acted or no ; add to that the little
care they take to have their Plays review'd and repeated in the prefence of intelligent perfons, before
they come to be acted publickly. For there is no
fmall difficulty to judg of the fuccefs of a Play, by
the reading of it alone; for very often thofe Plays
which read worft, are the beft, when they come to
be reprefented ; and on the contrary, likewife thofe
which feem admirable to the Reader, are often very
defective upon the Stage, and the reafon of this is,
the difference that there is between conceiving an
Action as you read, and feeing the fame thing reprefented to your Eyes. Things fine to fay are not
always fo to fee ; and the pleafure of Reading makes

some things agreeable, which the vehemency of
Action makes otherwise; as likewise some that appear weak in reading, are strengthened by Action;
all which faults in the representation, as they lessen
the Excellency of the Plays, so they discredit both
Poets and Actors, and keep the people in the Opinion that the Stage is not capable of much improve-
ment.

The fifth Cause about the *Decorations* is likewise
important among the Antients, the Magistrates, and
other great Men, who us'd to give publick Spectacles to the people, either by the obligation of
their place, or to gain publick favour, us'd to be
at the charge of the Decorations, the Players contributing nothing towards it, and by that means
those Ornaments were not only magnificent, but
perfectly answer'd the Poets Intentions. But now,
that our Players, though not very well in their
Affairs, nevertheless must undergo all the charge;
they cannot be blam'd if they endeavour to do it
as cheap as may be; but then the Decorations must
be imperfect, and altogether below the dignity of
the Poets Invention.

As for the Disorders of the Spectators, we may
consider, that nothing was more safe and quiet,than
the Antient Theatres, the Magistrates being always
present, and every thing done by their orders; but
amongst us there is no order at all, but any sorts of
people wear Swords in the Pit, and other places, and
therewith attack very often many peaceable Spectators, who have no other defence than the Authority
of the Laws. Among the *Greeks* and *Romans,* the
Women were so safe in the publick Theatres, that
they often brought their Children with them;
but

but with us a company of young Debauchees come in, and commit a hundred Infolencies, frighting the Women, and often killing thofe who take their protection.

We may add to that, that the Seats of the Spectators were fo conveniently plac'd among the Antients, that every one was plac'd conveniently, and there could be no diforder in changing of place; whereas now the Pit and Boxes are equally inconvenient; the Pit having no rifing, nor no Seat, and the Boxes being too far off, and ill fituated; fo that what with the diforders of the Pit, and inconvenience of the Boxes, the Theatres are much forfaken by the better fort of people.

To remedy all thefe Diforders, it will be neceffary firft, that the King be pleas'd to fet forth a Declaration, which fhall fhew on one hand how that Plays being no longer an Act of Religion and Idolatry, as they were formerly, but only a publick diverfion; and on the other hand, that the Reprefentations being now perform'd with decency, and the Players themfelves living fober, and not of debauch'd lives, (as they were when the Edicts were made, by which they are declar'd infamous) His Majefty doth upon thefe confiderations make void all thofe former Laws, forbidding them ftill neverthelefs to do or fay any thing upon the Stage againft decency or good manners, under fuch and fuch penalties, as of being driven from the Stage, and reputed infamous again. And to preferve that Modefty which is neceffary, it fhall be likewife ordered, that no fingle Woman fhall act, if they have not their Father or Mother in the Company, and that all Widdows fhall be oblig'd to marry within fix

months

months after their year is out for mourning ; and in that year shall not act except they are married again.

And for the Execution of these orders his Majesty may be pleas'd to settle a person of probity and capacity to be as it were an Overseer, Intendant or great Master of the Theatres and other publick Entertainments in *France* who shall take care that the Stage be free from all Scandal, and shall likewise give an Account of the life and actions of the Players. By this means the two first causes which hinder the *Re-establishment* of the Stage must cease ; for all scandal and obscenities being banished, there will be no scruple of Conscience in assisting at Plays ; and the Players will besides be in so good a reputation, as not to fear any reproaches from the sober sort of people. It was by such a declaration as this that the *Roman* Emperours re-est ablish'd the Theater when it was fallen into Corruption.

The third cause must likewise cease, for the profession of Actor being once made reputable, all those who have any Inclination that way will the easily er take to it ; and besides, the Overseer may himself select out of the Schools, and the Companys of Country Players such as shall be fitting, and oblige them to study the representation of spectacles as well as the Recitals and Expressions of the Poet, that so the whole action may be perfect ; and to this end none shall be admitted but by the Kings Letters Patents delivered to the Actor by the Intendant General of the Theatres, who shall give a certificate of his capacity and probity, after having tryed him in many ways. By this means there will always be excellent Actors, and the Representations will no longer be defective.   The

The 4th cause which regards the Poets themselves does require some distinction for those of them who have already the approbation of the publick by the Excellency and number of their works, shall be obliged onely to shew their Plays to the Overseer General to see that there be no *Obscenities* nor any thing against decency in them, all the rest to remain untouched, at the hazard of the reputation they have already acquired.

But as for the new Poets, their plays shall be throughly Examin'd by the Overseer and reformed according to his orders, by which means the Stage will not be loaded with ill *Dramma's*, nor the Players burdened with rewarding such as afterwards can be of no use to them.

As for the *Decorations*, they shall be perform'd by the care of the same Overseer, who shall employ understanding and able Workmen at the publick charge, and not at the Players costs, who shall have no Expence to bear but that of their clothes, and the reward they shall give the Authors.

As for the sixth Cause, which concerns the conveniency and safety of the Spectators, the King shall forbid all Pages and Footmen to enter the Play-house upon pain of death, and prohibit likewise all other persons, of what quality soever, to wear their Swords there, nor any offensive Arms, upon the same penalty, it being reasonable that that safety which cannot be had here, out of respect to the place, as it is in Churches and Pallaces, be obtain'd by the equality of the Assistants; and for this reason some of the Kings Guards shall be plac'd at the doors of the Play house, to take notice of any that shall go about to contravene this Order.

And

And for the greater conveniency of the Spectators, the Pit fhall be rais'd, and fill'd with Seats, that fhall overlook the Stage, which will hinder the quarrelling of the *Hectors*, there being not room for them to fight.

But to perfect the magnificence of the Stage, the Overfeer fhall look out a fpot of ground, fpacious and convenient to build one according to the Model of the Antients, fo that it be capable of the nobleft Reprefentations, and the Seats fo diftinguifh'd, as that the common people need not mingle with thofe of the beft fafhion; and round about which fhall be built houfes to lodg two Troups or Companies of Players *gratis*, which I fuppofe may be enough for the City of *Paris*.

And for the buying of the place, conftruction of the Theatre, lodging the Players, charge of the Decorations, and the Penfions of the two Houfes, as the King now gives them, with a Sallary For the Overfeer, and other fuch charges, there will a Fund be provided, without touching any of the Kings ftanding Revenue.

Thus there will be Remedys found for all the defects of the Theatre, which will be magnificent in all its parts, and worthy of the greatnefs of the Court of *France*, and the City of *Paris*, and the people will likewife have fome *Idæa* of thofe marvellous Reprefentations which have been upon the Stage of the *Palais Cardinal*, and that of the *little Bourbon*, and by confequent will be lefs envious and difcontented at the magnificent pleafures of the Court, and the great people.

F I N I S.

www.ingramcontent.com/pod-product-compliance
Lightning Source LLC
Chambersburg PA
CBHW021216270326

41929CB00010B/1153